THE FEDERALIZATION OF SPAIN

THE CASS SERIES IN REGIONAL AND FEDERAL STUDIES
ISSN 1363-5670
General Editor: John Loughlin

This series brings together some of the foremost academics and theorists to examine the timely subject of regional and federal issues, which since the mid-1980s have become key questions in political analysis and practice.

THE FEDERALIZATION OF SPAIN

Luis Moreno

FRANK CASS
LONDON • PORTLAND, OR

First published in 2001 in Great Britain by
FRANK CASS PUBLISHERS
Crown House, 47 Chase Side
London N14 5BP

and in the United States of America by
FRANK CASS PUBLISHERS
c/o ISBS, 5824 N. E. Hassalo Street
Portland, Oregon 97213-3644

Website: http://www.frankcass.com

British Library Cataloguing in Publication Data

Moreno, Luis
  The federalization of Spain. – (The Cass series in regional
  and federal studies; no. 5)
  1. Federal government – Spain 2.Decentralization in
  government – Spain 3.National liberation movements – Spain
  4.Spain – Politics and government – 20th century
  I. Title
  321'.02'0946

ISBN 0-7146-5138-9
ISBN 0-7146-8164-4

Library of Congress Cataloging-in-Publication Data

Moreno, Luis (Moreno Fernández)
  [Federalización de España. English]
  The federalization of Spain / Luis Moreno.
    p. cm. – (The Cass series in regional and federal studies, ISSN 1363-5670; 5)
  Rev. translation of: La federalización de España.
  Includes bibliographical references and index.
  ISBN 0-7146-5138-9 (cloth) – ISBN 0-7146-8164-4 (pbk.)
    I. Federal government–Spain. 2. Regionalism–Spain. 3. Nationalism–Spain.
  I. Title. II. Series.

JN8231 .M6213 2000
320.946–dc21   00-047582

Printed in Great Britain by
MPG Books Ltd, Bodmin, Cornwall

Contents

Tables, Figures, Diagrams and Maps

Tables

Series Editor's Preface

The last couple of decades have witnessed far-reaching changes of state, economy and society which have affected the nature and functioning of political systems. The main forces bringing about these changes are various kinds of globalization – economic, financial, cultural – and technological change; increasing macroregional integration, for example, the strengthening of the European Union and the North American Free Trade Agreement accompanied by, paradoxically, more societal fragmentation. The end of the Cold War with the collapse of the Soviet Union have also changed the geopolitical context in which states now operate. One of the most striking features of this recent period of history has been the growing importance of regions, whether understood as political governments, administrative entities or as units of economic or cultural life. For a short period, at the end of the 1980s, the old federalist slogan of a 'Europe of the Regions' was resurrected and seemed for a while to herald a new political role for regions in a new federalized Europe. Although this has not come to pass and scholarly and political evaluation of the role of regions in a Europe polity is now more modest, nevertheless, regions have still managed to garner for themselves a new legitimacy and have become once again a focus of political activity and repositories of identity – not replacing nation-states, but alongside and nested within them and the overarching polity of the European Union. The success of the regional idea and regionalism as a political ideology might be gauged from the fact that, in western Europe at least, all of the large nation-states have regionalized – Italy, Spain, France and, most recently, the United Kingdom – while there are pressures on the smaller unitary states, such as Ireland, Portugal and Greece, traditionally resistant to regionalism, to follow suit.

It is less clear whether federalism, as a political philosophy and movement, has been as successful as regionalism. It is true that the largest European state, Germany (as well as Austria), has been a member of the democratic family of states at least partly because of its successfully functioning federal system. Nevertheless, federalism, as a political philosophy, and federations, as forms of political organization, form an important backdrop to current developments not just in Europe but in other parts of the world. Indeed, federalism constitutes part of the intellectual underpinnings of the European Union itself and has tended to be forgotten in current debates between neofunctionalists, neo-institutionalists, liberal inter-governmentalists and multilevel governance theorists. Furthermore, there is sometimes a fine line between regionalized states, such as Italy and Spain, and federal states. The United Kingdom is both devolving political power internally and evolving new relationships externally with the Republic of Ireland. These new internal and external relations are simultaneously regional, federal and confederal. In Italy, the recent constitutional reforms were initially labelled a form of federalism although it clearly has not become a traditional federation. The merit of *The Federalization of Spain* by Luis Moreno is that it examines the Spanish case from a federalist perspective and attempts in so doing to introduce some clarity into what has become a conceptually murky field. Moreno analyses the Spanish case through two important conceptual lenses: the debate on regionalism, nationalism and federalism; and the historical development of the Spanish state. His discussion of the theoretical debate allows him to formulate a number of concepts which can be usefully applied to Spain: 'devolutionary federalism'; 'competitive versus concurrential regionalism'; and, finally, the application of the notion of 'dual identity', which is Moreno's main previous contribution to the political science literature on the problem of federalism. The development and empirical application of these concepts will be useful not simply for the Spanish case but also for further comparative studies as contemporary states, such as the United Kingdom, struggle to adapt their territorial arrangements to meet the challenges of modern governance.

John Loughlin
University of Cardiff

Acknowledgements

My thanks go first to the Dirección General de Política Científica – Programa de Movilidad Temporal de Personal Investigador (Spanish Ministry of Education) for financial support. Likewise, I am grateful to the hospitality of the University of Colorado at Boulder and, in particular, to the Department of Political Science and the Center for Comparative Politics at the time I wrote the first manuscript of this book in Spanish.

I am grateful to Ricard Giner i Sariola, Kerstin Hamann, José Luis Luján and Barbara Stewart, who read early versions of this text and offered me valuable comments on it. I wish to express my special gratitude to Salvador Giner, as well as to Ana Arriba and Araceli Serrano, with whom I have collaborated on earlier works on centre and periphery and multiple identities in Spain.

I am indebted to Robert Agranoff, Henry Drucker, Alain-G. Gagnon, Michael Keating and William Safran who have provided me with ideas and suggestions, many of which have been incorporated into the text. My thanks go also to my colleagues of the IPSA research committees on 'Comparative Federation and Federalism' and 'Politics and Ethnicity'.

I would like to thank Siglo XXI Editores (publishers of the Spanish edition of this book) for their co-operation. *La federalización de España* was first published in 1997, and since then I have been encouraged to update the text, taking into account recent developments. I hope that this book will help readers to understand the complex process of devolution and 'home rule all round' in Spain.

Thanks also to my late parents, Joaquín and Luisa, and to my children, Magüi and Jorge, for their love and encouragement. This book is also the product of the care and support that my friends and loved ones – Barbara, Bob, Carmen, Christian, Eloína, Erio, Elke, John, Jorge, Mari Carmen, Marisa, Pat, Pete, Peter and Tina – offered me during the time I wrote this and related texts.

Abbreviations/Glossary

BNG — Bloque Nacionalista Galego (Galician Nationalist Block). Left-to-centre coalition of nationalists.

Caciquismo — Clientelist practices by local bosses, or *caciques*.

Cantonalismo — (cantonalism) Movement promoting federation 'from below' on the basis of pre-established constituent units (it developed during the First Spanish Republic, 1873).

Carlistas/Carlismo — Followers of Carlos, pretender of the Spanish throne. Reactionary Catholic political movement advocating the preservation of old *fueros*.

Catalanisme — Catalonia's home rule movement.

CDS — Centro Democrático y Social Centrist party created in 1982 (member of the Liberal International).

CiU — Convergència i Unió. Centre-right nationalist coalition (CDC-Liberals and UDC-Christian Democrats).

CC — Coalición Canaria. Multi-party nationalist coalition in the Canary Islands.

Comunidades Autónomas — (autonomous communities) Nationalities and regions comprising the Spanish *Estado de las Autonomías*.

EA — Eusko Alkartasuna (Basques' Reunion). Centre-left Basque nationalists. Breakaway party from PNV.

EE	Euskadiko Ezkerra (Basque Left). Left Basque nationalists who merged with PSE/PSOE in 1993.
ERC	Esquerra Republicana de Catalunya (Catalonia's Republican Left). Centre-left Basque nationalists. Breakaway party from PNV.
Estado de las Autonomías	Spain's decentralized 'State of Autonomies'.
ETA	Euzkadi ta Askatasuna (Homeland and Freedom). Basque secessionist (terrorist) group.
Fueros	Charters of medieval origin protecting local customs and autonomy.
HB	Herri Batasuna (People's Unity). Coalition of Basque secessionists and political arm of ETA.
IU	Izquierda Unida (United Left). Left coalition of PCE, radical socialists and independent leftists (European United Left).
LOAPA	*Ley Orgánica de Financiación de las Comunidades Autónomas* (Organic Law for the Financing of the Autonomous Communities).
PCE	Partido Comunista de España (Spanish Communist Party).
PNV-EAJ	Partido Nacionalista Vasco– Euzko Alderdi Jetzalea. Centre-right Basque nationalist party (founding member of the Christian Democrat International).

PA	Partido Andalucista. Centre-left Andalusian nationalist party.
Pactisme	(pactism). Movement based on ideas of democracy, home rule and freedom.
PAR	Partido Aragonesista. Centrist Aragonese nationalists.
PP	Partido Popular. Right-to-centre Spanish Popular Party (member of the Christian Democrat International).
PSC	Partit dels Socialistes de Catalunya. Catalonia's Socialists Party federated to the PSOE.
PSE	Partido Socialista de Euzkadi. Basque federated organization of the PSOE.
PSOE	Partido Socialista Obrero Español. Left-to-centre Spanish Socialist Party (member of the Socialist International).
Reconquista	Reconquest of Moorish (Muslim) Spanish territories from the eighth to the fifteenth centuries.
Tribunal Constitucional	(constitutional court) Highest court in Spain.
UCD	Unión de Centro Democrático. Centre-right coalition which led the transition after Franco. It disappeared after the 1982 General Election.
Valencianisme	Regional home rule movement in Valencia.

Introduction

Some countries face a national dilemma. Spain has rather a dilemma of nationalities. This is chiefly cultural and political with interregional disparities tending also to reinforce internal cleavages.

Despite its secular conflicts of internal ethnoterritorial accommodation, Spain is an entity clearly identifiable as a country of countries, or a nation of nations. This unity goes beyond the simple aggregation of territories and peoples with no other affinity than their coexistence under the rule of one common monarch or political power. However, the social and cultural cohesion that makes up Spain's unity does not obliterate its internal rivalries. As has happened in the past, concurrence among Spanish nationalities and regions has brought about an extra cultural incentive for creativity and civilization, but it has also been used as an excuse for open confrontation.

After a long hypercentralist dictatorship (1939–75), a peaceful transition to democracy (1975–79), and an active involvement in the process of Europeanization after its accession to the European Economic Community (1986), Spain has undergone deep and far-reaching social transformations. In economic terms, for instance, Spanish development has been spectacular. In 1959 the Spanish GDP per head was 58.3 per cent of the EC mean; in 1985 it increased to 70.6 per cent, and in 1998 it grew to 81.5 per cent.[1] No other country in the group of the advanced industrial democracies has achieved a 'catching-up' process of similar proportions.

With the death of General Franco, and the dissolution of his dictatorship, the rise of demands for regional self-government reaffirmed Spain's spontaneous inclination towards the autonomy of its nationalities and regions. The democratic parties had fought against Franco's attempts of cultural genocide, repression and reinvention of history, but did not have a clear-cut model for the type of decentralized state they broadly advocated. Nevertheless, they shared the conviction that the legitimacy of democratic power was inexorably linked to implementing home rule of the country's nationalities and regions.

The constitutional expression of such a strong platform presented a great political challenge, for Spanish modern history had witnessed tragic failures in the past when regional aspirations and the territorial sharing of power were concerned. However, the wide interparty political consensus that made possible the drawing up of the 1978 Constitution succeeded in overcoming old reticence and mistrust. It also brought with it an element of ambiguity in the formulation of the *Estado de las Autonomías* (State of Autonomies), the name given to the new democratic and decentralized state. Two different conceptions of Spain, which had traditionally confronted each other, were formulated. Subsequently, a *via media* was negotiated, which explicitly recognized one Spanish state as an ensemble of diverse peoples, historical nationalities and regions. A nation of nations, in other words, which has as supreme constitutional principles those of liberty, justice, equality and political pluralism.

The text of the 1978 Constitution reflected many of the tensions and political stumbling blocks that existed at the time of the inter-party discussion on the territorial organization of the state. However, the constitutional provisions also mirrored a widespread desire to reach political agreement. As a result, Title VIII of the 1978 Spanish Constitution made it possible for one, three, all or none of the *Comunidades Autónomas* (nationalities and regions) to be self-governed. It depended on the political will expressed by the inhabitants of each *Comunidad Autónoma* (autonomous community), or by their political representatives. It also made it possible for the degree of self-government to be wide or restricted according to the wishes of the nationalities and regions. With the passing of time, *de jure* asymmetries have somewhat evened out, although the exercise of self-government implies *de facto* political disparities and diverse policy outputs implemented by each *Comunidad Autónoma*.

The 'open model' of 'home rule all round' established by the 1978 Constitution has consequently evolved into a gradual process of top-down 'federalization'. Let us remember that the 1978 Spanish Constitution does not include the word 'federal' in any of its provisions. Nevertheless, the *Estado de las Autonomías* can be considered a case of 'devolutionary federalism', and as such is scrutinized in international academic conferences.[2]

MAP 1: SPANISH NATIONALITIES AND REGIONS (*Communidades Autónomas*)

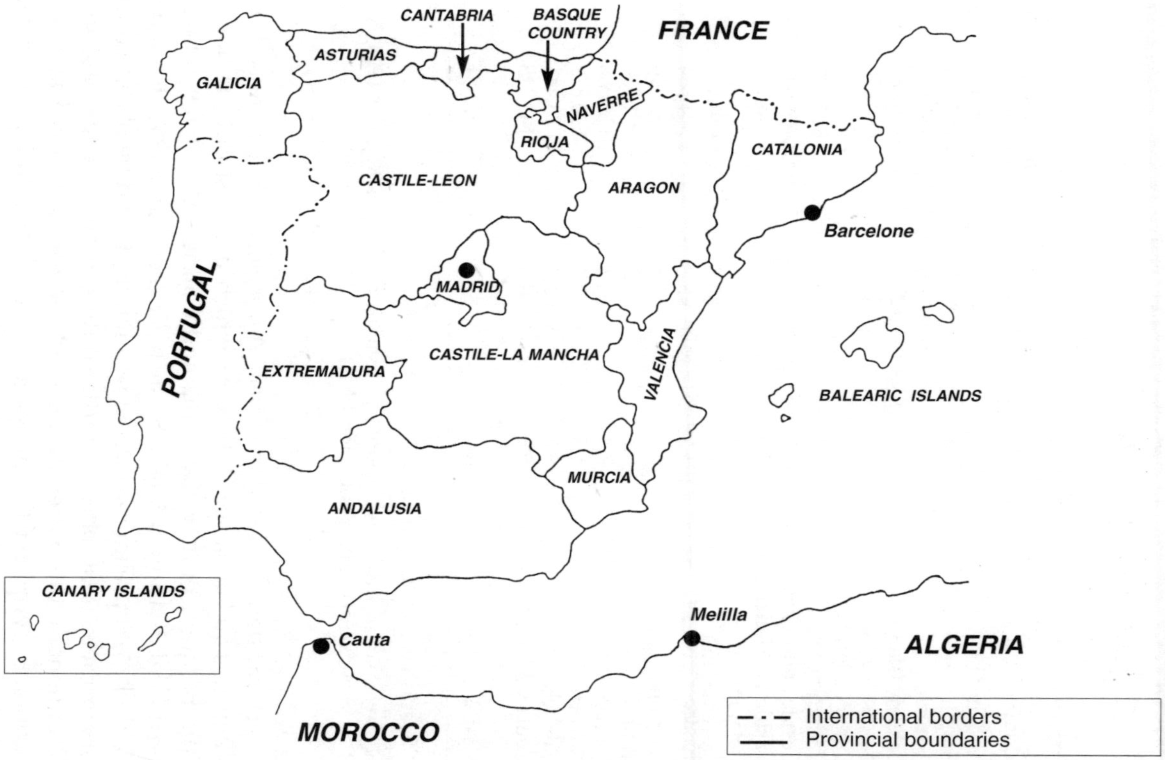

FRANCE

GALICIA

ASTURIAS
CANTABRIA
BASQUE COUNTRY
NAVERRE
RIOJA

CASTILE-LEON

PORTUGAL

MADRID

EXTREMADURA

CASTILE-LA MANCHA

ARAGON

CATALONIA

Barcelone

VALENCIA

BALEARIC ISLANDS

MURCIA

ANDALUSIA

Cauta

MOROCCO

Melilla

ALGERIA

CANARY ISLANDS

- - - International borders
——— Provincial boundaries

TABLE 1: SPANISH REGIONAL DATA

Comunidades Autónomas	% share of Spanish GDP	% per capita regional GDP European Union (mean=100)	Population 1998	
	1996	*1998*	*Inhabitants*	*% total*
Andalusia	13.3	58.9	7,236,459	18.2
Aragon	3.4	88.7	1,183,234	3
Asturias	2.5	69.5	1,081,834	2.7
Balearic Islands	2.5	125.8	796,483	2
Basque Country	6.1	93.4	2,098,628	5.3
Canary Islands	3.7	79.4	1,630,015	4.1
Cantabria	1.3	75.7	527,137	1.3
Castile and Leon	6.1	74.7	2,484,603	6.2
Castile-La Mancha	3.6	65.1	1,716,152	4.3
Catalonia	19.4	100.7	6,147,610	15.4
Extremadura	1.9	59.7	1,069,419	2.7
Galicia	5.5	68.7	2,724,544	6.8
La Rioja	0.7	91.5	263,644	0.7
Madrid	16.1	103	5,091,336	12.8
Murcia	2.4	65.1	1,115,068	2.8
Navarre	1.6	95.4	530,819	1.3
Valencia	9.6	81.3	4,023,441	10.1
Ceuta y Melilla*	0.3	60.3	132,225	0.3
SPAIN	100	81.5	39,852,651	100

* Spanish North African cities.

Source: Spanish Instituto Nacional de Estadística (Census Register 1998, National Accounts), and Fundación BBV (1999).

The Spanish *Estado de las Autonomías* is composed of 17 *Comunidades Autónomas*,[3] three of which are 'historical nationalities' (the Basque Country, Catalonia and Galicia). Map 1 reproduces the territorial division of Spain. Some basic regional data is also shown in Table 1. As a preliminary consideration, it should be observed that in Spain there is no abrupt north–south divide as is the case in Italy. Traditionally the hinterland around the capital Madrid has been an economic periphery (both Castiles, Extremadura and part of Aragon), while the geographical periphery in the north (Basque Country), and the east (the Balearic Islands, Catalonia, Valencia) have been important growth centres and industrial zones. Andalusia in the south and Galicia in the northwest have remained as poorer areas. Politically the geographical periphery has tended to be more European-looking and modernized. But Madrid and Andalusia have also been strongholds for progressive ideas and leaders.

After 20 years of the implementation of the first Statutes of Autonomy (Basque Country and Catalonia in 1979), the process of decentralization of power has consolidated and has achieved a higher degree of popular support.[4] Percentage changes in public expenditure clearly illustrate the proportions of the devolution of power in Spain. Between 1981 and 1998, central government expenditure dropped from 87 per cent to 54 per cent of the total, and regional spending rose from 3 per cent to 33 per cent. Local spending increased from 10 to 13 per cent.[5]

Federalization in Spain has developed in an inductive manner, step by step. Both Jacobin centralists encroached in sections of the public administration and in some influential Spanish parliamentary parties, together with representatives of the minority nationalisms (principally, Basque and Catalan) have favoured bilateral and *ad hoc* centre–periphery relationships. They have shown reluctance to encourage horizontal and multilateral processes of decision-making. This attitude is a major obstacle for the 'natural' unfolding of the *Estado de las Autonomías* into a federal-like system of government.

A minority of citizens in the 'historical nationalities', and in particular those in the Basque Country who align themselves with the ideas of ETA, advocate secession of their territories from the rest of Spain.[6] These separatists identify themselves exclusively as Basque. In the whole of Spain, however, more than two-thirds of its citizens express a *dual identity* or *compound nationality*. They incorporate both regional and state identities in various degrees and without apparent contradiction between them. As a result, Spanish citizens share their institutional loyalties at both meso and state levels of political legitimacy. Dual identity is at the root of the federalizing rationale of the *Estado de las Autonomías*, which has largely transcended past patterns of internal confrontation. Even for the Basque Country, where there is a high proportion of popular self-identification as 'only Basque' (around 27 per cent), the majority of citizens (around 57 per cent) express a degree of duality which tempers the viability of secessionist options.

Thus the peculiarities of both processes of state-formation and nation-building in modern Spain explain to a considerable degree how citizens express their territorial identities and institutional allegiances. Accordingly, it can be said that the most compelling variable for the future federalization of Spain rests upon the strengthening – or otherwise – of such duality of identities. The possibility of conflict is always present. However, in the period of time which elapsed since the inception of the 1978 Constitution ethnoterritorial co-operation and agreement in Spain has overcome old misunderstandings. It has also provided a deepening of democracy by means of a more effective access of civil society to political decision-making.

This book concentrates mainly on the territorial dimension of Spain's politics. Such a focus should not be misunderstood as a neglect of other functional concerns, many of which are closely linked to spatial policies and politics. Most research on Spain has concentrated on functional considerations. This book aims at filling an analytical gap regarding issues of regional autonomy, ethnoterritorial relations and internal accommodation within a state of plural composition. As a subject of research, Spain offers the possibility of formulating medium-range generalizations that can extrapolated to countries of analogous characteristics.

The first chapter of this book deals with theoretical concepts and assumptions related to the general discussion of territorial power: centre and periphery, decentralization, ethnic identity, federalism, nationalism, or self-government. Many of these notions have been subject to confusion and mystification. The review of such concepts aims at spelling out those epistemological considerations upon which subsequent analyses of Spain's reality are carried out. The general theoretical discussion deals primarily with the *ethnoterritorial* category with relation to a dimension of identity in which conflicts and political mobilization develop, and which has as main social actors those ethnic groups that possess a geographical underpinning.

History provides a good many arguments for the claiming of regional home rule in Spain. Most sub-state nationalisms and regionalisms find in the fertile and complex Spanish history reasons for the legitimization of their quest for autonomy and self-government. Chapter 2 examines Spain's history, focusing on territorial aspects related to its internal power structures, and the peculiarities of what was to become the first modern state in Europe at the end of the fifteenth century. A special reference is made to the dichotomy between particularism and universalism, which was gradually forged in the medieval period: such a relationship highly conditioned the early aggregation of the various territories of the Iberian Peninsula. Since then, the particular and the general have determined most aspirations, expectations and frustrations in the process of internal accommodation of Spain.

Chapter 3 examines plurality, asymmetry and nationalisms in Spain. An explanatory model for the understanding of the relations within decentralized Spain is put forward as *multiple ethnoterritorial concurrence*. Given the Spanish context of open interactions, concurrence is used to mean a simultaneous occurrence of events at both state and sub-state levels. The notion of concurrence should not be made equal to that of competition. Undoubtedly, there are numerous competitive actions between state and sub-state nationalisms and regionalisms. However, the underlying feature in the process of Spanish concurrence – mainly between central and meso levels – is the lack of compulsion to eliminate other concurrent participants. In some other instances, tragically exemplified in episodes in the former Yugoslavia and the former Soviet Union, the logic of competition leads to the elimination of the competitors.

The final chapter analyses in detail a sociological reality of the foremost importance in decentralized Spain: the duality in citizens' self-identification and the corresponding shared loyalties towards national and regional state institutions. A review of those areas susceptible to reform for the consolidation of the federal *modus operandi* is also carried out. In particular, the reform of the Senate as a genuine federal chamber, and the institutionalization of inter-governmental relations are subject to a critical analysis. Finally, the idea of *cosmopolitan localism*, shared by the Spanish mesogovernments, is put forward with relation to the process of European convergence and the principles of territorial subsidiarity and democratic accountability.

Throughout the book comparative references are made to situations and political phenomena in other advanced industrial democracies. As pointed out earlier, the case-study of Spain offers a paradigm of ethnoterritorial co-operation to other countries with similar characteristics. Within the Spanish context, special attention is paid to Catalonia. This 'historical nationality', with its values of civic tolerance and industrious creativity, is used frequently to exemplify a 'successful' stateless nation.

Internal developments may change in the future owing to the impact of such undemocratic factors as political violence and ETA actions. The ceasefire declared by the Basque terrorists in September 1998 was unilaterally revoked 14 months later. This announcement opened up a new situation of political challenges for both political parties and citizenship at large. Whether or not a democratic and peaceful compromise for the resolution of the conflict in the Basque Country can be achieved remains to be seen.

The ideas put forward in this book are not the result of a sudden interest in pluralist Spain. Rather, they are the result of a long process of intellectual maturation on the subject. I have aimed by descriptive and normative analyses to shed light on this intricate area of study. It is for the reader to assess the accomplishment of such tasks.

Madrid, December 1999

NOTES

1. Spain would reach the EU mean level of 100 per cent by the year 2025 if the annual 'catching-up' percentage of 0.8 per cent is maintained.
2. For instance, in the meetings of the Research Committees of the International Political Science Association (IPSA), 'Comparative Federation and Federalism' and 'Politics and Ethnicity' (de Villiers, 1994; Gagnon and Tully, 2001; Safran and Máiz, 2000).
3. The North African cities of Ceuta and Melilla also have chartered status as self-governed territories.
4. In 1996 two-thirds of Spaniards assessed the setting-up of the *Comunidades Autónomas* as 'positive' (see Table 2.5).
5. See Table 2.4.
6. In 1992 83 per cent of the voters of Herri Batasuna (political arm of ETA collecting around 17 per cent of the popular vote) declared themselves in favour of independence for the Basque Country. This percentage compares with 18 per cent and 21 per cent of Partido Nacionalista Vasco (PNV) and Eusko Alkartasuna (EA) voters showing preference for independence. These moderate and democratic nationalist parties collect around 28 per cent and 9 per cent of the popular vote, respectively. For the whole of the Basque Country, 19 per cent of the surveyed population was in favour of independence (see Table 2.7).

1

Concepts and Assumptions

In this Alice-in-Wonderland world in which nation usually means
state, in which nation-state usually means multination state, in which
nationalism usually means loyalty to the state, and in which
ethnicity, primordialism, pluralism, tribalism, regionalism,
communalism, parochialism, and subnationalism usually mean
loyalty to the nation, it should come as no surprise that the nature of
nationalism remains essentially unproved.

(Walker Connor)[1]

There is no lack of popular confusion – also observable at academic
level – in distinguishing and defining concepts such as race, ethnic
group, federalism, identity, nation, nationalism, state, or power and
territory. Theories related to these issues have frequently been limited
to the discussion of the efficiency or inefficiency of state institutions in
the provision of public services. Such partial treatment has minimized
the comprehensive study of: (a) the development of modern states
(state-formation, nation-building, mass democratization); (b) the
intergovernmental relations within the boundaries of the polity; (c) the
crisis in the legitimacy of the political institutions of the nation-state;
and (d) the impact of globalization in 'post-industrial' states.

This book concentrates on analyses dealing with many of these
concepts and notions. In order to articulate explanations for the
understanding of the process of federalization in Spain it is crucial, as
a preliminary step, to review those epistemological assumptions used
as tools for the interpretation of the phenomena under observation.

Some plausible theories concerned with our area of analysis have
been put forward by social scientists according to their particular
perspectives: political science, sociology, economy, anthropology,
history, public administration, or social psychology. As a result, the
emphasis in their interpretations has been affected by the disciplines
that they are most accustomed to handling: political actors and
institutions, economic variables, psychological attitudes, historical
trends and so forth. Commensurable explanations sought by
researchers remain attached to the scope and nature of their own

bodies of knowledge. The existence of a diversity of interpretations does not entail that the different theories are incompatible. In fact, social phenomena, far from being 'coherent' and 'uniform', are not only diverse but generally develop in mutually interdependent and interacting structures of a time-and-space nature.

One of the major obstacles for the understanding of ethnic phenomena has been the failed attempt by social scientists to develop a comprehensive explanatory theory. This task is associated with the development of a general theory of the cultural, psychological and social systems. In the absence of this, the best route to follow is that which facilitates the plausible construction of partial theories subject to factual verification.

Our analytical interest concentrates on those territories characterized by an emphasis on cultural and ethnic distinctiveness within plural societies in industrially advanced states. This analytical framework corresponds to Western multinational democracies such as, for example, Belgium, Canada or the United Kingdom. Political legitimacy in these countries rests primarily upon associative bases of a *Gesellschaft* type. According to the terminological differentiation made by Ferdinand Tönnies (1957), *Gesellschaft* bases are more 'mechanistic' and 'impersonal' than those corresponding to *Gemeins-chaft* polities. The latter are more homogeneous ethnically (for example, Denmark or Germany), and their social nexus is anchored in an intuitive presupposition of a common ascendancy. As a case-study, Spain offers an interesting subject of research, from which some generalizations can be extrapolated and applied to other countries.

In this chapter key concepts and assumptions related to the general discussion of our case-study will be explored and defined with the purpose of providing a better understanding of subsequent explanations and interpretations.

POWER AND TERRITORY

Power can be defined as the means by which one party is able to make – actively or by default – another party do something according to the wishes of the former. Territory, on the other hand, is the arena where the exercise of power between different political interests and institutions takes place. Thus the distribution/dispersion of power can be observed from two distinct perspectives: who wields the power and where the power is located within a territory.

Two main different approaches or paradigms have been considered in the study of power: elitist and pluralist. While the first contends that power is concentrated,[2] the second argues that power is scattered among diverse individuals, groups or agencies, and that an ample range of interests exists within different policy-making processes.

Power is distributed in functional and territorial terms. Regarding the former, the emerging industrial state in the nineteenth century created diverse functional units to accomplish its main economic goals of expansion and accumulation. This progressive functional division of the state and growth of government brought about an increasing trend towards *étatization*: bureaucratization, judicialization and central planning. Following this emphasis on functionally distributed power, mainstream sociologists and political scientists have argued persistently that spatial differences do not count as much as other functional cleavages in the running of the modern state. Such approaches have impinged upon academic interpretations in a rather spurious manner.

In fact, power has an inherent territorial dimension. It cannot be abstracted from its geographical component. The development of the industrial state inevitably involved a reallocation of the spatial division of power. Since the industrial revolution, and due mainly to a marked increase in the volume and scope of government activity, power has been distributed progressively according to meaningful geographical criteria. As a consequence of this, the issues of *dispersion–concentration*, *central–local relations*, and *state homogenization–regional diversity* have become crucial both for the configurations of the state institutions and the social transformations which can take place within the state.

State formation and nation-building

According to Max Weber, the state embodies the legal order of a given territory and exercises the monopoly of the legitimate use of force.[3] Inheritor of the ancient Greek concept of *politeia* (polity), the state in Europe was formed in various degrees and dynamics during the period from the twelfth to the eighteenth centuries. More concretely, the period 1485–1789 saw the building of most modern European nation-states, Spain being the first country to develop a modern state organization after 1492 (see Chapter 2, p. 37). According to Stein Rokkan, the second phase of nation-building, the subsequent processes of mass democratization and the construction of the welfare states completed the main four-phase process of political development in contemporary Europe (Flora *et al.*, 1999).

As a result of these historical developments, two broad models of state configuration can be identified:

Unitary
(a) Sovereign political power is undivided and rests upon an organic core of governmental responsibilities.
(b) Executive, legislative and judiciary operate on a state basis with some delegation of administrative functions to sub-state agencies or bodies.

Plural
(a) Territorial power distribution is distributed by consent among the different layers of government.
(b) Central, meso and local government can implement policies according to their own jurisdictions.

The unitary–plural typology finds expression in two corresponding systems of government: (a) *centralized*, where the *loci* of decision-making are concentrated in one core; and (b) *decentralized*, with a dispersion of power throughout distinct layers of government. States can be broken down into a further categorization of models as follows:

(1) where the central government is called sovereign, the system is said to be centralized;
(2) where neither central nor meso–local units of governments is sovereign, the model can be labelled federal;
(3) where the meso–local units of governments are called sovereign, the system is said to be confederal.

However, these three 'classical' types have evolved and adapted themselves to changing scenarios that have somewhat blurred their original 'yardsticks' or defining traits. For instance, although nominally confederal, Switzerland can be considered as a federal republic since the inception of the 1848 Constitution after the *Sonderbundskrieg* and, with this, the factual disappearance of the myth of the canton sovereignty. France has been cited regularly as the foremost example of a unitary and centralized system. Nonetheless, de-concentration has given way to the establishment of directly elected regional councils. Both Belgium and Canada were originally unitary countries that have transformed into formal federations within which some of their constituent parts have considered the possibility of secession.

The cases of Spain and the United Kingdom share some similarities as union– rather than nation-states. Their states developed in a peculiar manner, allowing degrees of autonomy of their constituent parts which were incorporated by means of treaty and agreement. While administrative centralization prevailed state-wide, the union structure entailed internal variations based on pre-union arrangements and rights (Rokkan and Urwin, 1983).

In these two European union-states, comprising minority nations and regions, the interrelationships between centre and periphery have been crucial in the structuring of their political cleavages and internal ethnoterritorial accommodation.

Centre and periphery

The centre–periphery relations of interdependence are of the utmost importance for the understanding of politics and policies in plural countries. Society has a centre, or central zone, that impinges in various ways upon those who live within the ecological domain in which the society exists. According to this 'diffusionist' approach, membership in the society is constituted by relationship to this central zone (Shils, 1975). Likewise, the centre is formed by a set of key decision-making powers that affect the relations of dominance and dependency, not only politically but also culturally and economically.

Centre–periphery relations, in any case, ought to be analysed from the double perspective of centralization and peripheral accentuation. Contemporary Spain offers a stark example of the noncongruence of political (Madrid) and economic (Barcelona) centres (Gourevitch, 1979), which highly conditioned the ambivalent action taken by nineteenth-century nation-builders. Attempts to impose by force such programmes of centralized nation-building contributed to a further delegitimization of political unitarism and an accentuation of periphery's distinctiveness (Díaz López, 1985; Giner and Moreno, 1990).

Theories of ethnocentrism and internal colonialism have stressed those abilities of state cores to implement programmes of national assimilation over peripheral areas. William Graham Sumner (1940) coined 'ethnocentrism' as the technical term for a view of things in which one's own group is the centre of everything, and all others are scaled down and rated with reference to it. Applied to territorial politics, ethnocentrism shows in the disregard displayed by the state core towards the economic development of the periphery.[4]

Internal colonialism is viewed as a structure of social relations based on domination and exploitation among culturally heterogeneous, distinct groups within the state (González Casanova, 1965). According to the internal colonialism theory, the superordinate, or centre, seeks to stabilize and monopolize its advantage over the subordinate, or periphery, by means of policies aimed at the institutionalization of a stratification system which is labelled as a 'cultural division of labour', and which produces a reaction heightening cultural/ethnoterritorial distinctiveness in both core and periphery.[5]

Neither ethnocentrist nor internal colonial theses are applicable to the case of Spain. Among other reasons, it would be wrong to consider the capital Madrid as being representative of a culturally homogenous political centre. For most of the nineteenth and twentieth centuries, Madrid has acted as the core institutional channel to privilege the interests of various Spanish territorial elites and oligarchies, which have often clashed with the objectives of some industrial peripheries. Thus no single ethnoterritorial group in Spain can be identified as constituting the political centre. This has rather been formed by contingent coalitions of regional elites (for example, Andalusian landowners, Castilian agrarian producers), which have counted on the traditional support provided by military officers and state officers recruited mainly from non-industrialized areas. Neither can it be argued that the centre has exploited a generally more prosperous Spanish periphery (Catalonia and the Basque Country).

The theory of ethnic competition fits more accurately in the explanation of the development of ethnoterritorial movements in Spain. It views ethnic mobilization as a consequence of competition between the diverse ethnoterritorial groups within the plural state all objectively pursuing the share of economic, political and social power. Ethnoterritorial conflict can also appear in the centre–periphery dichotomy when the economic and political yields are not subjectively considered as 'equitable' by the groups involved. In the case of Spain, a conceptual precision is made by distinguishing ethnoterritorial concurrence from competition (see Chapter 3, p. 91).

Modernization theory has pointed out that both processes of state-formation and nation-building were accelerated by the development of industrial capitalism in Europe in the nineteenth century. The enforcement of one central authority upon peripheral regions or subordinated political groups, often socially and culturally different, seemed to be necessary. As the case of Spain clearly shows, such centralization provoked a periphery accentuation, which took the option of 'voice' rather than those of 'loyalty' or 'exit' of other European countries (for example, France and Norway, respectively).[6]

The development of industrialization, urbanization and social communication has characterized in various degrees those processes of mass democratization in industrial societies. However, the cornerstone of national integration was seen as the creation of a common national identity throughout the territory under central state authority. Once again, such a programme is far from being accomplished in countries with a longstanding tradition of internal territorial cleavages and strong ethnoterritorial collective identities.

COLLECTIVE IDENTITY AND ETHNOTERRITORIALITY

The idea of an all-embracing state national identity rooted in both cultural and civic axes was brought about together with the idea of modernization. The social theory of functionalism, in particular, has insisted on its interpretation that internal territorial differences within nation-states had to disappear as a prerequisite for the extension of liberal democracy and mass politics. As communication of political, economic and cultural matters increased, the peoples of different regions would develop a new common identity, which would transcend their differences (Deutsch, 1966).[7]

The centre–periphery dichotomy was destined to decline in importance as society became 'modernized' by means of elite-initiated policies aimed at achieving social standardization (for example, common language and citizenship). Likewise, cultural identities of ethnic groups and minorities would be replaced by a set of class-orientated conflicts, or conflicts among interest groups. History has repeatedly falsified such analyses. In general, all-embracing identities are at present openly questioned and have become problematic.

Identity is the result of a process of synthesis by which the individual seeks to integrate various interactive elements (Epstein, 1978). Moreover, the discontinuity and dislocation of social arrangements allow different identities to relate to each other in quite an unpredictable manner (Melucci, 1989; Castells, 1997; McCrone, 1998). At present, identities are being corroded by the forces of globalization and are also subject to fragmentation, competition and overlapping elements of a multiple and diverse nature. Unquestionably, there is a noticeable strengthening of local, regional and national (sub-state) identities, which has coincided with an increasing challenge to the model of a centralized unitary state (Keating, 1988; 1992).

For social scientists a considerable problem arises in establishing boundaries and intensities of the various elements of citizens' self-identification, and in interpreting those causes for political mobilization related to territorial identities. In fact, identities are shared in various degrees by individuals and are subject to constant internalization by group members in different ways. Furthermore, supranational levels of ascription (for example, European) can integrate state and sub-state identities in apparent conflict among themselves.[8]

After the Second World War, and as a conceptual reaction against the tragic instrumentalization made by German Nazism on the concept of race, Ashley Montagu (1972) established the modern definition of ethnic groups. These are national, religious, geographic, linguistic or cultural groups which do not necessarily coincide with racial groups, and whose cultural traits have no demonstrated genetic connection with racial characteristics, but are based upon a subjective belief in a common ascendancy (Weber, 1961). Thus, membership of an ethnic group is voluntary whereas in a race it is not (Banton, 1983; Rex, 1986).

Our general theoretical discussion deals primarily with the concept of *ethnoterritoriality*, which refers to a dimension of identity in which conflicts and political mobilization develop and which has as its chief social actors those ethnic groups that possess a geographical underpinning. Such a spatial reference is identifiable within the boundaries of a polity, usually one of a compound or plural composition (Moreno, 1986; Rudolph and Thompson, 1992; Coakley, 1994).[9]

Taking into account its geographical underpinning within a state of a plural composition, an ethnoterritorial group can be defined syncretically as an historically formed aggregate of persons having an association with a given territory and possessing a shared cluster of beliefs and values connoting its distinctiveness in relation to similar groups coexisting in the polity and recognized as such by these other ethnic groups (Phadnis, 1989).

As pointed out earlier, individuals in plural societies are tied to cultural reference groups that might be in concurrence or interaction among themselves. This results in a multiplicity of sociopolitical identities, dynamic and often shared, which are not necessarily expressed explicitly. Identity markers are therefore malleable, and the intensity of their manifestation depends greatly upon contingent circumstances (Brass, 1991; Cohen, 1992). In Spain, the persistence of a *dual identity* (state–national and regional–ethnoterritorial) reveals the ambivalent nature of the internal ethnoterritorial relations that can coexist in plural societies (see Chapter 4, p. 110).

The emphasis on ethnic identity, or ethnicity, ought not to be placed merely on distinctiveness but also on those relationships of interaction.[10] Arguably, some authors consider that political accommodation to secure political and institutional stability in pluriethnic societies or polyarchies is almost impossible, and is bound to result in either the break-up of the state or the consolidation of a type of hegemonic authoritarianism for the control of the state's unity (Dahl, 1971; Horowitz, 1985).[11]

Contemporary liberal thinkers have greatly revitalized the debate regarding individual and collective rights. Most of them can be labelled 'liberal nationalists' (Tamir, 1993). Some have argued persuasively for the case of multiculturalism and the politics of recognition for minorities (Taylor, 1992; Kymlicka, 1995; Walzer, 1997). However, some of their normative analyses insist upon the 'unfeasibility' of accommodating ethnoterritorial groups within federations – as the case of Quebec and Canada would illustrate.[12]

However, ethnoterritorial co-operation and agreement may not only overcome conflicts and divergence within plural nation-states but can also provide a deepening of democracy by means of a more effective access of civil society to political decision-making – something which in the case of Spain overlaps with its internal ethnic and cultural diversity.

All things considered, the revival of ethnoterritorial political movements in the West can be explained in accordance with a shifting pattern of variables. The intertwining of these – all or some of them – have resulted in a set of diverse scenarios where ethnoterritorial mobilization adopts forms different in degree and outcome. The following can be identified among the most relevant ones:

(a) unequal distribution of resources and power among ethnoterritorial groups in polities of a plural composition;
(b) concurrence among ethnoterritorial groups in order to improve their relative positions of power within the plural state;
(c) general dissatisfaction of citizens with respect to the action of the central government;
(d) high degree of institutional patronage, which is a consequence of a diffusion of state power in decentralized political systems.

Indeed, ethnoterritorial mobilization is a result of a degree of policitization. It relates to both 'nationalist' and 'regionalist' movements in quest of self-government, whether claiming sovereignty for a new nation or within the framework of an existing state.

Nationalism and nations

Nationalism has been referred to as one form of politics or, rather, as politicized ethnicity (Smith, 1971; Gellner, 1983). As a powerful modern ideology, two main types of nationalism can be distinguished. Firstly, a *majority or state nationalism* forged by modernization and industrialization in the processes of state-formation and nation-building. This form of nationalism has aimed at integrating either ethnically homogeneous societies, such as Germany or Sweden, or heterogeneous ones, such as Italy or the United States. Secondly, a *minority or stateless nationalism* – also labelled as peripheral – present in countries such as Catalonia or Scotland, which has come to reassert pre-union identities in the form of political mobilization for democratic home rule (Beramendi *et al.*, 1994; Keating, 1996; Nairn, 1997; Guibernau, 1999). Both types of nationalisms are now briefly examined.

(a) *Majority or state nationalism* consolidated as an ideological force of mobilization against absolutist monarchy. In modern times the most dynamic sectors of the bourgeoisie and some elites of the peasantry also made use of this nationalist ideology in order to fight the old aristocratic privileges. The concept of citizenship drafted by the Glorious Revolution in England and articulated by both American and French revolutions became essential in the conformation of state nationalism during the nineteenth and twentieth centuries. Its final aim was none other than the building of nations where citizens would become peers with equal access to a set of universal rights and obligations. Thus, nations forged by this type of state nationalism were to become the embodiment of modernity (Greenfeld, 1992; Llobera, 1994; Hroch, 1985).

The initiative for nationalization generally corresponded to those hegemonic ethnoterritorial groups (*Volkstaat*), which implemented programmes of nation-building with varying results and outcomes (e.g. Castilians, English, Piedmontese or Prussians). In some instances such groups claimed to be the main or exclusive representatives of their states – an allegation which became difficult to maintain with the passing of time (e.g. the Walloons in the case of Belgium).

State or majority nationalism has been labelled 'civic' or 'unifying' as opposed to 'ethnic' or 'secessionist' minority nationalism. The former is widely considered to be a superior manifestation of human civilization and progress. The latter, instead, is viewed as a failed spin-off of history, which is bound to provoke permanent conflicts and violence. Recent collective tragedies in the Balkans seem to provide evidence to confirm such an axiological distinction. It should not be forgotten, however, that both forms of nationalism can be pathological in various degrees and scales. In fact, a good deal of the responsibilities for the two world wars in the twentieth century falls mostly on the irrationalities of some state nationalisms.

(b) *Minority or stateless nationalism* usually develops within plural states and is associated with demands for self-government.[13] These can range from a degree of home rule to the formation of a new independent state. This type of nationalism has often been made synonymous with that of regionalism. Indeed, both share three elements in most of their manifestations: (1) a collective identity and consciousness of community belonging; (2) a centre–periphery conflict; and (3) an existence of social mobilization and political organization for the achievement of their objectives.

As channels for ethnoterritorial movements, both regionalism and minority nationalisms are analogous and may be interchangeable in some instances. However, a distinction can be made between the two phenomena and this relates to those spatial units in plural states which either had a pre-union identity as self-governed territories prior to the configuration of the plural state (e.g. Spanish 'historical nationalities': the Basque Country, Catalonia and Galicia),[14] or which develop the political expression of their solidarity at a later stage in the process of state-formation (Castile–La Mancha or Extremadura, for example).[15] In any case, both types of minority nationalism and regionalism can share the same long-term objectives, and both owe much to the sequence reproduced in Figure 1.1.

Let us not forget that both ethnicity and nationalism are relational constructs. This is to say that ethnicity means nothing without the existence of ethnic groups or categories (Geertz, 1973; de Vos and Romanucci-Ross, 1975; Gellner, 1987; Roosens, 1989). They refer to tangible social phenomena, a consideration making the abstraction and gradation of their manifestations rather difficult outside the 'real' existence of collective groups. For this reason, and given the non-rational development of some forms of nationalism, as the cases of the former Yugoslavia and the former Soviet Union illustrate clearly, it remains a challenge for scholars and specialists to describe the political dimensions and the institutional outcomes of the development in contemporary times of so-called 'national fundamentalism'.

There are several theories for the explanation of the phenomenon of the nation. Nevertheless, two main approaches for the theorizing of the nation can be identified: *deterministic* and *functional*. Following this broad epistemological distinction, several school and sub-schools of thought have attempted to account for the national phenomena and can be grouped according to Figure 1.2.[16] They are now examined schematically.

FIGURE 1.1
ELEMENTS OF ETHNOTERRITORIAL MOBILIZATION

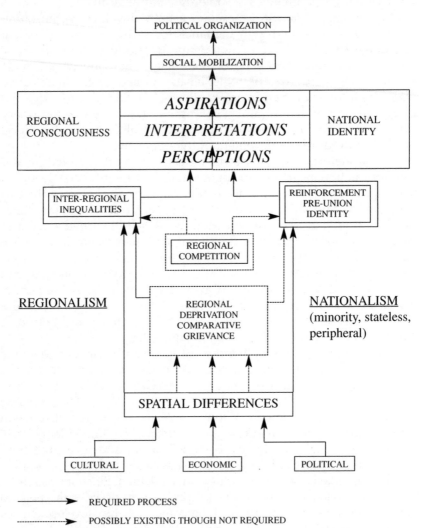

Source: Based on an idea of López-Aranguren (1983: p. 59).

FIGURE 1.2
THEORIES OF THE NATION

Assimilationist Marxist Diffusionist	K.W. Deutsch V.I. Lenin R. Dahl	Functional
Instrumentalist Elitist Rational choice	D. Horowitz C. Tilly M. Hechter	
Modernist Jacobin Structuralist	E. Gellner E. Renan E.J. Hobsbawm	
Historicist Organicist Pluralist	A.D. Smith J.G. Herder A. de Tocqueville	Deterministic
Socio-anthopolitical Psychologist Biologist	F. Barth B. Anderson P.L. van den Berghe	

(1) *The deterministic approach.* In general terms, this school of thought maintains that nations are historical products or evolving social organisms possessing a unique and distinct collective spirit.[17] Cultural elements such as beliefs, folklore, language or social memory and myths have moulded the collective consciousness of the various national communities.[18] All national cultures are legitimate, can be preserved and should develop as expressions of human existence (Berlin, 1976).[19] The destruction of the nation could lead, consequently, to the suppression of an essential entity for the achievement of human aspirations, including that of popular sovereignty (Mazzini, 1891).[20]

Deterministic primordialism points out that there is an inexorable relationship between the individual and the nation. Accordingly, life-courses of individuals are tied in with the past of the nation to which they belong. Past, present and future visions are conditioned by attitudes and knowledge rooted in the national collective. Eventually this approach tends to conclude that ethnic groups and nations are natural units of history and integral elements of human experience. Tradition can be invented as it mainly corresponds to a psychosocial dimension (Anderson, 1983). For determinists, however, whether it is 'artificial' or 'natural' the important factor is that the nation creates a relationship between individual destiny and the collective future. Such a continuum of attitudes is preserved by ethnic carriers and greatly shapes individual and group life trajectories (Nash, 1989). As a sub-variant of the socio-anthropological approach, *biologists* maintain that ethnicity and national development are the results of a sequential prolongation of kinship in the struggle for survival and the accomplishment of collective goals (van den Berghe, 1978).

Pluralists place emphasis not merely on ethnic distinctiveness but rather on the relationships of interaction between the different groups or nations within the framework of a compound state. Pluralists stress social heterogeneity but also propose the organization of such diversity. They refuse to admit the inevitability of institutional and political turmoil because of cultural fragmentation. Alexis de Tocqueville regarded the multiplicity of 'secondary groups' in a democracy as providing the best means for a healthier dispersion of power and to avoid social alienation.

As a critique to the deterministic view on the nation, it can be argued that despite the crucial importance of history in understanding ethnic sociopolitical mobilization, identity can be seen as a necessary but not sufficient prerequisite to explain the politicization of ethnicity for nation-building. Besides, 'cultural markers' of nations are subject to constant modifications and realignments (Barth, 1969; Thom, 1995). Historical 'perennialism' (Smith, 1986)[21] has made a theoretical contribution to the debate on the idea of the nation contesting many views put forward by modernization theories. However, it says little about the significant moments of co-operation and conflict between ethnic groups and nations during the various development of human history. Thus the difficulty is that of establishing who were the ancestors of the modern nations, when they took full awareness of their social existence, which type of cultural manifestations they expressed, how these were transmitted from generation to generation and which were the interactions that were formalized in their contact with external groups. These questions remain as the main theoretical challenges to be answered in a comparative perspective.

(2) *The functional approach*. This sees nations as modern phenomena resulting from industrial development and associated with the economic, political and social requirements of modernization processes. Functional *modernists* consider that nations and nationalism are the product of bureaucracy, capitalism and secular utilitarianism (Gellner, 1983). According to such a view, nations are contingent and do not derive from an immutable sense of history or human nature. Emergence of nations is dated around the second half of the eighteenth century. Any other national entity prior to that period of time is to be taken cautiously. Modernist *structuralists*, in turn, argue that nations respond to the 'logic of capitalism' and the needs of the modern economy (Hobsbawm, 1990). Functional *instrumentalists*, and in particular those holding an elitist understanding of the nation, underline sociopolitical factors as paramount for the maintenance of the interests and status of the national elites (Tilly, 1975; Brass, 1994).

For *assimilationists*, represented by both schools of diffusionist functionalism and 'orthodox' Marxism,[22] the extension of bourgeois liberalism during the eighteenth and nineteenth centuries resulted in a detribalization of 'pre-modern' societies. Both advocates of the American school of comparative politics and 'historicist' Marxists regard nation-states as functional to universal human progress.[23] In this respect, culture and language are dependent variables of nation-building and political assimilation within the state.

Rational choice theory views ethnic groups and nations as instrumental entities for maximizing the well-being of individuals. Group solidarity within the nation provides citizens with advantages that otherwise they could not possibly have by themselves (Hechter,

1987). Such improvements are made possible by selective incentives and positive discrimination with respect to other ethnic groups or nations (Olson, 1982).

In discussing the functional theories of nation, it comes as no surprise that 'rationalist' theoreticians of the social contract, individualism, materialism and functionalist thinkers are uneasy with concepts such as that of ethnicity. For them the notion of a universal and immutable human nature is a value far superior to those of ethnic groups or collectives. Nevertheless, their theoretical constructions (the rational citizen or the *homo economicus*) are also myths susceptible to analytical reification. Furthermore, advocates of modernization theories do not account generally for pre-modern collective identities that are in the genesis of modern nations (ancient Greek and Roman worlds, Celts, Normands or the Germanic peoples in the High Middle Ages). To confine the emergence of the nations to a relatively short period of time in human history is an exercise of reductionism in a complex area of study for the social scientist.

The deterministic/functional axis, or in other words the primordialist/modernist perspective, seems to draw an epistemological line between these two more representative groups of academics dealing with theories of nation. As a final general comment on both main approaches, it can be pointed out that (a) very few scholars would refuse to accept the existence of 'proto-nations' (Catalonia, Scotland) prior to the Modern Age, or that the notion of collective identity played an important role in the shaping of contemporary nationalism; and (b) it would be awkward to regard the phenomena of nationalism as a 'natural' product of history immune to the impacts of modern bureaucratization, colonization, industrialization and urbanization. However, (c) attempts to reconcile these two positions are rare – something which hinders the possibility of carrying out comparative research across countries.

In this discussion of the functional theory of the nation, the reader may have noticed that no explicit reference has been made to Jacobinism. Because of its direct and contrasting relationship with federalism we shall review this movement in our final conceptual section.

THE FEDERAL IDEA

Federalist philosophy has often been considered as most appropriate for the constitution of modern federations. But both federalism and federation are not equal terms. The former implies a combination of self- and shared-government. However, the institutionalization of such principles manifests itself not only in federations but also in federal-like systems of government of a diverse outlook. Variants of the federal idea range from ethnically homogenous polities (Germany),[24] to ethnically heterogeneous ones with no territorial ascription (the United States), or polities with ethnoterritorial diversity (Switzerland). A common feature of these three examples is an institutional arrangement based upon the essential federalist principle: the conciliation of unity and diversity by means of political pact.

Therefore, federalism and federation are concomitant concepts but cannot be made synonymous (Marc and Aron, 1948; King, 1982; Elazar, 1987; Watts, 1994). A federation is an institutional expression of the federal idea in a state constituted by intermediate territorial entities and by a general common administration. Both meso and central layers of government are accountable to citizens at each level of administration and with respect to their own competencies, powers and responsibilities. The main attributes of federal political systems are (a) the existence of a written constitution establishing a territorial division of powers that allows each level of government to have the 'last say' in some activities (Riker, 1975); (b) a bicameral legislature with a territorial senate; (c) the participation of the constituent units in the general process of decision-making; and (d) a decentralized system of government.

Empirically, federalism is manifested in policy outputs elaborated and implemented through political negotiation among sub-state units and central/federal general administration. Confederations (Switzerland), federations (Germany), federacies or associated states (Puerto Rico), consociations (Netherlands), unions (Italy),[25] leagues (Benelux), joint functional authorities (NATO) or condominiums (former Andorra) are also institutional expressions of the federalist philosophy. In 1991, Daniel Elazar concluded that nearly 40 per cent of the world's population lived in countries formally self-labelled as federations, while a further 33 per cent were states that had adopted federal forms and practices.[26]

Federal-like countries, therefore, share a political culture of intergovernmental pact and of territorial autonomy (central, regional, local) in the development of public policies. The 1978 Spanish Constitution does not include the word 'federal' in any of its provisions. Nevertheless, the *Estado de las Autonomías* can be considered an example of 'devolutionary federalism', and as such is scrutinized in international academic conferences. Federalism can also be regarded as a response to the stimuli of the diversity or plurality of society, comprising ethnoterritorial groups with differences of history, language, religion or traditions. Spain, with marked territorial cleavages, incorporates plural qualities that can be better accommodated within federal-like state institutions (Armet *et al.*, 1988).

Federalist proposals have been criticized for their propensity to centrifugal and dispersing tendencies. Not surprisingly, advocates of Jacobinism can be identified as long-standing opponents of federalism. Let us bear in mind that the most relevant contemporary implementation of the federal idea (the United States) coincided temporarily with the extension of Jacobinism and its conception of the centralized and unitary nation-state. The United States has consolidated for more than two centuries as a 'successful' system of democratic government by consent in contrast to that of centralized France. Both countries can claim to be heirs to the revolutionary spirit of the Enlightenment. Thus, a critique of French Jacobinism as compared with American federalism is useful to gain perspective in regard to a country (Spain) highly influenced by Jacobin ideas during most of the nineteenth and twentieth centuries.

Jacobin supporters of the French Revolution proclaimed their proposals of universal rights for all human beings. As Safran argues: 'In their efforts at promoting universal justice, progress, reason, democracy, and equality, the Jacobins saw an irreconcilable conflict between the rights of the individual – viewed as a socially autonomous unit – and the traditional rights of social groups or collectivities' (Safran, 1987: p. 2).

Nevertheless, Jacobin ideas took shape in the nation-state, which was defined in rational but non-historical terms. The nation-state was, therefore, the institutional result of citizens' daily communion. According to Ernest Renan, the prerequisite for constituting a people's community was the common desire to do things together and to achieve common glories (*Qu'est-ce qu'une nation?*, 1947). Revolutionary France was to represent the quintessential expression of Jacobin ideas, with nation-building developed according to a hierarchical, Parisian-centred and unitary mould. This political approach towards regimented centralization was not new in French history. In contrast with the Spanish case, the historian Américo Castro pointed out that since the eleventh century the aim of French ruling classes was none other than the establishment of a united nation (*grande nation*) under the uncontested and central royal authority, and which would integrate what civilization and language had already been conquering ... Arts and public life followed strict norms. One day rationalism decided that heads were to be decapitated, beginning with that of the King, and so it was done. Later, the geographical division, the education, the habits and even the manners were uniformed. French history, in its essential features, has been drawn with a compass and a ruler.

(Castro, 1984: pp. 24–5)

The ideas of the French Jacobins had a great influence on their Spanish followers during the nineteenth century (Hyslop, 1950). The main reason for the relative failure of the Jacobin programme in Spain was the absence among the Spanish liberal elites of a political rationality similar to that of the French. Furthermore, French Jacobins succeeded in making equivalent the concepts of reason and homogeneity – a relationship difficult to establish in Spain due to the marked heterogeneity of its peoples. Indeed, territorial disparities were also present in revolutionary France, and centralizing Jacobins eliminated alternative views such as those of other revolutionaries (e.g. the Girondins). As a result of Jacobinism, the nation-state came to be composed exclusively of individuals and not of ethnoterritorial communities (such as Alsatian, Breton, Catalan, Corsican, Gaul, Occitanian or Basque). By eliminating the intermediate territorial instance in France, the Jacobins contributed paradoxically to the *étatisation* of politics and the growing precariousness of individual liberties. A movement that had developed proclaiming the defence of the 'universal human being' ended with a glorification of the state.[27]

By contrast, the American revolutionaries were in the main committed federalists. They were in favour of a territorial division of governmental functions and powers:

In the compound republic of America, the power surrendered by the people is first divided between two distinct governments, and then the portion allotted to each subdivided among distinct and separate departments. Hence a double security arises to the rights of the people. The different governments will control each other, at the same time that each will be controlled by itself.

(Madison, 1788, *The Federalist Papers*, 1961[28])

Alexis de Tocqueville praised the achievements and qualities of the US system of government in his seminal *The Democracy in America* (1954). He considered optimal the distribution of competencies between central and intermediate layers of governments. At this point it is important to underline that the institutional translation of federalism is not aseptic or neutral. Already in the early stages of the American Revolution two divergent approaches confronted each other in relation to the degree of decentralization to be implemented for the consolidation of a legitimate and effective system of government.[29]

A substantial element of the federalist philosophy is revealed in its own etymological origin. The Latin word *foedus* means pact or agreement. This idea of covenant providing the basis for the federal government is its fundamental characteristic. In contrast with the ideas of Jean-Jacques Rosseau, Pierre-Joseph Proudhon based his notion of the social contract on the agreement between individuals. Contracts were to range from the most elementary social spheres to the general social order of a country as a whole. Laws, according to Proudhon, ought to be substituted by contracts. In other words, the abstract general should be replaced by a concrete will reflected in agreements among citizens.

The federalist ideas of Francisco Pi i Margall (1824–1901) can be regarded as the most elaborate and original of Spain's modern political history. Like Proudhon, Pi i Margall maintained that the main goal of federalism was not the disappearance of the parties involved in a pact but its continuing existence following a mutual agreement. This antonymical dialectic was at odds with the Hegelian monism, by which both affirmation (thesis) and negation (antithesis) were to disappear into an emergent synthesis. In this way Pi i Margall's idea of consent was to complement, or even to replace, that of hierarchical power. For him, federal organizations were the most sophisticated political expression of political contracts. These were based on the free will of the parties involved and thus, 'they cannot be dissolved by a unilateral decision. By mutual consent were established and only by mutual dissent can be undone, once they are unable to achieve the goals for which they were agreed upon' (Pi i Margall, 1911: p. 196).

For Valentí Almirall (1841–1904), as well as for Pi i Margall, federalism was intimately related to the notion of autonomy (Trías Vejarano, 1975). A federal system, according to him, allows the diverse autonomous territories to come together and to render to a federal (central) government those common functions that respond to a common interest. Spanish Krausistas[30] advocated an organic federalism according to an understanding of society as a social compound. Using a biological instance, however, organic federalism finds difficulties in dealing with the 'subordination' of parts of the politic body to one core, or in establishing which functions are to be considered bilateral or multilateral.

Discussions on the duality of the federal system of government have been approached by the diverse versions of federalism. _Dual federalism_ conforms with the idea of _dual sovereignty_ (federal government and federated states) formulated by Hamilton and Tocqueville. Difficulties arise because such a notion assumes a 'legal fiction' by proclaiming the establishment of two 'sovereignties' that can encourage territorial state power relations. Besides, in the contemporary world it is extraordinarily difficult to set exact boundaries between the competencies of the federal and federated layers of government, or even to preserve exclusive contexts for governmental action at each territorial level. In this respect, the debate of the so-called 'implicit powers' and the principle of subsidiarity have come to the fore of the political discussions in the process of Europeanization (see Chapter 4, p. 147).

Co-operative federalism, the second main variant of the applied federal theory, puts forward the idea that relations between central and meso levels of government should be based on collaboration.[31] Such practices are viewed as providing an antidote to the changing political colours of both federal and federated administrations, and as the best means for maximizing administrative interdependence. However, co-operative practices are best suited to countries with a policy culture of mutual trust and/or with a low degree of internal ethnoterritorial heterogeneity (e.g. Germany and its _Bundestreue_, or the case of the United States' 'melting pot'). [32]

There are other variants of federalism such as _creative federalism_,[33] _new federalism_,[34] _executive federalism_,[35] or _nominal federalism_.[36] They differ basically in their leanings towards a greater political emphasis for the central–federal or the mesofederated levels of action. In recent times the notion of intergovernmental relations has sought to combine different federalist approaches by underlying the contingency of policy-making in the three-tier systems of governments. Such processes often required multilateral agreement and concerted 'situational logic' to optimize the public provision of goods and services.

Intergovernmental relations based on democratically elected representatives of central, meso and local layers of government aim at making effective the principle of accountability – a basic pillar in the current process of Europeanization. Some countries, like Britain and France, have a tradition of hierarchical policy centralization that is at odds with democratic intergovernmental relations. The proliferation of 'quangos',[37] and of non-elected public bodies, or the concentration of power on an elitist class of public officials (*enarches*),[38] makes the operationalization of the principle of democratic accountability very difficult. Not surprisingly, bureaucratic and political practices based on meritocratic excellence and hierarchy are increasingly seen as being responsible for the encroachment of the so-called 'democratic deficit' in European political life.

Federalism can be viewed both in its political and in its societal dimensions. As for the latter, asymmetries are of the foremost importance in countries such as Spain. In fact, all societies are asymmetrical to a certain degree. However, analyses and prescriptions of asymmetrical federalism were first formulated according to the dictum of American functionalists. These considered 'undesirable' and 'inharmonious' a plurality that could be conducive to dispersion. Accordingly, diversity needed further centralization if federal systems were to become fully operational (Tarlton, 1965).[39]

All things considered, federalism enshrines differences and underlines the meaning of diversity.[40] It is certainly not a mechanism for 'disguising' internal oppositions, although it can be instrumental in such a purpose. Attempts to implement constitutional reforms, nominally federal, which seek to even out internal asymmetries have sometimes been attempted on behalf of the federal principle. The distinction between *de jure* and *de facto* asymmetrical federalism is crucial at this point. Lawyers and experts on constitutional law have concentrated on *de jure* interpretations and legal normative analyses. Political scientists and sociologists have tended to focus instead on *de facto* differences. A reasonable combination of the two is needed in order to gain a true perspective.

Elements that can be measured allow for comparative analyses to be grounded on the basis of patterned inference. These exercises of quantifiable contrasts in turn facilitate the formulation of plausible generalizations. But social reality cannot be constrained within digits and numbers set by the social scientist. In our field of study, for instance, the degree of autonomy or shared rule cannot be reduced to fixed quantities of *de jure* arrangements. In fact, federalism tries to capture an apparent contradiction between unity and diversity, which requires considerable flexibility in the understanding of the social phenomena under observation.

California, for example, elects two members to the US Senate – the same number as Wyoming. The populations of both states show the widest disparity (31 million and 0.5 million inhabitants, respectively). In India a similar situation exists in the case of Uttar Pradesh (110 million) and Sikkim (0.5 million). However, and despite their equal senatorial representation, the more important political 'weight' of the former territories when compared with the latter is undeniable. The underrepresentation of the most populated federated units in the US and Indian territorial chambers indicates not only a *de facto* asymmetry but also a *de jure* symmetry. Dialectics between *de jure* and *de facto* become a crucial area of study with such plurinational federations as Belgium, Canada, Malaysia or Russia.[41]

In the case of plural Spain, *de jure* and *de facto* asymmetries happen together with a combination of the two in various degrees and manners (see Chapter 4, p. 127). The 1978 Spanish Constitution established a major asymmetry in distinguishing 'nationalities' from 'regions'. With the passing of time early disparities in terms of number and amount of devolved powers have been equalized among all 17 *Comunidades Autónomas*. However, as levels of asymmetry have been closely related to the exercise of the principle of autonomy, no automatic disappearance of asymmetries can be expected. By the same token, nothing prevents asymmetries from being internally accommodated in Spain as a result of the aspirations and expectations of nationalities and regions.

Indeed, Spain offers an example of a federal-like country incorporating a considerable degree of internal diversity. The construction of the *Estado de las Autonomías* has engaged in the vast task of overcoming secular domestic differences by means of political negotiation and tolerance. Spain is clearly a country with a federal texture. The bases for such a statement are rooted in the characteristics of its historical development, which we shall discuss in the next chapter.

NOTES

1. This quotation corresponds to the article, 'A Nation is a Nation, is a State, is an Ethnic Group ...', first published in *Ethnic and Racial Studies* (October 1978), pp. 377–400, and later included in Connor (1994, pp. 111–12).
2. In the elitist-dominated society, the power deployed by the political institutions seeks to perpetuate the privileges of the elite (Hunter, 1953). As a sub-variant of this approach, Marxism regards power to be objectively structured to favour the interest of the capitalist/dominant class. For neo-Marxist views on power, see Poulantzas (1973) and Miliband (1973). For the pluralist view, see Dahl (1957, 1968).
3. In a more general sense, a political system (*politischer Verband*) is an organization that is structured in a hierarchical manner aiming at maintaining civic order in a defined territorial context (Weber, 1947; Bendix, 1962, 1964).
4. Arguably, a purely economic model can explain the development of the

railway in Victorian Britain with a meaningful ethnocentrist capitalist criteria (Cohn, 1982).
5. The case of modern Ireland has been cited as the prototype for the discussion of internal colonial developments. The origins of the Irish cultural division of labour were to be found in the Cromwellian Settlement of 1642 – a strategy which was a precursor of apartheid (Hechter, 1975, 1983).
6. Using the terminology coined by Albert Hirschmann (1970).
7. For William Safran, one of the prominent characteristics of American social science in general, and the behaviouralist–functionalist school of political science in particular, is its ahistoricist bias. History is rejected on two grounds: 'First ... as a succession of events that ... do not lend themselves to comparison and generalisation ... Second ... because it is associated with pre-modern (primitive) societies' (1987: p. 13). 'Mainstream' Marxists have traditionally taken a functional approach to the analysis of political integration and modernization (Connor, 1984).
8. Arguably, the fact that two identities can be referred to a larger entity does not preclude the possible incompatibility of their relationship (Pérez Agote, 1994). That would be the case, for example, of both Basque and Spanish exclusive forms of citizens' self-identification. However, the subsuming of those identities under the European confines implies a nexus – even though it is not explicitly sought – of congruence between both exclusive forms of self-identification.
9. The distinction between the 'territorial' and 'non-territorial' approaches to the study of ethnic political movements is somewhat analogous to that between *jus soli* and *jus sanguinis* in international public law.
10. This is underlined by the approach of cultural pluralists regarding the differentiation and structuring of the diverse ethnic communities living together in plural polities. Such a school of thought has subsequently evolved into the theses of multiculturalism (Glazer, 1997).
11. Robert Dahl's position is in line with the views of Ernest Barker who also regarded political secessionism and authoritarianism as the two viable options in pluriethnic polyarchies.
12. For Will Kymlicka ethnoterritorial accommodation would not constitute a stable political solution but a preliminary step to secession. Later on, he qualified his position, and it would be a misrepresentation to characterize him as being pessimistic about the viability of multinational federations (1998). Juan Linz's view is that federalism can consolidate liberal democracy in multinational states (1997).
13. It can also affect two or more neighbouring states, as the Basque or Kurdish cases illustrate.
14. As recognized in the 1978 Constitution. In general, it is not easy to distinguish conceptually the term 'nationality' from that of 'nation'. Such a terminological distinction was to a great extent a consequence of the dichotomy between 'nation-state' and 'state of the nationalities' as regards the cases of the Austro-Hungarian and Ottoman empires at the beginning of the twentieth century. In broad terms, nationality can be referred to as a minority nation which has acceded to a degree of institutional autonomy or independence within a multinational state and which concurs or coexists with a majority nation and/or other ethnoterritorial groups (Krejcí and Velímsky, 1981).
15. In Europe, examples of ethnoregionalism are also provided by the northeast

of England or Brussels, whereas Bavaria or Occitania could be included in the group of minority nations. As part of a more polemical proposition, territories such as Sicily, Sardinia or Corsica can be also included in this latter group, although in the past they did not exercise formal political independence or autonomy owing to their continuous domination by foreign powers. In any case, the changing nature of such external political domination (Arabic, Viking, Catalan–Aragonese, Spanish, French, Vatican, Italian) has fostered pre-union elements of territorial identification.

16. This classification could be further enlarged and subdivided. For instance, the influential school of Austro-Marxism developed historical, psychological and sociological analyses on the 'national question' (Bottomore, 1978). Austro-Marxists such as Max Adler, Otto Bauer, Rudolf Hilferding and Karl Renner, whom Lenin and Stalin fiercely opposed, do not fit adequately in any of the theories reproduced in Figure 1.2.

17. Giambattista Vico (1668–1744) systematically developed this 'organicist' doctrine and challenged the existence of a timeless natural law, in particular concerning social phenomena.

18. According to Friedrich Meinecke (1970), Germany exemplifies the 'cultural nation' in contrast with France, 'political nation' *par excellence*.

19. Johann Gottfried Herder (1744–1803) has been the most influential *organicist* thinker. Spurious use of his ideas led some authors to establish links between his ideas and the unfolding of aggressive nationalisms in France (Joseph de Maistre, Charles Maurras) and Nazi Germany.

20. Let us remember that advocates of the 'liberation' of Germany in the early nineteenth century, as well as those subsequent Slavic, Czech and Polish nationalists, claimed that their nations ought to be constitutional democracies. Wilhem von Humboldt (1767–1835), for example, fought against Bonapartist occupation while being a fervent political liberal.

21. The term 'perennialist' is used by Anthony Smith as an intermediate category between 'primordialist' and 'modernist'.

22. It has often been observed that Marxism and nationalism are 'incompatible' ideologies. This view has proved to be far from correct, as evidence of Marxist regimes during the twentieth century have shown (Connor, 1984).

23. For Joseph Stalin (1975), nations are to be based on a common language, a territory, and an economy and psychology expressed through a common culture. Accordingly, the Soviet dictator thought that Norwegians and Danes did not constitute a nation because although they had a common language the other requirements were not met.

24. In Germany, special constitutional charters protect ethnic minorities in the *Länder* of their residence (30,000 Danish, 12,000 Frisians and 65,000 Swabians). Let us bear in mind that Germany's population is about 80 million inhabitants. There are no 'special' provisions for immigrants, two million of whom are Turks and one million of Slavic origin.

25. A 'union' allows the constituent entities of a compound polity (*regioni*) to preserve their respective integrities primarily through the common organs of the general government rather than through dual government structures (Elazar, 1991: p. xvi). Given the dynamic nature of federal arrangements, the transformation of a union into a federal-like system of government can be achieved without major constitutional change.

26. With the disappearance of the Soviet Union and Yugoslavia the figures cited

should be revised. However, Russia maintained its political organization as a federation. Other countries, such as Belgium, Spain or South Africa, have joined both sub-categories as federations or federal-like countries.

27. Besides, Bonapartist cultural imperialism tried to instrumentalize French revolutionary values. It aimed to impose such values by force all over Europe, 'just as the heirs of Lenin were later to promote Russian imperialism in the guise of world revolution' (Safran, 1987: p. 3).

28. *The Federalist Papers* (1961) were written by Alexander Hamilton, James Madison and John Jay. Under the pseudonym of 'Publius', the three authors prepared 85 articles, which together with the Declaration of Independence, the Constitution and the Bill of Rights are considered to provide the political foundations of the United States of America. The *Anti-Federalists* (1967) argued that the American Constitution would lead to a 'consolidated system' of government which would destroy republican government and individual liberty as well as the independence of the states.

29. Such a dichotomy was reflected in Thomas Jefferson's ideas in favour of a primacy of the rights of the federated states and a deeper degree of decentralization, as opposed to the view of Alexander Hamilton, who advocated a more centralizing federalism that could foster the national economy. Decades later such political positions clashed on the battlefield during the American Civil War (1861–65).

30. Krausistas were followers of the ideas of the German philosopher Karl Christian Krause, who advocated a programme of 'harmonic rationalism' for the beneficial coexistence of social and economic classes, and as an alternative to traditional conservatism, *laissez-faire*, Catholic corporativism and revolutionary collectivism. They also claimed the strengthening of intermediate social 'mufflings' between the individuals and the central state.

31. Ivo Duchacek (1970) has pointed out that, in general terms, federal experiences have proved to be more fruitful in countries with political cultures grounded on values of pact, negotiation and tolerance.

32. Let us remember that the great American ethnic diversity is mainly non-territorial. Most ethnic conflicts are expressed in functional terms similar to the competition among 'interest groups' (Glazer and Moynihan, 1963). At the end of the 1960s, however, Stokely Carmichael (Kwame Ture) and Malcolm X (El-Hajj Malik El-Shabazz) pondered the creation of an independent state for Afro-Americans in the 'Southern Black Belt' where there is a higher territorial concentration for members of this ethnic group.

33. Developed under the auspices of the Johnson federal administration (1963–68). It aimed at a more fluid relationship between federal and local levels, without the necessary participation of the states of the union as 'go-between' intermediaries. 'Great Society' programmes sought to encourage civil society organizations to provide goods and services.

34. Formulated as a reaction to *creative federalism* and the so-called 'Big Government'. It has advocated a realignment of powers in favour of the federated states. The term was first coined by the Nixon administration in 1969. The Reagan administrations (1980–88) gave it an impulse in an attempt to 'devolve' functions to both states and individuals and to reduce federal public expenditure.

35. Which seeks to transfer administrative and executive responsibilities to each corresponding level of legislation. Australia offers an example of how

federated states and territories can provide the main bulk of public services (Galligan, 1995).

36. Where there is an implicit subordination of the federated units to the central–federal political decision-making. This is the case of some federal Latin American countries.

37. A 'quango', or 'quasi-nongovernmental organization', is generally created and appointed by the government. It can also refer to private-sector bodies carrying out functions for government. In 1984 the Thatcher government calculated that there were 1,680 such bodies and aimed – with no apparent success – at introducing a minimal public control of their finances (*Financial Times*, 19 October 1984).

38. Or graduates of the prestigious National School of Administration (École National d'Administration, ENA). By extension, *enarchie* refers to those trainees in the *grandes écoles*, particularly the ENA, the École Polytechnique and the École Normale Supérieure. Politicians such as Jacques Chirac, Alain Juppé, Laurent Fabius and Lionel Jospin are *énarques*. Most significantly, prominent officials of the *énarchie* have provided France with intellectual and political leadership. Their code of conduct has traditionally been based on a high level of excellence in public service and decision-making taken 'behind closed doors'. However, the elitism and arrogance of the *énarchie* is increasingly resented (Safran, 1998: pp. 267–9).

39. The 'societal approach' put forward by W.S. Livingston (1952, 1956) was to have a considerable influence on later federalist studies, Tarlton's included. He emphasized social diversity in contrast with what he considered an obsessive 'legalistic' approach towards asymmetries.

40. In this respect it can be said that federalism makes possible the institutionalization of the diversity (Burgess, 1993).

41. Asymmetries of a diverse nature are also referred to as intergovernmental processes, powers to constitutional reform, implementation of fundamental rights and liberties, statutory provisions of sub-state units (Watts, 1994; Fossas and Requejo, 1999; Máiz, 2000).

2

The Development of the Spanish National State

Both the grandeur and the *misère* of Spain, its readily recognizable tragic dimension and the equally identifiable tawdriness of much of its traditional social life owe much to the tensions bred by centre and periphery in its own soil.

(Salvador Giner)[1]

Spain is a compound national state that incorporates various degrees of internal ethnoterritorial plurality, including minority nations and regions. Given the fact that its modern political unification took place by means of a dynastic union under the Catholic Kings in 1469,[2] rather than as a consequence of a unitary process of territorial association, its constituent territories (crowns, kingdoms, principalities, dominions) maintained their existence. Besides, the incorporation of such territories into the Hispanic monarchy was achieved at an early stage of the European Modern Age, centuries before the processes of national homogenization carried out by other European monarchies.

In this chapter, historical events, myths and beliefs related to both plural composition and ethnoterritorial processes in Spanish history are analysed. I have selected those historical elements that I consider relevant for the understanding of state-formation and nation-building in Spain. The examination of such developments is necessary in order to gain perspective for the subsequent discussion on the nature of internal Spanish territorial politics. Historical interpretations form the bases upon which the normative analysis of the federalization of the Spanish *Estado de las Autonomías* is put forward subsequently.

The way in which ideologies and political actions manifest themselves in contemporary Spain are strongly forged by the forces of history. For a country which in 1492 was to become the first modern state in Europe, historical interpretations remain central reference points in its secular co-ordinates of conflict and co-operation. The analysis of events which have influenced the processes of state-formation and nation-building in Spain becomes thus indispensable in any prescriptive exercise concerning the future of its territorial political organization and its potential federal development.

The main criterion adopted in this chapter for the historical analysis is, therefore, its concomitance with the ethnoterritorial composition of Spain, which is carried out from a sociopolitical perspective. Other aspects, such as class conflicts, give way to those of an ethnic and territorial nature. This should not be understood as neglecting the functional dimension of society as vital in all aspects of human organization. However, the lesser attention paid to the elements of ethnicity and territory has often made it difficult to understand Spanish politics. In this book a special emphasis is therefore laid on ethnoterritorial peculiarities.

The review of the historical events which I have selected reflects my own interpretative approach. Exhaustive and detailed accounts of facts are avoided; thus we have a somewhat impressionistic picture of a complex social reality.

DYNASTIC UNION, THE *FUEROS*, AND THE HOMOGENIZATION OF THE BOURBONS

After the annihilation of the last Iberian stronghold in Spain (Numancia, 133 BC), the Roman presence in Hispania lasted for five and a half centuries. Both from the 'general' and the 'particular'[3] historical views of Spain, the autochthonous features of the peoples living in the Iberian peninsula remained latent despite the domination of the Romans. However, during this period political unity was moulded by the action of this external force.[4]

The barbarian invasions opened up a new process of political unification, strengthened by the occupying Visigoths from AD 540 onwards. This process only began to unfold towards the end of the occupation. Although Visigoth rule was crumbling, King Chindasvinto (r. 642–9) and his son Recesvinto (r. 649–72) were able to codify the Visigothic laws in the *Liber iudiciorum* or *Lex Wisigothorum*, which became applicable to the whole of the peninsular territory. For the second time in Hispanic history, and owing to the political action of a foreign lineage, a political bonding of the Iberian peoples was forged, enabling them to live under the same god, king and common laws. However, according to the historian Américo Castro, 'Visigothic life established nothing of an incontestably Spanish character'.[5]

For most of the eight centuries of the *Reconquista*,[6] certain parts of the peninsula acquired distinct forms of social organization. Some had diffuse political origins and, at the same time, themselves became the origins of the entities that evolved into a number of today's regions and nationalities. They shared a common mission, as Christians, to defeat the Moors,[7] to which end they established and dissolved numerous alliances. However, it was not only a struggle between Muslims and Christians. There were numerous treaties, interchanges, intrigues and, even cases of 'good neighbourliness'.

Throughout the medieval period, and parallel to the tendency towards warring and expansionism, the habit of making pacts with and respecting the rights of the defeated, whose cultural and technical knowledge was generally superior to that of the victors, was consolidated. Thus, with the growth of the Christian kingdoms, the 'reconquered' communities (Mozarab, Mudejar[8] and Jewish) obtained statutes or *fueros* that protected the integrity of their customs and ways of life. In this manner, in a country which was then a fertile mix of civilization for the Christian, Muslim and Jewish civilizations, the future significance of pacts as structural precursors of modern Spain was established. In general, social relations in medieval Spain were run by a complex web of statutory privileges that contributed indirectly to the consolidation of the very character of each of the territories and communities subject to the pacts.

In the period between the seventh and twelfth centuries, geography was a decisive factor in the political disaggregation[9] of the *Reconquista*. In Christian Spain, a number of kingdoms claimed to be the political heirs of Visigothic Spain, but their actions resulted in the constitution of peninsular 'sub-kingdoms', such as those of Asturias (739), Leon (866), Navarre (905), Aragon (1035), Castile (1037) and Galicia (1065), or that of Portugal in 1139.[10] For its part, Moorish Spain suffered the breakdown of the *taifa* kingdoms,[11] resulting in an intensification of both alliances and confrontations between Christians and Muslims.

During the Middle Ages,[12] a dichotomy between particularism and universalism gradually took root in Spain. On the one hand, the historical dynamic that generated autonomous kingdoms and territories strengthened the attachment to developing autochthonous customs and cultural traits. On the other hand, the crusading spirit against the common Muslim adversary, and, fundamentally, the unity of the Christian faith, ensured a high degree of mutual understanding and the useful 'recollection' of Roman Hispania and Visigothic Spain. Thus, two essential features characterized the political aggregation of the various territories of the Iberian peninsula during the Middle Ages: (1) the practice of pact-making, which aimed to universalize; and (2) the *fueros*, which tended to particularize.

The constitution of the Crown of Aragon better represented the will to integrate. In 1137, the Count of Barcelona, Ramon Berenguer IV, established, in the style of a confederation, the political unity of the Catalan counties and the kingdom of Aragon. Later, James I, 'the Conqueror' (1214–76), occupied the lands of Valencia and the Balearic Islands (1229–39). The Catalan–Aragonese king ceded the kingdom of Murcia to the Castilian king, Alphonse X, 'the Sage' (1252–84), putting an end to the peninsular expansion of the Catalan–Aragonese confederation, which turned its attention to the Mediterranean openings.[13]

The lands belonging to the Crown of Aragon led and guided by Catalonia and its capital, Barcelona, had fully self-governing institutions and experienced enormous economic growth during the thirteenth and fourteenth centuries. The dominions of the Mediterranean Catalan–Aragonese area of influence stretched to the French Languedoc and Provence, and further to Naples, southern Italy and Sicily, Athens, Neopatria and numerous enclaves.

At the same time, the ambition of the Castilian princes, through conquests and royal marriages, brought about the unification of Leon and Castile (1230), as well as the incorporation of the Basque provinces of Guipuzcoa (1200), Alava (1332) and Biscay (1379).[14] The *Compromiso de Caspe* took place in 1412, in which representatives of the Catalan, Aragonese and Valencian parliaments agreed to elect Ferdinand I of Antequera (r. 1412–16) as heir to the Crown of Aragon. This event was to become the origin of the marriage between Ferdinand of Aragon, grandson of Ferdinand I, and Isabella of Castile, in 1469. In 1436, and after a lengthy dispute with the Kingdom of Portugal, Castile obtained the recognition of its sovereignty over the Canary Islands from Pope Eugene IV.[15]

In 1479, the pacification of the Catalan *Remençes* by the future Catholic King Ferdinand of Aragon revitalized the pactist practices within the Catalan–Aragonese confederation. Such a course of action deviated from the model of patrimonial monarchy characteristic of the Renaissance in Europe, and which was later to be deployed by the first Habsburg king, Charles I.[16]

The highest point of the Reconquista was reached during the reign of the Catholic monarchs Ferdinand and Isabella, with the conquest of the Kingdom of Granada in 1492.[17] In 1515 Ferdinand, who beyond the Iberian peninsula was known as 'the King of Spain', added the Kingdom of Navarre to his crown. Thus the territorial unification of the various Spanish communities was consummated.[18] Nevertheless, the majority preserved their political organization and, in particular, their *fueros* which acted as vehicles for political relations with the monarchy, and formed the basis of the idiosyncratic make-up of the modern Spanish state. The *fueros* originated in legal statutes awarded to towns or cities by monarchs as rewards for services rendered in the struggles against the Muslims. They were codes that dictated the norms pertaining to the administrative, civil, penal and political life of the cities and territories under their jurisdiction. These minor constitutions were generally written by representatives of the communities involved, who, before presenting them to the monarch, would take care to include the protection of their practices and customs – to wit, their 'rights'.[19]

Larger territories, such as the feudal estate of Guipuzcoa in 1200, or the Kingdom of Navarre in 1234, would demand that the king accept their *fueros*. This custom, followed also by the Aragonese, the Catalans, the Castilians, the Portuguese and the Valencians, became a general norm of government between the monarch and his various subjects. A doubtful centralizing policy for royalty that imposed legislation limiting regional particularity and founded on Roman law was often violently rejected by the affected territories.[20]

By the turn of the Modern Age (1581), having become the Portuguese monarch, Philip II knelt and swore to maintain the *fueros*, privileges, practices, customs and rights which previous monarchs in Portugal had allowed and respected.[21] However, the Andalusian lands – the last to be 'reconquered' and occupied by Castilian nobles and *hidalgos*[22] – came to be governed directly from the Crown of Castile, which ordered their social life according to Castilian laws. In spite of this, the southern territories of the peninsula, home of Andalusia, kept the distinct traits and idiosyncrasies that resulted from almost eight centuries of Muslim and Jewish presence in the region.

Despite the strong opposition of Portugal, the Kingdom of Spain became the most powerful political unit in the sixteenth century. It was feared for its expansionism and extended its influence throughout the five continents, while consolidating its own empire in Europe through a peculiar form of obedience to the King of Spain. Allegiance to the King of Spain united the discordant variety of Hispanic peoples. Moreover, the Spanish monarchy encapsulated the ideal of national honour, founded on religious unity and the unquestionable stateliness of royalty, without which wealth and national well-being were meaningless.[23]

In foreign policy, the monarchs of the House of Habsburg favoured the formula of both political unity and territorial autonomy, and in general they maintained this attitude throughout their entire dynasty. The precedents for these were the political pacts of the Catalan–Aragonese confederation, adopted also by the Austrian branch of the same dynasty.[24] 'The universalistic imperial aspirations that Spain and the House of Habsburg represented ... rested entirely on local autonomy and inclined towards federative combinations' (Hintze, 1975: p. 99).

The Habsburg formula of multilateral territorial government was eventually confounded by the more centralized and better organized European states, as well as by the secessionist tendencies of its own political units. Nevertheless, the territories of the Iberian peninsula bore no meaningful comparison with the various nations that later on made up the Austrian Empire, given that their mutual ethnic and cultural affinities, especially those relating to church and religion, had been much greater. The role of the Catholic Church was crucial in constructing a symbolic universe common to all Spaniards and beyond autochthonous differences in culture, traditions and beliefs.

The splendour of Spain in the sixteenth century was mainly the result of the conquest of the Americas. This ran parallel to the political, economic and social decline of the Mediterranean:[25] the natural course of expansion for the Crown of Aragon. Such an unfolding of events confirmed the leading role of Castile in running government affairs in the Spanish domain. However, the state-formation brought about by the last Habsburgs was highly conditioned by their ambivalent vision of Spain. Imperial development in the sixteenth and seventeenth centuries focused on affairs beyond the frontiers of the Iberian peninsula. Attempts by courtiers and royal favourites in Madrid to assimilate the peoples of Spain,[26] provoking the Catalan Reapers' Revolt[27] and the independence of Portugal (1640), reflected the absence of a clear model of territorial structuring and the difficulties of governing so vast an empire as Spain's. Ultimately, the beginning of a generalized decline, sealed by the Treaty of Westphalia,[28] made the enforced homogenization of the political and institutional diversity of the peninsular territories of Spain not only inadvisable, but also highly improbable.

Over the two centuries of imperial splendour, the process of state-formation in Spain followed a different course from those of other European countries such as France or Britain. After the Protestant Reformation, the obsession with preserving the Catholic order and the ecclesiastical authority of Rome compelled Spain to invest bigger and better efforts in a host of armed conflicts. This resulted in an inflationary economic policy that took the country to the threshold of bankruptcy. Paradoxically, villains flourished in the world's most powerful country – as the authors of the Golden Age of Spanish literature so masterfully showed.[29]

The Habsburgs did not unite Spain by homogenizing the cultures, laws and customs of its lands. For the historian Claudio Sánchez-Albornoz, this was a serious mistake that burdened the country's subsequent development. According to this view, a simpler hierarchical government, evidenced particularly in the management of overseas affairs, was associated with a 'Castilianization' of Spain. The country's courtly elites participated in the important state enterprise of colonizing the Americas, with the exception of those who represented the traditional Mediterranean communities.

The development of a powerful bureaucracy afforded the institutions of the Spanish Crown the prime requirement for the formation of a modern European state. However, the Habsburg conception of the direct relation between the Crown and the institutions representing the interests of its territories was not easily reconciled with the idea of an assimilated unitary Spain. Distinctive active languages, laws and institutions maintained their active presence in the peninsula's communities. Ultimately, a poorly co-ordinated foreign policy, and the insistence upon belligerence abroad on numerous fronts, irretrievably marred all chances of developing an articulated and balanced domestic policy.

During the eighteenth century, and aiming to reflect the French absolutist model of state monarchy, the leading figures of the Enlightenment advocated the building of a Spanish nation above and beyond the internal boundaries of kingdoms, principalities and lordly estates (Domínguez Ortiz, 1976). This process had been attempted, with different degrees of success, in other old European states: witness France's imposed 'gallicization' and Britain's 'anglicization' of most of its territory. In any case, the 'Spanish mosaic' persisted formally throughout the Old Regime (during the seventeenth and eighteenth centuries). The writer José Cadalso described such diversity in his celebrated *Cartas Marruecas* (Moroccan Letters):

> ... an Andalusian has nothing in common with a Biscayan, a Catalan is totally different from a Galician; much the same happens between the inhabitants of Valencia and Cantabria. This Peninsula, divided during so many centuries into various kingdoms, has always displayed a variety of costumes, laws, languages and currencies.
>
> (Cadalso, 1978: p. 85)

Not surprisingly, the territorial division into 31 provinces, which was set down by Floridablanca in 1789, followed the lines of the traditional distribution of lands and territories. This was also the case with the Crown of Castile whose last parliamentary session was held in 1789. The meeting was convened assembling the representatives of the Kingdom of Galicia and the province of Extremadura, and making a distinction between the delegates of the capitals of the old kingdoms of Leon, Granada, Toledo, Seville, Cordoba, Murcia and Jaen, and the remaining cities.[30]

When the Bourbon dynasty took the Spanish throne, there began a long period of mirrored responses to the political actions of the neighbouring country of France. Philip V, grandson of the French King Louis XIV, abolished the Catalan *fueros* in 1714 after the War of Succession (1700–15). The political decline of Aragon, and especially Catalonia, during the eighteenth century occurred alongside a major commercial and economic development through the Catalan access to overseas markets.

Despotismo ilustrado (enlightened despotism) stimulated the regional meritocracy and encouraged its presence in parliament in Madrid. The efficient functioning of Charles III's government (1759–88) found its tragicomic counterpoint in the ineptitude of his successor, Charles IV (1788–1808), which extended even more to the reign of Ferdinand VII (1814–33), and to the Spanish monarchs of the House of Bourbon throughout the nineteenth century. Foremost among the decisive factors that determined the political

underdevelopment and social unrest of Spain in the nineteenth
century, were the actions of the Bourbon monarchy and its
supporters: the aristocracy, the Catholic Church, the landowning
classes and the unproductive wealthy.

THE WEAKNESS OF NINETEENTH-CENTURY MODERNIZING LIBERALISM

Napoleonic Spain aimed to amalgamate monarchic despotism,
enlightened or not, with the Jacobin ideals of the French Revolution.
The popular rising of 1808 against Napoleonic occupation was
a general affair across the whole of the peninsula. With the War
of Independence,[31] Spain reaffirmed its cohesion as a national state
in an emergency situation. Paradoxically, the popular uprisings to
expel the foreign troops were led in many cases by the very advocates
of the enlightened programmes on the French policy of seeking
uniformity.

The War of Independence was an historical landmark whose
resolution, broadly speaking, would determine the peculiar processes
of nation-building and modernization in Spain, not only in the
nineteenth century, but in most of the twentieth century as well.
During the conflict with the French (1808–14), the diverse territories of
the Spanish peninsula fought separately, but united in a common aim
to free themselves from those who illegitimately occupied their land.

The co-ordination between the various regional governments
constituted a *de facto* federal-like government.[32] Politically, this was the
most significant fact to contribute to the defeat of the Napoleonic
troops. However, the liberal Constitution of Cadiz (1812) designed a
centralizing unitary state very different to other liberal models of
territorial organization. In this respect, it is worth mentioning the case
of the American Revolution, precursor of the French Revolution, and
the United States' Constitution. Despite the obvious disparity
between their historical trajectories, certain parallels can be drawn
between the American struggle for emancipation from the England of
George III, and the war in Spain for independence from Napoleonic
France. Both conflicts involved a combination of territorial diversity
and shared interests. But both countries followed subsequently
different paths in the organization of their respective states.[33]

Ironically, the ideas which governed the nation-building of liberal

Spain were no more than a transposition of the French Jacobin programme: a centralized bureaucracy, an internal market, common taxation, and judicial and cultural homogenization. These aims were held by the Spanish political elites, which lacked the administrative rationale of their French peers. For the liberals who promoted the Constitution of Cadiz and their political heirs, the provinces (formerly kingdoms, principalities, lordly regions or dominions) were territorial entities tied to a feudal past.[34] This was judged to be the source of the backwardness and apparently irreversible decline of Spain in its relations with foreign powers – a decline that would worsen with the gradual loss of Spain's colonial power.

The Spanish liberals identified with the Constitution of Cadiz advocated a centralized and unitary Spain with a higher degree of equal access for all Spaniards regardless of the institutional particularities of their territories of residence.[35] Their plans for reform were nevertheless more theoretical than practical. Besides, the pressure exerted by the powerful reactionary forces of the Old Regime considerably limited the implementation of their proposals. For instance, the 1812 Constitution accepted the declaration of Spain as a 'confessional state', but the privileges of the old classes and estates remained untouched. Both these aspects played a key role in the political evolution of the nineteenth century.

The 1812 Constitution, as well as the provisions of the Three-Year Liberal Period (1820–23), advocated a local government structure with a wide electoral base, ánd with substantial powers for municipal councils. But, in the end, its ability to distribute authority along territorial lines was enfeebled by the views of the Spanish *moderate* liberal governments, which supported the appointment rather than the election of political posts.[36] After the promulgation of the Royal Statute of 1834, anti-centralist peripheral reactions became increasingly explicit all over the peninsula.[37]

The *liberales* wanted to build the Spanish nation by applying a unifying programme in a country half-way towards bourgeois modernization.[38] They imitated the hypercentralist practices and strategies of their French counterparts, with the result that the nineteenth century did not witness political integration of the diverse Spanish polity. This was reflected in the creation of a highly ingenious provincial administration: on 30 November 1833 two decrees prepared by Javier de Burgos[39] established the province as an administrative unit. The idea was to design a uniform state administration. Although the criteria for geographical delimitation were reminiscent of the French *départements* of a clearly centralist tendency, they were notably feeble.

Many territories of Spain, particularly those with a strong historical identity and a tradition of self-government, perceived liberal centralism as unnatural and stifling. This, in turn, provoked these regions to demand the restitution of their ancient rights to autonomy. Navarre, the Basque provinces and Catalonia contested attempts at centralist reform most vehemently. The circumstances of the time ensured that the Carlists and those reactionaries who supported the *ancien régime* were able to benefit from the peripheral hostility towards parliament in Madrid.[40]

In its early stages Carlism encapsulated collective sentiments that sought the imposition of a Catholic traditionalism of a rural, integrist, Pope-fearing, monarchic and regionalist character. Carlism ('God, King and Country') broke out in 1822 through a dispute over dynastic inheritance,[41] proclaiming the supremacy of history and, in the name of a virulent anti-liberalism, fuelled by a frantic fear of secularization, rationalism and modernity. In the nineteenth century, three Carlist civil wars ripped Spain apart: 1833–40, 1846–48, and 1872–75. It was significant that the Carlist movement should triumph precisely in the rural areas of the first industrial regions in Spain: the Basque Country and Catalonia. It may well be that Carlism at that time owed its strength to a combination of the remoteness of central government and the proximity of industrial production, superimposed on the strong ethnicity of those regions.[42]

In nineteenth-century Spain, the royal court in Madrid became the distributive centre of political favours and financial perks. Government action was mainly orientated towards maintaining and gaining support. During the reign of Isabella II (1833–68), and in particular during the period of authoritarian liberalism headed by General Narváez, corruption, favouritism, intrigue and privilege flourished. Accusations from the periphery denounced the representatives of the parasitical feudal and military classes in the capital of the kingdom as responsible for the country's underdevelopment.

The liberals were incapable of consolidating either their political reforms or their 'national revolution'. This was due not only to the conflict between the forces of pre-modernity and those of the *ancien régime*, but also to their own political contradictions. Most notable among these was the individualism and party fractionalism they practised, which quite clearly contradicted the conception of Spain they claimed to embrace.

The political history of nineteenth-century Spain is riddled with conspiracies involving groups and leaders advocating, in many cases, identical concepts and forms of government. Throughout the century, a myriad of 'big shots' and opportunists came and went, hoping to take part in guiding the country and producing only convulsions, decadence and instability. Ultimately, the failure of the *Revolución Gloriosa* (the bourgeois Glorious Revolution) after the deposition of Isabella II in 1868, sealed Spain's backwardness and sociopolitical maladjustment with respect to its European neighbours.

An episode towards the end of the period heralded by the Glorious Revolution is especially relevant: the experience of the First (Federal) Republic of 1873 and the phenomenon of *cantonalismo*.[43] In general terms, the republicans were federalists. However, most of their parliamentary representatives and political leaders shared the same individualistic and intolerant attitudes as their political opponents.

After the 1873 elections, the constituent assemblies, in their first parliamentary session, solemnly ratified the Federal Republic as the form of state. The political and programmatic credibility of republicanism was tainted by the incapacity of its leading figures to reach political agreements.[44] Personal misunderstandings among leaders, and shameless ambition and vanity combined with the continuous harassment of conservatives and reactionaries, prevented the establishment of a republican and democratic 'hispanicism' (Henessy, 1962).

This chaotic climate, caused by the political weakness of parliament and the central institutions, was set against the feverish activity of those supporting a federalism from the periphery. This was the manifestation of a *cantonalismo* in a moment of considerable tension dominated by the Carlist and Cuban conflicts.[45] Personal rivalries between republican leaders, who were incapable of articulating the demands of their provincial supporters, were the prelude to the unilateral *cantonalista* demands for home rule – an untimely attempt to form a 'bottom–up' Spanish federation.

The *cantonalista* experience caused alarm because of its centrifugal character and its potential for creating uncertainty. Again, force was used: the military coup of Generals Pavía and Martínez Campos 'simplified' the political situation and forced the restoration of the Bourbon monarchy with Alfonso XII (1874–85).

The governing bodies that led the country from 1808 onwards and the most radical federalist movements were not manifestations of territorial disintegration but rather attempts to constitute a laterally vertebrated Spain, away from an inefficient centralized and hierarchical system. With the exception of some political theorists and activists (such as Pi i Margall), the *doctrinarismo arbitrista* (arbitrist doctrinarianism) deployed by most of the politicians during the nineteenth century was the manifestation of a lack of originality and impotence in the institutional construction of a plural Spain. Indeed, the processes of unification in Germany and Italy, together with the colonial achievements of unitary states such as France and the United Kingdom, confounded the political leaders of a decadent Spain who were also facing growing tensions. The history of Spain seemed to deviate from the path taken by the leading European nations.

All things considered, the nation-building and political modernization that took place in Spain during the nineteenth century achieved some of the intended goals. Formal education extended throughout the country, as did the use of the Spanish language (Castilian). The internal market also consolidated, together with a centralized bureaucracy, a homogenization of the juridical life and the accomplishment of a national network of communication and transport.[46] The 'romantic historiography' also had an important input in the nationalization of Spanish life, as happened in other European countries. The reinterpretation of historical events, viewed from the perspective of Spain as a whole, was often aimed at playing down internal differences and supporting the idea of a single, unified nation-state, as opposed to a mosaic of peoples and territories.[47] However, the problems for the internal territorial accommodation would remain for years to come. If the struggle against centralism can be considered as the single most constant factor in Spain during the nineteenth century, the territorial malintegration of its constituent territories would continue to be an unresolved problem for most of the twentieth century.

THE INCONGRUITIES OF CENTRE AND PERIPHERY IN POST-COLONIAL SPAIN

With the Restoration of the monarchy between 1876 and 1923 and the centralizing dictatorship of Primo de Rivera (1923–30) which followed, a new statist and nationalistic attempt to impose a uniformity on the country reared its head, but ended in failure. Ultimately, the reigns of Alphonse XII and XIII expressed not only a contradiction between monarchy and democracy but also between unity and plurality.

During the 'peaceful' period of the Restoration two main dynastic parties, conservative and liberal, shared in turn the responsibilities of government. The architect of parliamentary procedure was Cánovas del Castillo (1828–97), who used the Westminster system as a model of reference. The Restoration regime, nevertheless, was far from being a formal democracy. In practice, it was immersed in the generalized clientelism of the local political chiefs[48] of the two parties (*caciquismo*) and widespread institutional corruption. The regime managed to survive for a long period, but problems of modernization remained unsolved and created deep social tensions. Thus Restoration proved incapable of emulating the programmes of nationalization of the Third French Republic. Unlike the situation in some other European countries, there was no democratic and mass organization capable of inducing a constitutional change in order to limit the direct intervention of the king, to democratize the Upper House or Senate, or to control the army's growing power of veto.

An awareness of the incongruous situation which characterized the political centre of Spain (Madrid) and the peripheral economic centres of Barcelona and Bilbao is of central importance to an understanding of the country's problems of ethnoterritorial accommodation before the Second Republic (1931–39). This situation substantially contributed to the industrial periphery's inability to assimilate the 'hispanicist' values embraced by the pre-modern rural oligarchies, the conspicuous bureaucratic classes and the frustrated military hierarchies which ran the country after the so-called '*Desastre del 98*' (disaster of 1898). In this year, after the humiliating defeat in the Spanish–American War (February–December 1898), resulting in the loss of the colonies of the Philippines, Cuba and Puerto Rico, Spain abandoned its status as one of the world's colonial powers. The country plunged into a deep and widespread social depression. The long period of intellectual absorption and the movement away from the European trend towards economic modernization, which had begun in the early nineteenth century, became even more acute.

Internal tensions underlined the structural weaknesses of the unitary state model. In particular, the so-called 'Catalan problem' was, from 1898 to 1923, a constant concern of each successive government, and the real axis on which Spanish politics revolved. In the end, the champions of authoritarian Spanish nationalism welcomed the military solution (the Primo de Rivera dictatorship) to suppress demands which grew in intensity after the advent of the Second Republic.

A combination of disparity in Catalonia's social structures[49] and impoverished rural Spain was cause of the rise of *Catalanisme*[50] and Catalan nationalism. In particular, the differences between Spain's two major cities, Madrid and Barcelona, became increasingly evident. Between 1877 and 1920, the proportion of workers in Madrid working in industry over the city's total working population grew considerably (from 18.4 to 42.5 per cent), but in this respect remained behind Barcelona, with 37.1 per cent in 1877 to 54 per cent in 1920. Perhaps it was more significant that the proportion of 'unproductive' middle classes in Madrid, consisting of civil servants, members of the armed forces and domestic staff (23.6 per cent in 1877 and 15.3 per cent in 1920) was greater than that of Barcelona (5.9 per cent in 1877 and 5 per cent in 1920).[51]

The establishment of universal male suffrage in 1890 placed Catalanism squarely in the Spanish political scene. In 1901 the electoral alliance of the Centre Nacional Català and the Unió Regionalista achieved a resounding electoral success. Soon afterwards the Lliga Regionalista was created: a party which attracted considerable support from the Catalan bourgeoisie and the dynamic middle classes, putting an end to the monolithic centralism of both conservatives and liberals.[52]

In 1906 the electoral platform Solidaridat Catalana was composed of Carlists, Catalanists, Republicans, Socialists and the Lliga. It achieved great electoral success and placed Catalan demands high on the political agenda. Let us remember that in the elections of 1908 the candidates of the Solidaritat obtained in Catalonia 31 out of the contested 34 parliamentary seats (see Table 2.1). A year later came the *Semana Trágica de Barcelona* (the so-called Tragic Week). This was a popular uprising sparked off by the refusal of *reservistas*[53] to join the army in the Moroccan War. The Spanish army were highly repressive towards this spontaneous and peripheral movement, and continued to be so in the years to come.

TABLE 2.1
DISTRIBUTION OF SEATS IN THE SPANISH PARLIAMENT
(LOWER HOUSE) (1910–20)

	1910	1914	1916	1918	1919	1920
Liberals	210	119	218	154	132	111
Conservatives	107	211	108	148	192	218
Reformists	—	12	12	9	6	9
Republicans,	37	—	17	15	18	15
and socialists	—	21	1	6	6	4
Regionalists and nationalists	8	13	15	31	18	19
Jaimistas, integrists, traditionalists	11	7	10	9	7	5
Catholics, agrarians, independents and others	11	11	0	9	11	14
TOTAL	384	394	381	381	390	395

Source: Linz (1967: p. 210).

The 'Tragic Week' was the result of a combination of factors, notably an anti-war sentiment and the action of the anarchists, but also of a powerful anti-centralist sentiment on the part of the Barcelona population in general. Sections of the Catalan bourgeoisie reacted with panic to both revolutionary action and maximalist nationalism. Parallel to this, the central government reversed its earlier resistance to co-opt Catalan politicians, and moreover awarded important economic concessions to the Catalan industrial sector. As a consequence, the wide coalition of Catalanists started to crumble and began to show its inherent conservatism.[54] However, the Lliga of Cambó y Prat de la Riba accomplished an important political goal with the establishment of the Mancomunitat in 1914. This was the first Catalan governmental institution since 1714, and although its functions were merely administrative, it had an important symbolic value as its jurisdiction covered the whole territory of Catalonia. But the frustrations generated by the coup of Primo de Rivera (1921) and the subsequent dismantling of the Mancomunitat set the limits of the pragmatic strategy taken by the Lliga. Later on, other radical nationalist parties and leftist organizations (Esquerra Republicana and Estat Català) would replace the Lliga in the electoral preferences of the Catalans and would hold the political initiative after the proclamation of the Second Republic.

The Partido Nacionalista Vasco–Euzko Alderdi Jetzalea (PNV-EAJ: Basque Nationalist Party), founded by Sabino de Arana Goiri in 1895,[55] was less successful than the Catalanist Lliga in obtaining pan-class support,[56] partly because of its religious emphasis and its ethnocentric claims. Early Basque nationalism stressed traditional community values that were opposed to bourgeois industrial society, the effects of which involved a considerable influx into the Basque Country of migrants from the rest of Spain. Primitive Basque essentialism of a racist character was the ideological basis of early Basque nationalism, which combined with powerful populist elements and ethnoreligious exclusivism to produce a discourse quite distinct from that of Catalan nationalism. This latter ideology was more intellectual and less folkloric, and has always been less separatist. It may have provoked greater resistance than Basque nationalism because it offered an alternative view of Spain, something which the Basques frequently ignored. Both nationalisms, however, could be seen as political manifestations of a vigorous and prosperous periphery, which contrasted with the inept and parasitical centralism of the Spanish state to which it was subordinated.

In other Spanish territories regionalism came in different forms, in many cases stimulated by the Catalan and Basque movements. Partly as a consequence of the federal experience of the First Republic (1873), there were clamours for recognition in Galicia.[57] Later on, the ideas of Manuel Murgía and Alfredo Brañas laid the ideological foundations of contemporary *galeguismo* with a dual approach: liberal represented by the Liga Galega in Coruña, and traditionalist in the case of the Liga Galega in Santiago. In 1922 Vicente Risco was elected *conselleiro supremo* (supreme councillor) of the Irmandade Nazionalista Galega (Galician Nationalist Brotherhood).[58]

Valencian regionalism also found expression in the discourse of Faustí Barberà i Martí pronounced in 1902 in *Lo Rat Penat*.[59] In 1908 the Unió Valencianista Regional discussed a strategy for *valencianisme* between pro-Catalan and centralist options. Andalusian regionalism made itself known in 1907 during the celebration of the Floral Games in Seville. In 1915 the local leader, Blas Infante, published a doctrinal manifesto in defence of the Andalusian nation. The Ronda Congress of 1918 was the source of a movement backing Andalusian home rule which would be accommodated into a federal Spain. After the First World War, Asturias also gave birth to a regionalist movement related to the concerns of the local coal industry.[60] In 1924 the Nationalist Party of the Canary Islands was also founded.[61]

Chronologically, the appearance of explicit claims for regional autonomy in contemporary Spanish politics occurred just before and just after the beginning of the twentieth century. The main reason for the dissemination of autonomist demands in Spanish at this time lies in the poor, if not absent, legitimacy of the regime of the Restoration, and in the disparity between the official version of what Spain was, and what it really was.

During the Restoration a widespread distrust and hostility against the central government fuelled regional sentiments. While the dynastic parties (conservative and liberal) promised justice and equal opportunities for all, clientelist political bosses or rough local clientelist political bosses (*caciques*) were often their main supporters. Not only peasants, day-labourers and unskilled workers, but also members of the middle classes and significant sections of the intellectual elites had a perception of state institutions as alien, remote and brutal. Frequent recourse to brutality to repress popular demands was considered necessary by the dominant and unproductive classes of the conservative bourgeoisie so that revolution and separatism could be neutralized.

For some skilled workers and other members of the middle classes state institutions were also regarded as the main providers of political positions and stable jobs in the army and civil administration. Perceptions and sentiments towards the Spanish state could thus be both hostile and favourable, depending not only on social class but also on place of residence within Spain. As regards the latter, inhabitants of large areas of Castile and Andalusia, and even of a historical nationality such as Galicia, regarded state institutions as the main source of life opportunities and eventually adopted a strong Spanish identity. This would translate into a centralist and homogenizing understanding of Spain's social reality. As a consequence, administrative, juridical, military and political officers became increasingly hostile to the idea of Spanish plurality, something which was to have far-reaching effects in subsequent civil and political conflicts.

THE SECOND REPUBLIC, THE CIVIL WAR, AND THE FRANCO DICTATORSHIP

In spite of its short duration, the Second Republic (1931–39) made a significant contribution to the resolution of ethnoterritorial conflicts, among other achievements. The most notable improvement was the constitutional design of state as a regional model, situated somewhere between a unitary and a federal state.[62] This led to statutes of autonomy for Catalonia, the Basque Country and Galicia. However, anti-clericalism and the regional autonomy question played a fundamental part in the political polarization process before the Civil War (1936–39). The issue of regionalism versus centralism created innumerable controversies within the Republican forces themselves (see Table 2.2 for the distribution of parliamentary seats during the Second Republic). A good proportion of these had inherited the Jacobinist ideas of the nineteenth century. Ultimately, the enemies of republican democracy destroyed all chances of setting up a territorially structured state during the 1930s, and after the Civil War the country fell firmly into the hands of a deeply centralist reactionary coalition, which also had 'imperialist' pretensions. The end of the dictatorship did not occur until General Franco died in 1975.

TABLE 2.2
DISTRIBUTION OF SEATS IN THE SPANISH PARLIAMENT
(SECOND REPUBLIC)

	1931	1933	1936
Traditionalists, Fascists	4	40	22
Conservatives, Agrarian	40	164	104
Right Republicans	21	26	4
Right Radicals	70	100	4
Left Radicals	28	4	93
Left Republicans	136	9	39
Regionalists and Nationalists	63	64	58
Socialists	105	61	99
Communists	—	1	18
Others	3	5	22
TOTAL	470	474	463

Source: Linz (1967: p. 260) and author's own elaboration.

On 14 April 1931 the Spanish Second Republic was proclaimed. On the same day, the Catalan nationalist, Francesc Macià, leader of Estat Catalá, declared a Catalan Republic and the creation of an Iberian Confederation. After negotiations with a provisional republican government, the Generalitat[63] was re-established, and references to a 'Catalan state' were dropped. It was settled that Catalonia would be granted a Statute of Autonomy, approved by referendum in August of the same year and passed by the Spanish parliament the following year.[64] This development encouraged the Basque Country and Galicia to seek similar forms of self-government. By the end of the Second Republic, a good number of Spain's regions had showed an eagerness for autonomy such as had been granted to Catalonia.

Three days after the proclamation of the Second Republic, an assembly of Basque mayors gathered by José Antonio Aguirre (leader of the Basque Nationalist Party) claimed their right to autonomy within a Spanish federal republic, by the legendary Oak of Gernika. Months later, another assembly of mayors met in the city of Estella (Lizarra) and passed the proposal for a statute of autonomy, ratified also by the Navarran local councils and the Carlist representatives. Nevertheless, obtaining approval of the proposal from the Spanish parliament was more difficult than for the Catalan statute. The fact that the Basque nationalists had not participated in the San Sebastian Pact, a party-wide agreement to accept the Republican regime, and that neither socialists nor left-wing republicans had taken part in the Estella meeting, both contributed to this delay. The thorniest issue of the interparty negotiations had been the claims made by the Basque nationalists to establish an independent and bilateral relationship between Euskadi and the Catholic Church.[65]

A new statute project for the Basque Country was prepared in 1932, but rejected by the Navarran local councils. By the end of the following year, the statutory project did not include Navarre and was supported in a referendum by 47 per cent of Alavese and almost 90 per cent of Biscayans and Guipuzcoans. The proposal was put forward in the Spanish parliament in December of 1933, but two years later it had still not been passed. After the left-wing victory of the Popular Front in the February 1936 elections, the members of parliament for the Basque Country presented the proposal approved by referendum in October 1933 once more to parliament. By the beginning of the Civil War, the Parliamentary Commission had practically completed its approval. On 1 October 1936 the Basque statute of autonomy was passed, with similar rights and powers to that of Catalonia.[66]

In Galicia the Organización Regional Gallega Autónoma (ORGA: Autonomous Regional Organization of Galicia), led by Santiago Casares Quiroga, had instigated the drafting of a proposal for autonomy. It was of an openly federal character, and thus incompatible with the provisions of the Republican Constitution of 1931. A second initiative lacked the party-wide support required for most of the republican period before the Civil War. Finally, with the support of political parties within and beyond the Popular Front, widespread approval by referendum was obtained, three weeks before the coup that provoked the Civil War, on 18 July 1936.[67]

Several regions of Spain had expressed autonomist claims by the time of the military uprising. Although many of them had not yet taken the legal steps required by the 1931 Republican Constitution, a significant number had begun some part of the process (Aragon, Andalusia, Asturias, the Balearic Islands, the Canary Islands, both Castiles, Leon and Valencia). The 'home rule all round' process, though incipient, was spreading throughout Spain by the time the Civil War broke out. With the victory of General Franco's forces, a long period of political centralization ensued, aimed once again at the creation of an artificially uniform Spain.

Two of the most notable pathological fixations of the Franco dictatorship (1939–75) were anti-communism and anti-separatism. On the one hand, communism, combined with an unfounded and paranoid supposed Jewish–Masonic conspiracy, posed not only an evil threat to Imperial Spain but to Christian Western civilization as a whole. On the other hand, the 'sacred unity of the homeland' was regarded as an indispensable unifying element and *raison d'être* of Franco's despotic dictatorship. To a large extent, Francoism justified itself through its ability to suppress and extirpate all forms of autonomism, regionalism and culturally different ethnoterritorial claims.[68] Any form of federalism or wish for regional home rule was understood by the Franco regime as 'separatism'.

The Francoist conception of national unity, at the expense of the cultural and ethnic variety of the people of Spain, degenerated into an obsessive dogma which became central to the ideology of the reactionary coalition which dominated the country uninterrupted from 1939 to 1976. Catch-phrases such as 'El Imperio hacia Dios' (God's Empire), or 'España, una unidad de destino en lo universal'

(Spain, a unit of destiny in the universal) together with a simulated 'timeless' culture pertaining to the whole of Spain, were used to attempt to destroy Spanish cultural and ethnoterritorial diversity. Francoism tried to articulate a futile campaign to implement a Spanish national uniformity. In reality, and somewhat ironically, the linguistic and cultural oppression of Francoism stimulated peripheral regionalism and nationalism in Spain. This oppression consisted in the obliteration of cultural differences, the mere existence of which appeared to question the Francoist conception of Spain. Of course, these differences not only disputed this conception, but also constituted clear evidence that it was erroneous. In spite of or because of this misconception, Franco set up and attempted to enforce a programme of 'national' homogenization.

For Francoist supporters 'eternal Spain' was the ideological expression of an old and unpolluted 'Castilian spirit' with a universal language and ideals beyond the limits of time and space – a Spain, in short, which had emerged victorious and misunderstood in the midst of a turbulent era for humankind. Francoism regarded Spanish ethnoterritorial peculiarities as quaint signs of the unique Spanish 'soul'. Any deviation from this Spanish *Volkgeist* was not only illegitimate but also dangerous and punishable. Spain was, however, very different from such a view. In fact, as Giner points out, the Franco dictatorship provoked the opposite effect to such centralist state-moulding:

> Even under the most extreme totalitarian circumstances such a task (e.g. Spanish 'national' homogenization and cultural assimilation) cannot be easily accomplished. One consequence of attempts to erode communal identities and national traits can be their intensification. External threats and conflicts often lead to both external cohesion and mobilization. They may also bring classes and interest groups together which otherwise have little in common with each other or whose aims are mutually antagonistic. That is why nationalism appeals to the solidarity of the non-solidary.
>
> (Giner, 1984: p. 87)

Throughout its long political life, Francoism nonetheless failed to eliminate Spain's internal ethnoterritorial differences. In fact, it achieved exactly the opposite. The governing classes had advocated a peculiar and artificial idea of Spanish nationalism that had little to do with the historical process of state-formation and nation-building in Spain, and which made unitary centralism and dictatorship concomitant concepts. Francoism supported Spanish nationalist values based on sectarianism and exclusion, bringing about a 'de-naturalization' of ethnoterritorial relations in the country. The result of this was that by the beginning of the democratic transition in the 1970s, the very concept of anything Spanish was regarded by the democratic and progressive forces as synonymous with repression, cultural hegemonic imposition and fear of Spain's plural reality.

From the 1960s onwards, Francoism reinforced its assimilationist policies through the use of television and modern mass media. This was carried out despite the multilingual character of Spain – an incontestable fact that worked against the viability of attempting to impose one single language throughout the country.[69] A platform for popular grievances began to grow, though in different degrees. Regions that had previously shown only weak aspirations for autonomism or home rule found reasons to claim these rights by the end of the 1970s. From the Canaries to the Balearics, from Asturias to Extremadura, the regions of Spain 'discovered' regional identities and the attractions of self-government.

The autonomist boom, which reached the lands of Castile and Leon, owed much of its emergence to the nature of Francoism.[70] During the final years of its existence, the opposition to the Franco dictatorship developed a compact programme for democratic rights and for the political decentralization of the Spanish state. In the so-called 'historical nationalities' in particular (Catalonia, the Basque Country and Galicia), the forces opposed to Francoism were able to articulate a highly coherent political discourse denouncing the absence of democracy and the continuous official attacks on their identities. In these communities, democratic and ethnoterritorial vindication became analogous. Every time that Basque and Catalan opposition groups negotiated secretly in exile with other democratic forces, the demand for one thing was invariably tied to the assertion of the other. In this way the ideology of autonomism and political decentralization made its way into Spanish democratic political consciousness.

Thus Francoism provided the atmosphere necessary for today's regionalism, autonomism and nationalism, although it remains true that, strictly speaking, separatism and federalism have more ancient roots. The ability of sub-state nationalism to overcome ideological and political divisions manifested itself in cases of substantial consensus among the forces opposing the Franco regime. The most emblematic may be the Assamblea de Catalunya (Catalan Assembly), founded in 1971, and based on the notion of *pactisme* (pactism) a component of the Catalan way of life.[71] With admirable efficiency, the Catalan Assembly was capable of organizing an illegal, persecuted and heterogeneous political opposition. Its activities were based on a simple four-point programme: (1) political amnesty; (2) freedom; (3) a statute of autonomy; and (4) democracy.[72] It gathered together representatives of various political groups (Christian Democrats, Socialists, Communists), trade union leaders and representatives of local movements from Barcelona, groups of university students and teachers, as well as intellectuals and citizens in general, in a clandestine movement opposed to the Franco regime. It was highly representative of Catalan society in the 1970s. Its ability to create a democratically legitimate alternative to the Franco regime in Catalonia constituted a unique precedent for the peaceful transition to liberal democracy the whole country was later to enjoy.

In the Basque Country, the separatist guerrilla group ETA found considerable popular support, and given the oppressive political circumstances it became intertwined with the democratic movement. In 1973, ETA assassinated Admiral Carrero Blanco, Franco's prime minister and his intended political heir.[73] At that time, those who advocated political violence against the Franco dictatorship were regarded sympathetically by many sectors of the population, and not only in the Basque Country. With the advent of liberal democracy, many of these people would eventually distance themselves from ETA and its methods, and indeed the paradoxical intensification of its actions. The military nucleus of ETA continued to insist that the militants of the Basque national liberation movement were the only victims of police torturers and of the representatives of centralist oppression (Letamendía, 1994).

The disparity of Franco's regime and Spanish society led to the fracture of state institutions. Francoism was incapable of dealing with the industrialized Spain of the 1970s: by that time as highly urbanized and sociologically patterned as the rest of Western Europe. Towards the end of the Franco regime (1960s and early 1970s), the activities of some 'underground' sectors of the Justicia Democrática (the judiciary) and the Unión Militar Democrática (armed forces) reflected a lack of confidence of Francoism as the ruling ideology of the Spanish state. Also significant was the fact that sections of the Catholic Church, whose hierarchy had 'blessed' the victory of Generalísimo Franco in the National Crusade (the Civil War) and advocated National-Catholicism for the new regime, moved into new directions especially after the Second Vatican Council of 1962.

The active opposition of the workers' organizations, also from within the system, through their infiltration in the official Francoist 'vertical' trade unions, accelerated the weakness of the authoritarian state to cope with both democratic and autonomist claims. Despite this, however, it was not until Franco's death that the Spaniards realized the irrefutable fact that the regime could no longer survive without the presence of the dictator.

THE 1978 CONSTITUTION AND THE DECENTRALIZATION OF POWER

After Franco's death in 1975 the transitional process to democracy began in earnest. There was general agreement among the democratic parties that decentralization was essential. However, the specific model to be adopted was unclear. The constitutional expression of such a strong platform for home rule was a major political challenge, for Spanish modern history had witnessed tragic failures where ethnicity and the territorial sharing of power were concerned.

The broad party political consensus which made the drawing up of the 1978 Constitution possible also brought with it an element of ambiguity in the formulation of the territorial organization of the Spanish state. In fact, two different conceptions of Spain, which had traditionally confronted each other, were given expression in the document. On the one hand, there was the idea of an indivisible Spanish nation-state; while on the other was the notion of Spain as an ensemble of diverse peoples, historic nations and regions. A middle way between these two visions of Spain would thus need to be negotiated and explicitly recognized by the Constitution.

The text of the 1978 Constitution reflects many of the tensions and political dilemmas that existed in the discussion of such territorial provisions. However, it also reflects a widespread desire to reach political agreement among all the constituent political parties that were involved in the process of negotiation. An open model of decentralization was the consequent result for the territorial organization of democratic Spain.

The starting-point for the process of decentralization lay in the provisions of Title VIII of the 1978 Constitution. In the first instance, the constitutional provisions permitted any number of the *Comunidades Autónomas* to be self-governing, depending on the will expressed by either the inhabitants of each nationality or region, or their political representatives. The Constitution also made it possible for the degree of self-government to be wide or restricted, according to the wishes of each nationality and/or region:

> Title VIII [of the Constitution] allows Spain one autonomy, or three, or a few, or all, or none, according to the will expressed by the people or the representatives of a given territory, and allows that autonomy to be wide or restricted, and that different communities should have the same or different degrees of autonomy, and that they organize themselves homogeneously or heterogeneously, and for the mistakes made in the process to be rectified.
>
> (García de Añoveros, 1984)[74]

In the end, conservatives, centrists, nationalists, socialists and communists ended up hammering out an agreement for the implementation of the federalizing *Estado de las Autonomías*, which would not jeopardize the constitutional consensus on the issue of decentralization. The accepted solution took the form of an unwritten pledge to extend the procedures of political dialogue and consociationalism into the future. This open model of asymmetrical decentralization did not presuppose the ways and means by which the different spatial entities could finally be articulated. Thus, an implicit desire was expressed by the 'Fathers' of the 1978 Constitution to provide the procedures and degrees of self-government to be pursued by the nationalities and regions while allowing them a high degree of flexibility.[75] The formulation of a clear division of powers based upon 'orthodox' federal techniques was, however, avoided.

The arbitrating role of the *Tribunal Constitucional* (Constitutional Court),[76] the highest court in Spain, has been of paramount importance for the subsequent implementation of the *Estado de las Autonomías*. It has among its attributes the capacity to decide in legal conflicts between the state (central government) and the

TABLE 2.3: SPANISH GENERAL ELECTION RESULTS (CHAMBER OF DEPUTIES, 1977–2000)

	1977		1979		1982		1986		1989		1993		1996		2000	
	Popular vote (%)	MPs (no.)	Popular vote (%)	MPs (no.)	Popular vote (%)	MPs (no.)	Popular vote (%)	MPs (no.)	Popular vote (%)	MPs (no.)	Popular vote (%)	MPs (no.)	Popular vote (%)	MPs (no.)	Popular vote (%)	MPs (no.)
Socialist Party (PSOE)	29.3	118	30.4	121	48.1	202	44.1	184	39.6	176	38.8	159	37.5	141	34.1	125
Popular Party (AP/PP)	8.2	16	6.0	9	26.4	107	26.0	105	25.8	106	34.8	141	38.9	156	44.5	183
Union of Democratic Centre (UCD)	34.4	166	34.8	168	6.8	11	—	—	—	—	—	—	—	—	—	—
Democratic and Social Centre (CDS)	—	—	—	—	2.9	2	9.2	19	7.9	14	1.8	—	—	—	—	—
Communist Party/United Left (PCE/IU)	9.3	19	10.8	23	4	4	4.6	7	9.1	17	9.6	18	10.6	21	5.5	8
Convergence and Union (CiU)	2.8	11	2.7	8	3.7	12	5	18	5.1	18	4.9	17	4.6	16	4.2	15
Basque Nationalist Party (PNV)	1.6	8	1.6	7	1.9	8	1.5	6	1.3	5	1.2	5	1.3	5	1.5	7
People's Unity (HB)	—	—	1.0	3	1	2	1.2	5	1.1	4	0.9	2	0.7	2	—	—
Basque Left (EE)	0.3	1	0.5	1	0.5	1	0.5	2	0.5	2	—	—	—	—	—	—
Basques' Reunion (EA)	—	—	—	—	—	—	—	—	0.7	2	0.6	1	0.5	1	0.4	1
Republican Left of Catalonia (ERC)	0.8	1	0.7	1	0.7	1	—	—	—	—	0.8	1	0.7	1	0.8	1
Andalusian Party (PSA/PA)	—	—	1.8	5	—	—	—	—	1.0	2	—	—	—	—	0.9	—
Aragonese Party (PAR)	—	—	0.2	1	—	—	0.4	1	0.4	1	0.6	1	—	—	—	—
Valencian Union (UV)	—	—	—	—	—	—	0.3	1	0.7	2	0.5	1	0.4	1	—	—
Canary Coalition (AIC/CC)	—	—	—	—	—	—	0.3	1	0.3	1	0.9	4	0.9	4	1.1	4
National Galician Block (BNG)	—	—	—	—	—	—	—	—	—	—	—	—	0.9	2	1.3	3
Others	13.3	10	9.5	3	4.0	—	6.9	1	6.5	—	4.6	—	3.0	—	4.9*	—
TOTAL	100	350	100	350	100	350	100	350	100	350	100	350	100	350	100	350

Source: Spanish Ministerio del Interior and Junta Electoral Central.

* The Chunta Aragonesista (left-to-centre Aragonese nationalists) and Iniciativa per Catalunya-Verds (Catalan leftists and greens) obtained 0.3% (1 MP) and 0.5% (1 MP) of the votes, respectively.

(Table 2.3 continued)
PSOE: Left-to-centre Spanish Socialist Party (Socialist International).
PP: Right-to-centre Spanish Popular Party (Christian Democrat International).
UCD: Centrist coalition which disappeared after the 1982 general election.
CDS: Centrist party created in 1982 (Liberal International).
PCE/IU: Spanish Communist Party/ left coalition of PCE, radical socialists and independent leftists (European United Left).
CiU: Centre-right Catalan nationalist coalition (CDC–Liberals and UDC–Christian Democrats).
PNV: Centre-right Basque nationalist party (Christian Democrat International).
HB: Coalition of Basque secessionists and political arm of ETA.
EE: Left Basque nationalists who merged with PSE/PSOE in 1993.
EA: Centre-left Basque nationalists. Breakaway party from PNV.
PA: Centre-left Andalusian nationalist party.
PAR: Centrist Aragonese nationalists.
UV: Right-to-centre Valencian nationalists.
CC: Multiparty nationalist coalition in the Canary Islands.
ERC: Centre-left Catalan pro-independence party.
BNC: Left-to-centre coalition of nationalists.

Comunidades Autónomas, or even in conflicts among the latter. There is a need for compromise on the nomination of candidates to the *Tribunal Constitucional*. Owing to the Spanish system of proportional representation – D'Hont rule (a form of electoral proportional representation) on provincial constituencies for the election of the MPs to the Chamber of Deputies or lower house – it is highly unlikely that a single political party could ever achieve the required three-fifths of the total members of both houses of parliament (see Table 2.3 for electoral results during 1977–2000). This stipulation provides the highest court with a great deal of authority and independence. Some critics have pointed out that the role of the *Tribunal Constitucional* in solving disputes relating to governmental powers places electoral bodies in a position which is subordinate to the judiciary. Consequently, they argue, there is a risk that judges may become political and that their known political views are taken into account when they are appointed.

In Spain, the need for a pact between government and opposition in the election of the members of the *Tribunal Constitucional* has so far proved to be a barrier against open political sectarianism in the nomination of the candidates. For instance, the important judgment of the Court (5 August 1983) on the LOAPA Act ('Organic Law on the Harmonization of the Autonomy Process'), passed by the Spanish parliament, reinforced the open and federalizing interpretation of the 1978 Constitution very much against the views of centre-right UCD and centre-left PSOE governments, which in the early 1980s were highly conditioned by the turbulent political situation.

Let us remember that in the late 1970s, early Catalan and Basque moves towards self-government sparked off similar initiatives by other Spanish nationalities and regions which did not wish to be left behind. In the summer of 1981, and after the attempted military coup of 23 February 1981, both the UCD government and the main PSOE parliamentary opposition felt the need to 'harmonize' the process of decentralization along the lines of the German model of co-operative federalism. This UCD–PSOE pact sought the unilateral co-ordination of the decentralization process from the central administration – a political view which turned out to be a massive miscalculation.

When the legislative inception of the LOAPA law was attempted (1981–82), the Basque and Catalan nationalists, together with the communists and, to a much lesser extent, the conservatives, were fiercely opposed to it. Indeed, the timing and content of such harmonizing policies from the centre, when the structure of the centralist Francoist state still remained largely untouched, was inopportune and inappropriate. It is important to point out that if any type of federal-like arrangements were to succeed in the future in Spain, the gravity in the centre–periphery political relationship could not be placed exclusively in the core of the polity. This is a general consideration in a country where all non-democratic regimes had been centralist and where the economically powerful periphery had traditionally been neglected in the process of political decision-making.

In the general process of decentralization during the 1980s, the case of the southern region of Andalusia is of particular relevance. In 1982 political leaders and the population at large in Andalusia opted for the same 'fast route' procedure and degree of home rule previously pursued by the three historical nationalities of Catalonia, the Basque Country and Galicia. The result of the popular referendum[77] held in Andalusia ratified these wishes and the 'demonstration effect' sparked off a sense of ethnoterritorial concurrence for other regions in pursuit of equal access to home rule (see Chapter 3, p. 90). This development brought about a crucial element of heterogeneity that modified the model, implicitly accepted by some Catalan and Basque nationalists, of implementing home rule only in the Spanish historical nationalities while the rest of the regions would merely be granted administrative decentralization (de-concentration). Since then, nationalists in the three 'historical nationalities' have tried to establish a 'political differential' with respect to the rest of the *Comunidades Autónomas*. This attitude is reflected in the so-called 'Declaration of Barcelona'. On 16 July 1998 the Basque Partido Nacionalista Vasco, the Catalan Convergència i Unió, and the Galician Bloque Nacionalista Galego claimed the establishment of a confederal model of political accommodation in Spain and put forward the idea of 'shared sovereignty' of their nationalities within the Spanish state.

On 12 September 1998 the *Pacto de Lizarra* (Estella) (inspired by the 1998 Good Friday Agreement in Northern Ireland) was signed by the Basque nationalist parties (Partido Nacionalista Vasco–Euzko Alderdi Jetzalea, Herri Batasuna and Eusko Alkartasuna), together with the Basque branch of the Spanish coalition of United Left (IU), and 19 political and social associations in the Basque Country and Navarre. Neither of the main Spanish political parties (PP and PSOE) participated in such a forum. The main claim of the pact was to articulate a negotiation with the Spanish central institution issues of political sovereignty, territoriality and self-determination. The pact was an initiative prior to the declaration of a truce by ETA, which took place five days later. Since then political dialogue and negotiations among the Basque political forces themselves, and those with the central government, have proved to be difficult. However, timid measures such as a limited transfer of some ETA inmates to prisons near the Basque Country were accomplished. In the meantime, the results of the Basque elections held on 25 October 1998 simply reproduced a somewhat stalemate political situation. The nationalist parties (PNV-EAJ, Euskal Herritarrok[78] and EA) collected fewer votes (54.5 per cent of the popular vote for parties with elected members of the Basque parliament) than in the 1994 elections (56.3 per cent), as compared to the non-nationalists (PP, PSOE, IU and Unidad Alavesa)[79] with 44.4 and 43.3 per cent, respectively.

The ceasefire declared by the Basque terrorists in September 1998 was unilaterally revoked 14 months later. This announcement opened up a new situation of political challenges for both political parties and the citizenship at large. However, whether or not a democratic and peaceful compromise for the resolution of the conflict in the Basque Country can be achieved remains to be seen.

The construction of the *Estado de las Autonomías* had to follow a 'top–down' process of decentralization. This way of doing things is just one of the options available in the development of federal-like systems. The result at the beginning of the twenty-first century is not much more than a series of practices of a federal nature involving a series of politically concurrent units. The full development of multilateral decision-making, or a genuine common exercise of three-tier government action (at central, regional and local levels simultaneously), will require a gradual process of adjustment.

The decentralization process embodied in the 1978 Spanish Constitution has undergone a long period of consolidation, with the result that the Spanish nationalities and regions now have a considerable degree of autonomy. This is illustrated by the evolution of the distribution of public expenditure in the three-tier system of government, reproduced in Table 2.4.

TABLE 2.4
TERRITORIAL DISTRIBUTION OF PUBLIC EXPENDITURE IN SPAIN
(percentage)

	1981[1]	1984	1987	1990	1992	1997	1999[2]
Central	87.3	75.6	72.6	66.2	63.0	59.5	54
Regional	3.0	12.2	14.6	20.5	23.2	26.9	33
Local	9.7	12.1	12.8	13.3	13.8	13.6	13

[1] Beginning of the process of devolution.
[2] Government's estimates.

Source: Spanish Ministry of Public Administrations.

Support for autonomy, apart from the Basque and Catalan communities, has been particularly strong in Andalusia and other regions (the Canary Islands, Galicia and Valencia). Certainly some regions were 'encouraged' by their most prominent political parties to enter into the *autonomist* process. Some areas with no self-governing tradition whatsoever were suddenly inspired to claim home-rule rights. These were mainly uniprovincial communities lacking ethnoterritorial specificity, unless they recognized their origins elsewhere: Cantabria, La Rioja, and even the province of Madrid, for instance. For some provinces and counties the decentralization process entailed a shift away from their ethnoterritorial bases. One of the consequences of this was the creation of hybrids such as Castile–La Mancha or Castile and Leon.[80]

The cases of Navarre and the *Països Catalans*[81] exemplify the difficulties in setting clear boundaries in certain regions. For radical Basque separatists, Navarre is an integral part of their country which can never be given up. This is the claim made by both Herri Batasuna (the political branch of ETA), the Basque terrorist separatists and ETA itself. However, it is quite clear that a majority of the people of Navarre[82] believe that the old kingdom has as much right to its own constitution as a *fuero*. The Catalan countries are perceived as a whole, with a composite identity, deserving political treatment as such not only by pan-Catalanist parties, but by the usually more cautious President of the Catalan Government, Jordi Pujol, in his federalist understanding of Spain: 'In the specific case of Spain I could conceivably be a federalist, if the federation was based on genuine and authentic nationalities of the state, viz. Euskadi [Basque Country], Galicia, the whole of Castile, and the Catalan Countries (or just Catalonia, if Valencia and the Islands ... rejected being associated with the Principate)' (J. Pujol, 1980: p. 26).[83]

While for some communities autonomy meant the greatest possible degree of self-government and the narrowest possible gap between the people and power, for others it entailed a greater emphasis on support from the central administration against unemployment, underdevelopment, or outright poverty.[84] A certain dichotomy has thus arisen between the political perception of the exercise of self-government and the understanding of the concept of solidarity with the aim of achieving greater equality.

TABLE 2.5
ASSESSMENT OF THE SETTING-UP OF THE *COMUNIDADES AUTÓNOMAS*
(percentage of respondents)

	October 1994	*March 1996*
Positive	51	67
Negative	19	13
Neither positive nor negative	11	8
'Don't knows'	10	16

Source: Spanish Centro de Investigaciones Sociológicas (Opinion Data No. 5)

The socialization and internalization of values related to the territorial structuring of the *Estado de las Autonomías* has deepened as compared to the beginning of the process. In 1996 the assessment of the setting-up of the *Comunidades Autónomas* was judged 'positive' by two-thirds of Spaniards (see Table 2.5). Other figures are also very significant: (1) in 1996, 3 per cent of Spaniards were in favour of a state without *Comunidades Autónomas*, as compared to 9 per cent in 1994; (2) in the same period the support for the same type of *Estado de las Autonomías* grew from 31 to 47 per cent; (3) there was an increase of support for the maintenance of the *Comunidades Autónomas* with a higher degree of home rule (from 20 to 22 per cent) (see Table 2.6). This data further legitimates continued political decentralization.

TABLE 2.6
PREFERENCES FOR THE TERRITORIAL ORGANIZATION
OF THE SPANISH STATE
(percentage of respondents)

	November 1984	December 1990	March 1996
Central government without *Comunidades Autónomas*	9	7	3
Comunidades Autónomas as at present	31	41	47
Comunidades Autónomas with more home rule	20	19	22
Comunidades Autónomas with possibility of secession	10	7	7
'Don't knows'	19	16	11

Source: Spanish Centro de Investigaciones Sociológicas (Opinion Data, No. 5).

A minority of citizens in the 'historical nationalities', and in particular those in the Basque Country who support ETA's proposals, advocate the secession of their territories from the rest of Spain. According to the data reproduced in Table 2.7, around a fifth of the PNV and Convergència i Unió (CiU: centre-right nationalist coalition) voters were in favour of independence for the Basque Country and Catalonia, respectively. Xabier Arzallus, leader of the PNV, was of the opinion that just 51 per cent of 'yes' votes in a hypothetical referendum for independence would be enough to claim secession of the Basque Country from the rest of Spain.[85] In such an eventuality the PNV would expect its voters to vote in favour of independence.

TABLE 2.7: PREFERENCES FOR THE TERRITORIAL ORGANIZATION IN
THE 'HISTORICAL NATIONALITIES'
(percentage of voters)

	Basque Country	PNV	EA	HB	Catalonia	CiU	ERC	Galicia	BNG
Centralized	6	5	1	—	11	5	1	14	4
Autonomy as current	34	33	21	2	34	27	4	39	12
More autonomy	22	35	42	9	28	42	25	20	51
Independence	19	18	21	83	17	20	67	4	27
'Don't knows'	19	8	15	5	10	7	2	24	5
N	1,615	309	69	143	2,470	734	112	2,192	110

N = Number of people surveyed.

Source: Spanish Centro de Investigaciones Sociológicas and Pallarés *et al.* (1997: Table 10).

All things considered, at the turn of the millennium the tendency towards decentralization has permeated the consciousness of most Spaniards. In the future, if this 'home rule all round' process is to be geared towards federal-like arrangements it needs to adapt itself to new forms of intergovernmental relations, especially at the level of institutional collaboration.[86] The articulation of institutional relations involving shared powers and responsibilities lies at the very base of the federalizing relations of Spain. This mode of relations is one of *multiple ethnoterritorial concurrence* and is analysed in the next chapter.

NOTES

1. Giner, 1984: p. 79.
2. Date of the marriage of the future heirs to the Kingdom of Castile and the Crown of Aragon. In 1474 and 1479, the Catholic Kings took effective possession of the thrones of Castile and Aragon, respectively.
3. From the 'particular' perspective of a Catalan nationalist, Enric Prat de la Riba described how, in the sixth century BC, Phoenician explorers found the Iberian *etnos* stretching from Murcia (in the southeast of the peninsula) to the River Rhone in France. This was 'the first link in the chain of generations that have forged the Catalan soul' (1917: pp. 99–102).
4. The Roman *Hispania* came to an end with the invasion of the Suevians, Vandals and Alani in AD 404. Note that Roman control of the Iberian

peninsula was not completed until AD 19, the year in which the troops of
Agrippa took control of the last strongholds of the native rebels in Cantabria.
However, rebels in Asturias rose in rebellion in AD 58.

5. 'In the year 1000, however, Christian Spain was essentially what it would be
   in 1600, and could be clearly distinguished from France and Italy' (A. Castro,
   1984: p. 13). For de Riquer and Ucelay-Da Cal (1994), a sense of national
   community was already detectable in Spain before the eighteenth century.
6. The Christian recovery of the land occupied by the Moors, which lasted from
   718 until 1492.
7. The Reconquista was a Christian 'holy war' in which the figure of Apostle
   Saint James (*Santiago Apostol*) was a referential myth of the utmost
   importance. '*Santiago y cierra España!*' (St James and Spain together!) was a
   rallying cry for the peninsular Christian troops.
8. The Mozarabs were Christians under Moorish rule allowed by the Moors to
   practise their faith in return for their allegiance. The Mudejars were Muslims
   allowed to carry on with their culture and religion under Christian rule.
9. While the northeast of Spain, structured around the values of Christianity and
   the figure of St James, and the Castilians rebelled against the old kingdom of
   Leon-Asturias, Catalonia had remained part of the Carolingian Empire since
   987 as the 'Hispanic Landmark' (*Marca Hispánica*). According to historian
   Américo Castro, 'Catalonia neither belonged completely to Spain, nor ceased
   to be part of it'. Catalan nationalists, including Jordi Pujol himself, have
   identified the Carolingian Frankish origins of the *Comtats* as the founding basis
   of modern Catalonia, and as such different from the rest of the Spanish lands.
10. This was the year of the ascension of Alphonse I to the throne of Portugal, a
    would-be kingdom that refused to remain as a mere earldom pertaining to
    the Crown of Castile. The Middle Ages saw the unification and separation of
    a diversity of the peninsula's territories 'according to royal marriages and
    successions' (Vilar, 1986: p. 31).
11. After the dissolution of Cordoba's Caliphate, Moorish Spain was divided into
    Muslim states known as *taifas*.
12. According to Ortega y Gasset, 'the secret of the great Spanish problems is to
    be searched for in the Middles Ages … when Spain was constituted' (1989: p.
    142). For historians such as Claudio Sánchez-Albornoz (1956) and Angus
    MacKay (1977), during the long medieval period, and in contrast to the rest
    of Europe, the concepts of border and reconquest became essential symbolic
    and actual referents in the historical development of the country. Later they
    would be replaced by the enterprise of the Spanish Empire and the
    expansion overseas.
13. According to Francesc Cambó, leader of the Catalan League in the twentieth
    century, this was the great mistake of the Catalan–Aragonese foreign policy
    at that time. For James I and his heirs the Iberian peninsula 'was foreign land
    … and, thus, Catalonia forgot about Spain. Castile took advantage of it and,
    without opposition, became the uncontested power within the Iberian
    peninsula. Castilian hegemony and the consequent unification of Spain were
    the inexorable consequences of the extra-peninsular foreign policy adopted
    by James I' (Cambo, 1927: pp. 64–5).
14. For Salvador de Madariaga the three Basque provinces were not constituent
    of the Basque Country. This was a modern political creation (1979). In any
    case, all three provinces took good care of their *fueros*, before and after they

joined the Castilian Crown: 'They would not recognize Lord or King without the prior and solemn pledge for honouring their *fueros*' (Pi i Margall, 1911: p. 251).

15. Towards the end of the fourteenth century, Castilians, Portuguese and Catalans undertook numerous expeditions to the Canary Islands for economic reasons (to obtain slaves and dyes). In 1402 the first occupation of the archipelago took place, involving French and Norman mariners in the service of Castile. Portugal's frustrated attempt to capture the islands was in some way compensated by the occupation of Madeira (1419) and the Azores (1427). Finally, in 1480 the Kingdom of Portugal recognized Castilian sovereignty over the Canaries.

16. On the occasion of the rebellion of the local *Comuneros* in Castile (1521) and *Germanías* in Valencia (1522) and Majorca (1523).

17. The very year when two other major events took place in Spain: the first expedition to the American continent and the expelling of the Jews.

18. This diversity was vividly described by Don Alonso de Cartagena, Bishop of Burgos, before the Council of Basle in 1434: 'the Castilians and the Galicians and the Biscayans are of diverse nations, and speak altogether different tongues' (Castro, 1984: p. 28)

19. According to Pi i Margall, 'The peoples remained the same in their lands with different lords. They did not experience changes in their everyday life and they were rather indifferent to the union of kingdoms in which they did not participate directly' (1911: p. 213).

20. The *Usatges*, codified *c.* 1159 as the fundamental text of Catalan law, emphasized the figure of the prince as sovereign of land and subjects, although his duties towards his vassals, and certain limitations on his powers, remained (MacKay, 1977: pp. 112–13, *passim*).

21. After the battle of Aljubarrota in 1411, the Kingdom of Portugal had forced a truce with Castile consolidating Portugal's political independence. Later, Portugal embarked on a formidable overseas expansion.

22. The *hidalgo* (*hijo de algo*, 'son of something') was a figure of great historical importance during the Spanish Middle Ages, the subsequent Reconquista and the empire-building period. The *hidalgos* composed the lower ranks of the nobility and carried out activities as sort of royal civil servants. In modern times the *hidalgos*, under various fashions and appearances, continued to reflect the singularity of a certain Hispanic individualism, at times with an entrepreneurial nature but often in a self-complacent and self-centred way (Castro, 1984; Vilar, 1986).

23. This explains, at least partially, the contempt of old Christians for the virtues of work, technical and administrative capacity, and for the economic wealth of the Jews and the Muslims (the latter also expelled from Spain in 1609).

24. Both the Spanish and the Austrian political structures represented the *ordo Romano-Hispanicum*, also known as the *iugum Romano-Hispanicum* in the Europe of the time, for the Dutch Calvinists who rebelled against the Spanish Crown (Giner and Moreno, 1990).

25. The conquest of Constantinople by the Turks (1453) and the discovery of America by Columbus (1492) are the main historical referents of the economic decline of the Crown of Aragon. The political and economic strategic attention of the European powers turned from the eastern Mediterranean to the Americas.

26. Among these, the weakness of the Duke of Olivares in his confrontation with Cardinal Richelieu stands out. The Duke (1587–1645) governed Spain for 22 years under Philip IV. The royal troops were incapable of defending the Low Countries, or the route from Barcelona to Genoa, or Burgundy, previously consolidated by the Duke of Alba (Elliot, 1970, 1984).

27. In a confidential memorandum of 25 December 1620, the Duke of Olivares advised Philip IV to become King of Spain, and not to remain content with being King of Portugal, Aragon and Valencia, and Count of Barcelona: 'You should see to it that these kingdoms of which Spain is composed are ruled by the laws and in the manner of Castile. In doing so, your Majesty would become the world's most powerful sovereign' (reproduced in J. Linz, 1973: p. 43). The attempt resulted in the eventual banishment of the Duke in 1643, and Catalonia's loss of Roussillon and Sardinia. The Catalan national anthem, '*Els Segadors*' (The Reapers) evokes the events of 1640.

28. The treaty was finally signed in the German city of Münster on 24 October 1648. After 70 years of conflict, the Spanish Crown recognized the full independence and sovereignty of the Low Countries.

29. Or *Siglo de Oro* (Golden Century), which refers to the period that extended from approximately 1550 to 1650. The villains' purpose was to procure a way of life for themselves in an increasingly impoverished society, and this was often sought in cunning and artful ways.

30. 'It is worth noting that there were no direct representatives of the kingdom of Navarre, the dominions of Biscay, Alava and Guipuzcoa and the principality of Asturias. The latter was still considered a part of the kingdom of Leon in Floridablanca's territorial division' (Olábarri Gortazar, 1985: p. 77).

31. Known by the British as the 'Peninsular War'.

32. The territories elected two representatives to the Central Junta, supreme unit of governance in occupied Spain. Besides those functions of general action (co-ordination of war activities, colonial and foreign relations, and general services), the rest of the administrative affairs were run at the regional level.

33. The federative North American experience had a notable influence in the ideas of the Spanish democrats, radicals and republicans during the period 1820–70. José Canga Argüelles was the author of the *Cartas de un americano sobre las ventajas de los gobiernos republicanos federativos* (Letters of an American on the Advantages of the Federative Republican Governments). This booklet was published in 1826 by the London Spanish Press and had a great impact among the intellectuals and politicians mentioned (Elorza, 1975).

34. Article 324 of the 1812 Constitution established that 'the political government in each and every one of the provinces will be the responsibility of the supreme chief appointed by the King'. Centralism was a concept made equal to that of *modernidad* (modernity).

35. In the case of Catalonia, such a course of action meant the abolition of its own penal code (1822), prohibition of the use of the Catalan language in schools (1825), and the dismantling of Catalonia's regional administration (Madariaga, 1979).

36. Liberal *progresistas* demanded more democratization for local councils. Once in power they eventually adopted the same clientelist practices as the *moderados* in order to secure their electoral bases (Hennessy, 1962: pp. 2–3).

37. The revolution of the *juntas*, which proved to be successful in 1808 and 1820, was the main political instrument of the urban bourgeoisie in peripheral

Spain to achieve reforms in line with industrialized Europe. Many were the provincial 'revolutions' initiated by the *juntas*, particularly in Catalonia and Valencia. Their struggle to attain democratic reforms was systematically repressed by the central state – a pattern repeated until the Second Republic (1936–39) (Linz, 1973; Giner, 1980).

38. This concept is related to the industrialization processes backed by the liberal economic elites, which were virtually ineffective in the Spanish civil society of the time. During the nineteenth century, Spain, in a sense, ceased to be a traditional society without becoming a modern one. On the failure of the industrial revolution in Spain during the 1900s, see Nadal (1980).

39. The francophile Javier de Burgos, promoter of provincial reform, had been subprefect of Almeria during the reign of Joseph Bonaparte, the sovereign imposed upon the Spaniards by his brother Napoleon.

40. However, it is inappropriate to draw a simple dichotomy between centralist liberals and Carlist *foralistas* (supporters of the old *fueros*). In the Basque provinces, for example, the vast majority of the liberal forces fought simultaneously for the Spanish liberal Constitution and for the Basque *fueros*.

41. In 1713 Philip V had established the *Ley Sálica* (Salic Law), by which men took precedence over women in the line of royal succession. In 1833 Ferdinand VII repealed the law in order for his daughter to become the future queen (Isabella II). The followers of the Pretender Charles (brother of Ferdinand VII) rebelled. The Carlistas or *tradicionalistas* remained active in Spanish history even after the Civil War (1936–39), during which time they joined Franco's forces.

42. It is possible that this strength is not altogether dead in the Basque Country. The Basque separatist movement (ETA, HB, KAS, EH) is still characterized by an emotional and messianic style which is not so far removed from the Carlist traditionalism which preceded it, and which it has now to a large extent replaced (Giner and Moreno, 1990).

43. The expression is derived from the Swiss federal-like division of its land into cantons.

44. 'These Republicans needed an antagonist force. As they did not have a strong opposition from the non-Republican parties, they divided and fought each other' (Trujillo, 1967: p. 188).

45. The Cuban war of independence from Spain lasted from 1868 to 1878.

46. Some other key dates in the process of Spanish modern nation-building include the establishment of the Stock Exchange in Madrid (1831), the Guardia Civil (Civil Guard, or rural police, with a presence in most of the Spanish towns: 1844), the national system of secondary and advanced education (1845 and 1857), the implementation of national penal codes (1848 and 1870) and civil code (1870, 1889), and the establishment of the Banco de España (Central Bank) in 1856.

47. An example of which is the voluminous *Historia General de España* (General History of Spain) published by Modesto Lafuente during 1877–82.

48. These were supported, and sometimes co-opted, by the parliamentary leaders and government officials in Madrid. For Gumersindo de Azcárate, both *caciquismo* and centralism were the two worst diseases of Spain. Hidden behind the facade of representative institutions 'there was a mean, hypocritical and bastard oligarchy'. Joaquín Costa (1844–1911) proposed *Regeneracionismo* (Regenerationism), a movement of liberal organicism with an 'iron hand' to repress 'pitilessly and unabatedly both *caciques* and

oligarchs'. (Both quotations from Tuñón de Lara, 1986: pp. 22 and 85, respectively.)

49. On the social structure of Catalonia, see Giner's monograph (1980).

50. Catalanism was the name given to the movement led by Catalan nationalists and disenchanted republicans who wished Catalonia to rebuild the Spanish state on a federal basis. Valentí Almirall, disciple of Pi i Margall, was a key figure who prepared the *Memorial de Greuges* (Memorial of Grievances). This was submitted to King Alphonse XII with no tangible consequences. In 1892 Enric Prat de la Riba, secretary of the Unió Catalanista (Catalanist Union) prepared the *Bases de Manresa*, a political programme of Catalanism. On the figure of Almirall, see Trías Vejarano (1975). On the political thought of Prat de la Riba, see his *La nacionalitat catalana* (1917).

51. Data taken from J. Linz (1967: p. 209).

52. The Lliga Catalana, later Lliga Regionalista, was a Catalanist political party founded in 1901, later influential in Spain under the leadership of Francesc Cambó. Both dynastic or monarchical parties opposed the inclusion of any Catalan in their governments during the early twentieth century. Francesc Cambó, leader of the Lliga, and later a very influential political leader in Madrid, described the situation in a parliamentary intervention in 1914: 'Since the accession of the King Alphonse XIII [in May of 1902] until now, 180 ministers have sworn as cabinet members. None of them was Catalan' (see Vidal-Folch, 1994: p. 109).

53. Many of them veterans who had completed their military service and were on 'reserve'. In 1887 the Lliga de Catalunya had already presented a memorandum to the Regent María Cristina (mother of Alphonse XII) in which they claimed that 'the numbers of soldiers required for the needs of the Army in Catalonia should be established locally, not by means of conscription or selection at random. They should be recruited on a voluntary basis and should be paid a stipend' (see Jover, 1983: p. 379).

54. It then became clear that not only were entrepreneurs, urban traders or intellectuals part of the Catalanist bourgeois conglomerate. There were also rural landowners and industrialists, dependent on Spanish protectionism and internal markets, who were fearful of risking their economic positions in order to take a leading role in the modernization and progress of Catalonia and Spain (Solé Tura, 1967).

55. In its early stages Arana's nationalist proposals developed in the province of Biscay with the label of *bizkaitarrismo*. In 1893 Arana published *Bizcaya por su independencia* (Independence for Biscay).

56. In 1907 the first nationalist was elected mayor of Bilbao. Ten years later the PNV–EAJ (Basque Nationalist Party) representatives took control of the powerful *Diputación* of the Biscay province.

57. In 1887 the Federal Assembly of Galicia gathered in Lugo and approved 'a constitutional project for a Galician state' (Jover, 1983: p. 381).

58. This was the heir organization to the *Irmandades de Fala* (Language Brotherhoods), which since the early twentieth century aimed at revitalizing Galician as a cultivated language (Beramendi and Núñez-Seixas, 1995). Risco recreated the traditional catholic ideas of Brañas, incorporating elements of Murguía's Celtic mythology. Liberal connotations disappeared and were substituted by new ideas of reactionary European thought, such as some Aryan racist theses (Máiz, 1994).

59. This discourse signalled the transition from Valencian provincialism to regionalism (Cucó, 1971). Blasquismo, a regional movement inspired by the write Blasco Ibáñez, would later on articulate a strong political platform for a radical *valencianisme*.

60. Nicanor de las Alas Pumariño promoted the Liga pro-Asturias and, later on, the Junta de Fomento y Defensa de los Intereses de Asturias.

61. A precursor was the Partido Popular Autonomista (Autonomist Popular Party) created in 1901 in Santa Cruz de Tenerife by Secundido Delgado and José Cabrera. Both formations had a limited impact in the Islands, although they enjoyed some popularity among emigrants in the Americas.

62. Or *Estado Integral* (Integral State) according to the denomination of the republican constitutionalists, who envisaged a gradual decentralization of powers to Catalonia, the Basque Country and Galicia (Trujillo, 1967).

63. The Generalitat is Catalonia's government. Of medieval origin, it is housed in a fifteenth-century palace in the centre of Barcelona.

64. The *Estatut d'Autonomia* was supported by more than 90 per cent of those who voted at the referendum – three-quarters of the total electorate. Later, the Spanish parliament introduced some minor modifications after the intervention of and support by the prime minister, Manuel Azaña.

65. Many Basque nationalists, fervent Catholics, resented the anti-clerical republican climate. They proposed an independent concordat between the Basque Country and the Vatican. Note that at the end of 1931 the central government had decided to suspend 12 Basque newspapers because they were encouraging a popular uprising against civil authorities, so that 'the interests of the Catholic religion could be defended' (Madariaga, 1979: p. 331).

66. Representatives of all republican parties were present at the ceremony of the appointment of José Antonio Aguirre as *lehendakari*, or president of the Basque autonomous government. At the same time, Manuel Irujo became a member of the central government. Later on, during the Civil War,

> Basque governmental officials behaved as if they were running an independent state. Furthermore, they maintained secret bilateral contacts not only with Britain and the Vatican, but also with fascist Italy so that a separate armistice could be worked out [for the Basque Country] ... However, after Franco took control of the territories on the northern coast of Spain, the Basque leaders moved to Barcelona where they continued to participate in the Republican Government and to support the Republican Army [during the rest of the Civil War].
>
> (Olábarri Gortázar, 1985: p. 135)

67. On 28 June 1938 around 70 per cent of the Galician electorate voted. The final result was 991,476 votes for and 6,805 against autonomy (Tuñón de Lara, 1983).

68. Except for some local institutions in Alava and Navarre: provinces where large numbers of Carlists joined Franco's forces.

69. In the case of Catalonia, national identity had been essentially preserved by the survival of its language: 'cultural nationalism became a surrogate for political nationalism, when political nationalism was perforce a clandestine affair' (Carr and Fusi, 1979: p. 157). For the relation between language and politics in Francoist Spain, see J. Linz (1975).

70. The Spanish state under Franco was not just highly centralized and inefficient, but above all despotic. With such character it could not achieve its

unifying and homogenizing objectives. 'The civil rights which, in countries like Britain and France, compensate to some extent for excessive centralism were non-existent in Francoist Spain. Francoism, paradoxically, set up the conditions for regionalism, autonomism, federalism and ethnical nationalism' (Newton, 1983: p. 104).

71. *Pactisme* establishes that 'rules are made by parties entering into contracts of their own accord, and also that social life is the result of bargaining among people, and not of unilateral violence or imposition' (Giner, 1980: pp. 5–6).

72. The cry was '*Llibertat, Amnistia, Estatut d'Autonomia!*'

73. Curiously, this occurred only a few metres away from the US Embassy in Madrid and after several months, during which members of ETA had bored an underground tunnel below the public causeway.

74. Jaime García de Añoveros was Minister of Economy in the last centre-right Unión de Centro Democrático (UCD) governments during the period 1979–82.

75. The popular expression 'coffee for all' reflected this desire to avoid coercing the autonomist aspirations of the Spanish *Comunidades Autónomas*.

76. The Spanish Constitutional Court is inspired by the model proposed by Hans Kelsen for the Austrian Constitution of 1920, which was also adopted by the 1931 Spanish Constitution (Second Republic). It also incorporates several aspects of the 1948 Italian Constitution and the German Basic Law, or *Grundgesetz*.

77. The referendum was held on 28 February 1980, after 97 per cent of Andalusian towns and eight provincial councils had decided to pursue autonomy according to the provisions of Article 151 of the 1978 Constitution. The 64 per cent turnout was considered high. But the important requirement was that more than 50 per cent of the votes in each Andalusian province should be 'yes' votes. The results were somewhat controversial given that, in spite of the considerable support for autonomy in Andalusia as a whole, in the province of Almeria only 47 per cent of the inhabitants voted 'Yes'. Finally, the political situation that had arisen made it impossible to turn back on the 'fast route' of Article 151.

78. Electoral coalition promoted by Herri Batasuna to contest the 1998 Basque elections, and integrated with various political and social associations in the Basque Country and Navarre. This secessionist platform obtained 17.9 per cent of the popular vote and 14 members in the Basque parliament and increased the electoral results obtained by Herri Batasuna in 1994 (16.2 per cent and 11 per cent, respectively).

79. This centre-right party operates only in the province of Alava and claims a distinct political personality for this territory.

80. The historical personality of the old Kingdom of Leon has somewhat evaporated since the mid-nineteenth century when a 'new' Castile was reinvented covering the plains around the River Duero (Carretero, 1988). In fact the old Kingdom of Leon included the south of Asturias and the provinces of Leon, Zamora, Salamanca, Valladolid and Palencia. Likewise, La Mancha (or Toledo Country) did not originally include Castilian territories such as Guadalajara, part of the province of Cuenca and Albacete. The latter was a territory of the old kingdom of Murcia, but nowadays its socioeconomic structure is more akin to that of La Mancha.

81. 'Catalan countries'. Expression used by pan-Catalanists to denote the

Principate of Catalonia, the Kingdom of Valencia and the Balearic Islands. Frequently included is Rosselló (Roussillon), in southern France, where Catalan is also spoken.

82. According to González Navarro, 'Navarre is also a nation ... [The Navarrans] refuse to be confounded with the Aragonese, those inhabitants of the Rioja, or the contemporary Basques' (1993: pp. 173–4).

83. In accordance with such a view, the whole of Castile would include a disparity of regions such as Andalusia, Asturias, Extremadura, Murcia or Rioja, together with the traditional Castiles.

84. As in the case of Extremadura, the poorest region of Spain, whose political representatives have articulated a discourse from the perspective of social rejection to aspire to the prospect of massive depauperization in open competition with richer Spanish territories.

85. The same day this statement was made to the media, Iñaki Anasagasti, leader of the PNV parliamentary group, expressed a contrary view, saying that 'it would be politically absurd to propose an independent Basque Country in a united Europe' (*El País*, 14 December 1999).

86. According to 1990 data, most Spaniards considered that relations between autonomous governments and central government should be 'collaborative' (80.7 per cent), and involve 'shared responsibilities' (50.2 per cent) (García Ferrando *et al.*, 1994: p. 113).

3

The Mode of Relations within Decentralized Spain

In Italy, Holland, Portugal, Sweden and Norway, 99 per cent of the population of each of these states belong to one nationality; in Spain and Denmark 96 per cent of the population. Then there are three states with an almost homogeneous national composition: France, England and Germany.

(V.I. Lenin)[1]

The ethnic and linguistic[2] variety of Spain, a country governed by actors, institutions and political forces that have traditionally been both weak through inefficacy and strong through violence, has too often resulted in damage to its unity. Moreover, there has been a traditional lack of congruence or a 'noncongruence' between political and economic powers.[3] Catalonia and the Basque Country, the two northern peripheral Spanish communities with full ethnic potential, have remained as two of the three economically most dynamic territories of Spain, the third being the region of Madrid. This noncongruence has traditionally nourished the centrifugal tendencies present in modern Spanish history. Such tendencies have found expression in a number of armed conflicts: the Revolt of the Reapers (1640–52); the War of Spanish Succession (1701–14); the Carlist wars (1833–40, 1846–48 and 1872–75); the Tragic Week of Barcelona (1909) and, finally, the Civil War (1936–39).

Despite its secular ethnic conflicts, Spain is an entity clearly identifiable as a historical unity. This unity goes beyond the simple aggregation of territories and peoples with no other affinity than their coexistence under the rule of one common monarch or political power. In this respect the Iberian peninsula is not like the Balkan peninsula. The social and cultural cohesion that makes up its unity does not, however, obliterate internal opposition. As has happened in the past, territorial rivalries among Spanish nationalities and regions have brought about an extra, cultural incentive for creativity and civilization, but have also hindered social and economic progress and wasted much energy in certain periods of Spanish history.[4]

Since the fifteenth century, state development in Spain has been erratic and lacking in continuity, as shown in the previous chapter. Consequently, a lack of political accommodation within the Spanish state is noticeable together with the salience of its cultural and ethnoterritorial diversity. After the last failed attempt of imposed national homogenization by Franco's authoritarian regime, democratic Spain has resumed the challenge of reconciling its internal diversity.

After nearly 20 years of widespread decentralization, the political and spatial reorganization brought about by the progressive consolidation of the Spanish *Estado de las Autonomías* is in line with a model of *multiple ethnoterritorial concurrence*. This model relates sociopolitical ethnoterritorial mobilization to the interplay among Spanish nationalities and regions pursuing political and economic power, as well as to the achievement of legitimization for their institutional development. The constitutional order inaugurated in 1978 set the rules of an open and flexible territorial articulation in which autonomy and solidarity are key principles facilitating its political integration. Plurality, asymmetry, the role of majority and minority nationalism and the *multiple ethnoterritorial concurrence* are the objects of our subsequent analyses.

PLURALITY AND ASYMMETRY IN SPAIN

In contemporary times the *españolismo* (hispanicism)[5] expressed by prominent Spanish thinkers put the emphasis in the moral reconstruction of Spain as the premise for a new political revival (Ganivet, Ortega, Unamuno). The question of centralization versus decentralization was secondary (Fusi, 1989).[6]

The upsurge of peripheral nationalism in the late nineteenth century was regarded by the central political elites as the cause of the stagnation of the process of nation-building which began in the late eighteenth century (de Blas and Laborda, 1986). Some mystification surrounds attempts to explain the causes and effects of these historical developments. The misconception of considering an exclusive and homogeneous Spain as the pattern to which ideas and behaviours should conform has been the most common shortcomıng of both descriptive and normative analyses.

Problems and difficulties faced by Spain in modern times have primarily been those of internal accommodation. By negating internal plurality and asymmetries, contemporary Spain has had to face important political traumas which have remained a source of conflict until the late twentieth century. Complexity and fragmentation characterize social life in Spain. The 'standard' response by political actors has been based on a simplistic vision of the Spanish reality. This has been responsible for the persistence of a one-directional understanding of Spain which has fuelled political action based primarily on voluntarism.

All things considered, the Spanish case is not as exceptional as some analysts tend to suggest. Other European countries of analogous cultural and historical proportions, such as France or the United Kingdom, are regarded as having incorporated a higher degree of internal ethnoterritorial coalescence. This idea is, at the least, superficial.

It is useful to remember that modern France, the paradigmatic case of a centralized nation-state, was the result of a large-scale economic, political and social revolution (1789). But even before then,[7] during the _ancien régime_, a drive to homogenize culturally the French 'hexagon' was systematically carried out. In 1539 Francis I imposed by edict a sole language (_langue d'oîl_) to be used throughout his kingdom. Despite the fact that in vast regions of the Occitania the _langue d'oc_ was the autochthonous language, this took refuge in the households although its survival could not resist the passing of time. Both state and absolutist monarchy were made equal concepts.

The French Revolution and the Napoleonic Wars reinforced the congruity between national and political identities as the central core of the Jacobin ideology (Safran, 1991). But it took some time for the effects of the Revolution to be diffused throughout France. Eugen Weber (1976) points out that in 1870 the great majority of inhabitants in rural areas and small municipalities did not regarded themselves as members of the French nation. This perception of 'non-belonging' lasted until the First World War. In fact, it was only during the Third Republic (1875–1940) that communication and transport networks were extended nationwide, school provision was made compulsory and military conscription was established. These factors point to the consolidation of the process of nation-building in France. Even at the end of the twentieth century, however, the French state was still not immune from internal tensions and home rule demands in the so-called 'ethnic periphery' (Alsace, Basque Country, Brittany, Corsica, Occitania). It can be said, consequently, that the process of nation-building centred in Paris took over a century to be accomplished. Its apparent success is reflected in a favourable public perception of the actions pursued by the centralized state, although regional diversities persist in the French periphery.

Concerning the case of the United Kingdom, it seems more appropriate to concentrate on the state rather than on the nation. In fact the United Kingdom represents the case of a 'union-state' similar to some extent to that of Spain. Britain's nationalism has been manifested in a form of patriotism of its constituent nations, particularly during the numerous wars and colonial expansion (Crick, 1989). This sort of patriotism needs therefore to be qualified in contrast with the type of state nationalism characteristic of other European states (for example, Germany, Italy, the Netherlands).[8]

Let us remember that in 1536 Wales was annexed by England. After the death of Elizabeth I, James VI of Scotland took the throne of England in 1603, thus consummating the Union of the Crowns. In 1707 the Treaty of Union of the Scottish and English parliaments was signed, resulting in the political unification of Britain. Since then, however, Scottish civil society has enjoyed a considerable degree of autonomy and the effects of Scotland's 'anglicization' have been moderate (McCrone, 1992; Paterson, 1994). In fact, British nationalism during the nineteenth century manifested itself mainly in imperial expansion overseas. It hardly showed major concerns for domestic affairs regarding state homogenization and allowed Scotland the status of a 'junior' partner, taking care internally of such important affairs as education, law, local government and church relations. It was precisely with the loss of Britain's imperial power after the Second World War that a reassertion of the Welsh and Scottish identities brought about an asymmetry in the British electoral system and in the standardized mould of British politics.[9]

The 'old' French nationalism and the 'new' Italian and German unifying national movements were successful in their attempts to consolidate their modern nation-states. Spanish nationalism on the other hand was highly conditioned by its own weakness and development at a time of general decline and social instability. Besides, the higher degree of internal plurality in Spain showed a great resistance to the programmes of unitary nation-building pursued by the 'francophile' Spanish liberals during the nineteenth century. Their actions were also constrained by the powerful advocates of the 'old regime' and above all by their political inability to understand fully the nature of Spain's diversity, as well as by a general intellectual mediocrity within the country.[10]

As stated earlier, functionalist and diffusionist theories have persistently conveyed the idea that, together with the Industrial Revolution, the development of capitalism and the consolidation of the modern nation-state, processes of social convergence and boundary-building would eliminate internal differences between territories. Spain, together with other countries of multinational ethnoterritorial composition, offers a sound example of the inaccuracy of such presumptions.

In some cases the irruption of the modern nation-state exacerbated those internal problems of regional imbalances. In contrast with the neo-classical and Keynesian regional models which assume territorial equilibrium or self-balance, the persistent trend of regional inequality has to be considered as intrinsic to the capitalist mode of economic growth. Early 'orthodox' economic theory put the *where* under the *why*. According to this view, the location of industries should be determined by the cost factor and, consequently, citizens were expected to maximize wages by moving to those areas more profitable for increasing the general wealth of the country. The consequence of this economic approach was an agglomeration of financial and human resources in some geographical areas – processes of concentration and urbanization.

Market forces tend to open rather than close inequities among regions within the state.[11] They do so because economic growth is uneven. In advanced industrial (post-industrial) societies both national strategies of multinational corporations and their neocorporatist connivance with central governments have not had major impacts in altering the nature of the intrinsic regional imbalances within nation-states.

The institutional combination of capitalism, industrialization and nation-building has nevertheless been a key element in the structuring of contemporary democracies. In Spain, those internal forces opposing an homogenizing assimilation have recurrently re-emerged by means of ethnoterritorial movements of a sociopolitical nature. The intensification of the divergences caused by modernization and the development of peripheral nationalism is illustrated by the case of Catalonia, which we shall now analyse.

Catalonia's industrialization

Catalonia based its great industrial expansion of the nineteenth century on capital accumulation brought about by agricultural production and colonial trade with the Americas during the second half of the eighteenth century. Overseas trade in fact trebled between 1760 and 1780. In 1778, with the promulgation of the Decree of Free Trade by the Spanish central government, Catalan merchants saw the legal acknowledgement of a factual situation which was to be the starting point of modern Catalan prosperity.

The demographic increase of the population of Catalonia between 1787 and 1857 was nearly 90 per cent (from 875,388 to 1,652,291 inhabitants). Such figures correspond to 7.8 and 10.7 per cent of the total Spanish population. The city of Barcelona alone increased its population between 1830 and 1877 by 155 per cent (from 97,418 to 248,943 inhabitants).[12]

In 1832 the first factory in Spain to operate by steam engine was opened in Barcelona. Such industrial impetus was later fuelled by the capital brought in from America by Catalan businessmen whose wealth had been acquired through trading operations with Cuba and Puerto Rico.

During the mid-nineteenth century, the great Catalan industrial expansion in the textile sector was spectacular. The Basque Country, the other Spanish territory where a considerable industrial development was also taking place at that time, held the primacy in the metallurgical sector, and indeed frustrated the aspirations of Catalonia in this sphere.

Catalonia's industrial boom, as compared with the rest of Spain, is best illustrated by the fact that in 1862 41 per cent of the power produced in Spain for industrial use was located in Catalan territory. In 1851, very significantly, the College of Industry was founded in Barcelona and remained the only one of its kind in the whole of Spain until 1897. However, and despite all this panorama, it is rather inaccurate to speak of a genuine Catalan industrial revolution:

Even taking into consideration the consolidation of the cotton industry during Isabella II's reign (1843–1868), it is wrong to

> consider such expansion as constituting a Catalan industrial revolution or, otherwise, as a process of generalized mechanization ... in Barcelona (1866) the industrialists paid only 6.9 per cent of the direct-tax collection. [This] compared with the 49.6 per cent paid by the merchants and traders, 14.7 per cent by the craftsmen and manufacturing sector and 23.1 per cent by the financial companies ... The process of industrialization in Catalonia was very much focussed on the cotton-textile industries.
>
> (Balcells, 1983: p. 33)

Catalonia's economic development in the nineteenth century took place in the midst of strong protectionist policies instituted by the Spanish government. Thus, in order to defeat the liberals and free-trade supporters, the Catalan industrial bourgeoisie — the most dynamic section of the Spanish dominant class – was willing to join its interests with those of the most reactionary Spanish agrarian oligarchy. This subordination to the backward Spanish landowning economic and political forces was aimed at deterring the import of (amongst other things) British textile products, which were far more competitive that their Catalan counterparts.[13] The agrarian oligarchy in turn benefited from the oligopoly of its much less competitive cereals in both the Spanish and colonial markets.

Thus industrialization in Catalonia brought about an increase of the Spanish internal heterogeneity (Giner, 1984). *Catalanisme* built on this 'differential fact' a great deal of their programme of demands for home rule, although the perception of distinct origins and national characteristics (cultural, geography, history, law, language, politics and psychology) run parallel. This self-awareness also made acute the paradox that a politically subordinate territory of Spain had become the most vital centre of economic progress. Note that despite the fact that Arana's early Basque nationalism articulated itself against industrialization, a similar process to that of Catalonia's took place decades later in the Basque Country.

However, the limitations of Catalan capitalism and its marginal relationship with the centralist political and financial powers made its position somewhat ambivalent. This was a situation rather different from that which obtained in other territories in southern Europe, Piedmont and Lombardy for instance, to which Catalonia could be compared. But it should not be forgotten that in the case of Italy unification came about as the end-result of a process of aggregation together with a programme of national resurgence. Besides, this programme of nation-building was articulated from the north of the country. Within the Spanish context, when Catalonia peaked in terms of industrial development, Spain was a long-established state with entrenched vested interests in all parts of the country.[14]

Thus one of the paradoxes of contemporary Spain was that the nationalities with a full ethnoterritorial potential and more economically prosperous, Catalonia and the Basque Country, became richer and more in tune with the rest of industrial Europe than the other Spanish territories. But at the same time, a tension with the political ruling groups at the centre of the Spanish state bred a sort of schizophrenia among the Catalan modern industrialists. As a consequence their reformism became half-hearted and lacked the support of the more backward-looking, albeit more powerful, oligarchy based in Madrid.

The internal asymmetries of Spain have remained constant over the last two centuries, in spite of the authoritarian and dictatorial attempts at centralized nation-building, as well as those encouraged by liberal and progressive forces.[15] The *patrias chicas* (home towns or home areas)[16] continue to be social points of reference of the first order. At the same time, a certain 'regional specialization', as it were, has developed, corresponding to a deeper fragmentation of the traditional historical territories. Even the federalists of the First Republic (1873), facing the difficulty of how to fashion the intermediate communities, argued that there was no need to discriminate or to concede autonomy to some regions to the detriment of others.[17]

Throughout the modern period, the proliferation and subdivision of Spanish territories has been the consequence of two main factors: (1) rivalries, historic pride and the strength of autochthonous cultures, and (2) a rejection of a generally despotic and inefficient statism which has accompanied a long process of widespread decadence. In a country with a long and complex history such as Spain, there has been no lack of historical opportunities to legitimize identities or implement political programmes of action at sub-state level. It may be for this reason that minority nationalisms of the twentieth century (Basque, Catalan, Galician) 'rediscovered' the political value of their own cultural markers (chiefly language) to maintain different claims from the other Spanish ethnoterritorial movements. The Catalan nationalist thinker Enric Prat de la Riba reflected this vision in his criticism of the Catalanist autonomism put forward by Valentí Almirall:

> [Almirall] puts forward the idea that the constituent units of the [Spanish] compound state should be the large regions which used to be independent kingdoms: Castile, Leon, Galicia, Majorca, Catalonia, Aragon, Valencia, Asturias, Navarre. [However], putting together Castile, Catalonia, Valencia, Galicia, Leon, Biscay and Andalusia as members of one single unit without taking into account the larger or lesser differences that unite or separate them is untenable. Why Extremadura and why not La Mancha? Why Asturias and why not La Rioja? ... The differences separating Castile and Catalonia, Catalonia and Galicia, Andalusia and the Basque Country are broad, total and irreducible ... Language separates them ... Instead, how would it be justifiable to separate into two different units Castile and Leon, or Extremadura and Andalusia, where differences can be traced and can be found?[18]
>
> (Prat de la Riba, 1917: pp. 31–4)

In contemporary times, language has played a fundamental role in the revitalization of minority nationalisms, introducing a distinguishing element into the internal asymmetry of the Spanish national state.[19] However, the ethnoterritorial nationalist and regionalist movements that have emerged have also appealed to other cohesive factors, principally history and mythology. In this respect, few analysts would dare to affirm that Castile, at the beginning of the third millennium, is a national unity which groups together, for linguistic reasons, territories such as Cantabria, Murcia, La Rioja, or even Andalusia, to mention some of those which are historically Spanish Castilian-speaking.

Obviously, language, and to a lesser extent dialects, shared dialects and regional accents, can provide a solid base for ethnoterritorial self-assertion which is constantly present anyway in everyday life, alien to and unaffected by more sophisticated cultural constructions. Notwithstanding this, the recourse to history is, in the Spanish case, the principal source that feeds identity and sociopolitical mobilization. This is not only true at the ethnoterritorial level, but at the level of Spain as a whole. This last feature is often undervalued by some of the sub-state nationalisms and regionalisms, but it has remained a constant in the formation of the Spanish national character. Some of the most notable historical landmarks that illustrate this are the Reconquista of Spain, colonization of the Americas, the *Guerra de la Independencia* (Peninsular War) and, in tragic contrast, the Civil War.

The dichotomy between majority Spanish nationalism and minority peripheral nationalisms has often been the object of absurd historical misinterpretations and numerous political and social misunderstandings. For this reason, it is worth examining the question, albeit briefly. In any case, it illustrates effectively the ethnoterritorial heterogeneity that so characterizes Spain.[20]

MAJORITY AND MINORITY NATIONALISMS IN SPAIN

As we saw in Chapter 1, nationalism manifests itself broadly in two ways. The first is majority or state nationalism, in which nation and state are considered to be identical, or when a single nation clearly prevails in a plural state, acting with a view towards national assimilation. The second case, minority or peripheral nationalism, is often the result of an uneasy ethnic or ethnoterritorial integration in the processes of state-formation, and involves the desire of sub-state communities to possess political structures of self-government.

. By the end of the Peninsular War (1814), Spain was an 'aggregate monarchy', entering the liberal era with heterogeneous internal units, which lacked articulation (Elorza, 1975). Spanish nation-building in its early stages aimed to transfer sovereignty from the monarch to an institutionalized nation. This historical phase corresponded to the 'institutional nationalism' of the nineteenth century, having been preceded by the 'Bourbon nationalism' of the eighteenth century, and the 'Habsburg paleo-nationalism' of the sixteenth and seventeenth centuries (de Riquer and Ucelay-Da Cal, 1994).[21]

From the very beginning, the Spanish liberal nationalists undertook a task they thought historic: that of putting into practice a process for Spanish national construction. In Spain, the task of dismantling the cumbersome remains of the feudal past, supported by the efficiency of the French Jacobins, fell on the fragile shoulders of the nineteenth-century liberals. For them, centralism, liberalism, progress and uniformity were not only complementary but inseparable elements.[22] However, nothing like the French Revolution of 1789 was to occur on a national scale in Spain.

Throughout the nineteenth century, the inability of Spanish liberal nationalism to articulate a coherent strategy for the country's territorial particularities, in addition to the actions and reactions of the military *caudillos*, acted as a stimulus for federalism and regionalism, later peripheral nationalism and, eventually, separatism. In fact, during the nineteenth century in Spain, the authoritarian and arbitrary exercise of power was precisely the reason for the national state's becoming a vehicle of imposition and repression, and thus the prime cause of the peripheral reaction.

The Restoration period (1876–1923) was characterized by a tough ideological and political struggle between majority and minority nationalisms. For Antonio Cánovas del Castillo (1876–1923), the true architect of the longest-lasting political regime in contemporary Spanish politics, the various nationalities should converge towards a common centre, integrating their 'races' into one nation. Thus, the Spanish state should tend towards the absorption of 'the various nations which may constitute it'.[23]

The centralizing Spanish nationalism of the Restoration synthesized its political programme and vision through the concept of the homeland: 'nor should one ask the homeland why, if she so orders it that at the foot of her flag a man should give his life, for she is for ever right about this also'. Note that Cánovas del Castillo identifies the homeland with the Spanish nation. But in the political practice of his time, such patriotic designs ended up being determined by the sovereignty of a people whose representative institutions (government and parliament) were corrupt and the instruments of an illegitimate self-contained political class.[24] Furthermore, from the perspective of this Spanish nationalism, the concept of the nation-state went beyond temporal co-ordinates: it was by nature indissoluble. Not even the power of the ballot could threaten national unity. This is precisely the reason behind Spanish state nationalism's denial of the existence of peripheral nationalisms.

By the end of the nineteenth century, an 'ideal' Castilian conception of Spain predominated. The underdeveloped Castile also happens to lie at the very centre of the peninsula. It was the Catalanist Valentí Almirall who suggested the idea of a frustrating central plateau–periphery dichotomy, in which unitarism appeared to subject the more advanced regions to the standards of those which were underdeveloped (Trías Vejarano and Elorza, 1975). Bearing this in mind, it is hardly surprising that political Catalanism and Basque nationalism played with the idea of separatism as a viable option. Both regarded it as improbable that the constituent Spanish communities, dominated as they were by an artificial and suffocating Spanish state, would survive. The consequence of such a disparity of views was the disgraceful antagonism between centre and periphery during the first decades of the twentieth century:

> In the clash of misunderstandings between Spanish and peripheral nationalism, Catalan nationalism was not the least intransigent. It expressed maximalist disqualification[25] of any manifestation of Spanish [majority] nationalism, and denied the existence of any bases for it. Likewise, Spanish nationalism had a similar view with respect to Catalanism'.
>
> (de Blas, 1991: p. 100)

Late modernization, regional industrialization, peripheral nationalism, weak state institutions, deep class differences and poverty were among the main features of Spanish society in the early twentieth century. However, these aspects did not coalesce into the 'two Spains' to which the poet Antonio Machado alluded when referring to the internal confrontation that culminated in the Civil War (1936–39). Instead, class and territorial differences produced a set of multiple and interlocked conflicts. Collective interests and confrontations did not reflect a simple model of centre–periphery duality.

During its brief historical existence the Second Republic (1931–39) tried to solve the conflicts between majority and minority nationalisms. The Constitution of 1932 adopted a regional model of territorial organization which provided the framework for the subsequent granting of autonomy to Catalonia, the Basque Country and Galicia. Both anticlerical and ethnoterritorial issues played a crucial role in the process of political polarization prior to the Spanish Civil War; even within the republican forces the dilemma between regionalism and centralism created considerable controversy and turmoil. In the end, the enemies of liberal democracy in the Spain of the 1930s managed, by means of a military uprising, to destroy any possible consensus concerning the territorial articulation of the various Spanish nationalities and regions.

After the conflict, the victors eliminated every sign of the territorial structuring which the Second Republic had initiated. Under Franco

Spain was controlled by a coalition notable for its hypercentralism and for its imperialistic fantasies. Spain became 'one, great and free'.

In contemporary western European political history there has been virtually no greater concentration of power, for such a long period of time, than that held by General Franco's regime. In spite of this, the regime's obsession with a culturally regimented and politically uniform Spain merely served to stimulate and legitimize the struggle of minority nationalisms and regionalisms to assert themselves. We need to remember here that, seen from a more general perspective, attempts to erode or suppress national traits or collective communities often produce a reaction contrary to that desired by those in power. This is because nationalism, either in its state or minority manifestations, obtains the sympathy of the previously unsympathetic. And what is more, it tends to be legitimized by an external oppression or 'external adversary', and not a supposed national essence.[26]

The wide political consensus that made the elaboration and later popular plebiscite of the 1978 Constitution possible could be seen as a reflection of a more mature view of the old dichotomy between Spain's two conflicting kinds of nationalism. However, its dispositions towards the territorial organization of the state were left open to be dealt with by a later development: the gradual process of setting up the *Comunidades Autónomas*.

The progressive inception of the *Estado de las Autonomías* initiated in 1978 can be explained by the characterization of a model of *multiple ethnoterritorial concurrence*. To explain all-encompassing phenomena and political processes as complex as the decentralization of power in Spain since 1980 is a weighty task for the social scientist. The explanatory model put forward here aims at providing interpretations for the understanding of such an intricate political process. In the next section the guidelines which set the conceptual boundaries of this interpretative model are put forth.

MULTIPLE ETHNOTERRITORIAL CONCURRENCE

In Spain multiple ethnoterritorial concurrence relates to the interplay among Spanish regions and nationalities pursuing political and economic power, as well as the achievement of the legitimization of their institutional development. It incorporates in a dynamic manner the economic, political and political elements that are central to Spain's process of federalization (Moreno, 1994, 1995, 1997a).

Given the Spanish context of open interactions, *concurrence* is used to mean a simultaneous occurrence of events at both state and sub-state levels within plural Spain. However, the term *concurrence* should not be understood as being equivalent to that of *competition*. In decentralized Spain there are competitive actions between state and sub-state nationalisms and regionalisms, and between the latter amongst themselves. But the underlying feature in the process of Spanish concurrence – mainly between central and meso levels – is the lack of compulsion to eliminate other participants. In some other instances the logic of competition implies instead the aim of achieving the monopoly by means of the elimination of the competitors (Popper, 1976).[27]

Thus concurrence is associated with the eventual accomplishment of broad political agreements, though these do not arise necessarily, nor as a result of lineal processes. Underlying this semantic interpretation of *concurrence* there are, chiefly, elements of asymmetry, heterogeneity and plurality. Taken together they constitute the federalizing rationale in the process of setting up the *Estado de las Autonomías*.

To give a clear structure to our explanatory model of multiple ethnoterritorial concurrence it is worth adopting a sequential categorization as in the following framework. First, two axioms[28] related to the Spanish case, although they are generally applicable to most of the contemporary world's decentralized and federal-like systems: (a) *conflicting intergovernmental relations*; and (b) *politicizing of ethnoterritorial institutions*. Second, two premises dating from the pre-*Estado de las Autonomías* era will be analysed: (c) *differential fact*; and (d) *centralist inertia*. Third, three principles will be identified as fundamental pillars upon which the organizational rationale of the 1978 Constitution rests (explicitly or implicitly): (e) *democratic decentralization*; (f) *comparative grievance*; and (g) *interterritorial solidarity*. And finally, three rules will be shown to play a most important role in the social and political structuring of the progressive process of federalization in Spain: (h) *spatial centrifugal pressure*; (i) *ethnoterritorial mimesis*; and (j) *inductive allocation of powers*. We shall now consider each of these concepts in turn.

(a) The axiom of *conflicting intergovernmental relations* is shared by most of the plural systems of government. Usually, it is closely linked to the diversity in the political leanings and partisan affiliations present at all levels of government and other institutions representing territorial interests. Conflict and agreement are also present in intergovernmental relations in Spain as in any other federal-like state. Owing to the open nature of the provisions of the 1978 Constitution regarding state territorial organization, a climate of permanent political bargaining among local, regional and central governments is bound to remain as the most characteristic feature of the (as yet unfinished) Spanish process of decentralization (Agranoff, 1993).

It must be said that since 1980 criticisms of the degree of dispersion and fragmentation of political life have flourished in Spain. Advocates of unitary Spain have proposed new forms of centralization as 'solutions' to what is considered an 'unbearable' situation. Such criticisms come from those who feel threatened by a sense of uncertainty and the provisional nature of intergovernmental relations. These perceptions are not in tune with the constitutional precepts and their implications which have guided the development of the Spanish system of decentralized government.

In fact, intergovernmental conflict and agreement in Spain are inseparable from a spatial and open distribution of power provided for in Title VIII of the 1978 Constitution. The provisions contained in the Constitution owe their existence, in turn, to the broad political and social consensus in favour of democracy that was reached after the death of Franco. One must recognize that internal ethnoterritorial accommodation in Spain will never be free from the tensions and deals characteristic of federal-like systems.

The political culture of Spain has not yet fully assimilated the values which necessarily accompany the coexistence of political institutions led by different parties which also have disparate territorial interests. The interaction between the territorial levels of administration takes place with some friction. On occasions, such tensions are used to resolve individual struggles for power or to establish party control. There is in effect a certain confusion involving ideology and public policy which clouds Spaniards' perceptions of political life.

Nevertheless, in the last two decades, there has been widespread agreement over questions of major importance for the consolidation of the *Estado de las Autonomías*. In particular, the reform of the system for financing the 15 *Comunidades Autónomas* of the so-called 'common regime' has mounted the biggest challenge in recent times (see Chapter 4, p. 132). These negotiations between regional and central governments were set to provide a more stable and functional framework for public expenditure and fiscal co-responsibility, as well as to facilitate a more effective level of horizontal equalization so that economic disparities among regions could be reduced.

(b) The axiom of the *politicizing of ethnoterritorial institutions* is associated with the practices of political rivalry among the three layers of government in pursuit of maximizing their political image and performance. An example is that of 1992, when three major international events were held in Spain: the Olympic Games in Barcelona, Seville's World Fair, and the European Cultural Capital for Madrid. Each level of government directly involved in the organization of these events ran political publicity and marketing campaigns.[29] This exercise of governmental patronage is carried out not only for domestic purposes but, given the process of European convergence and the increasing interdependence of the world economy, also as a means of attracting interest and investment from abroad.

At the meso level, the consolidation and growing influence of regional elites have induced neocorporatist capacities for co-option and negotiation. This accretion of sub-state national power is commensurate with the growing capacity of regional elites for negotiation. Their practices are legitimized by the constitutional order and are grounded in the increasing budgetary manoeuvrability of the *Comunidades Autónomas* mesogovernments. Percentage changes in public expenditure in Spain illustrate this phenomenon explicitly: between 1981 and 1998, central government expenditure dropped from 87 per cent to 54 per cent of the total, and regional spending rose to 33 per cent. Local spending increased from 10 to 13 per cent (see Table 2.4, p. 66).

In any case, the European vocation made patent by all of the Spanish nationalities and regions is to be emphasized. In fact, some of the most powerful minority nationalisms in Spain (Basque, Catalan) regard the consolidation of the European Union as the most desirable scenario where the powers of central governments and the very idea of the nation-state would be in retreat. This European outlook is also symptomatic of a general desire to leave behind the long stagnation of the Franco era, during which Spain remained isolated from the process of European integration (see Chapter 4, p. 144 for the analysis of the development of a new *cosmopolitan localism* in Europe).

(c) The premise of *differential fact* is taken to refer to a feature, or rather a combination of features, which characterize one ethnic group or community as opposed to another. It is therefore a concept deriving much of its meaning from a rather subjective perspective rooted in the ethnicity or ethnic identity of a given people. It seems clear that the mobilization patterns of the 'historical nationalities' (Basque, Catalan, Galician) have been premised on this differential fact since the earliest stages of the decentralization process in Spain. This idea is directed towards the historical origins of the Basque Country, Catalonia and Galicia – sub-state nations whose own languages, which are different from Spanish (Castilian), are also 'official' according to the Constitution. Media and citizens in these nationalities use autochthonous languages, and their regional parliaments and governments have greatly encouraged the preservation and protection of this cultural legacy.

Self-awareness of their own *differential fact* is a permanent incentive for the Basque Country, Catalonia and Galicia to maintain their institutional distinctiveness in relation to the rest of the *Comunidades Autónomas*. The 'historical nationalities' claim a legitimate political advantage over the other regions for having had self-governing institutions during the Second Republic. Moreover, Basque and Catalan nationalisms, along with other democratic opposition forces, were especially active during the late Franco years, and during the process of transition to democracy in Spain after 1975.[30] Since the beginning of the process of decentralization in the late 1970s they have insisted on their 'distinct origin'.

However, it is worth remembering that the sociopolitical mobilization in Andalusia which led to the referendum of 28 February 1980, for achieving the same constitutional procedure and degree of self-government as previously pursued by the 'historical nationalities', brought a crucial element of heterogeneity to devolution and the 'home rule all round' process. This development influenced the model, implicitly accepted by Catalan and Basque nationalists, of implementing only home rule for the 'historical nationalities' while the rest of the regions would merely be granted administrative decentralization. The Andalusian 'demonstration effect' sparked off a desire to catch up from other regions in search of equal access to home rule. Since then, the premise of the *differential fact* has been closely linked to the principle of *comparative grievance* analysed below.

Most significantly, the *differential fact* also manifests itself in the form of powerful nationalist parties and political coalitions in the 'historical nationalities'. This is a key element in the articulation of a popular feeling of being distinct from the rest of the Spanish peoples. However, when the *differential fact* is seen in terms of politics and of the distribution of power, it displays an asymmetry which is not easy to interpret in the light of the future development of the Spanish *Estado de las Autonomías*.

One would think that the distinct origins of the 'historical nationalities' could become a reason for them to draw attention to their differences. It seems logical that they wish want to maintain their differences with other *Comunidades Autónomas* where certain traits are concerned (culture, geography, language, traditions). It remains to be seen whether such a desire is extensible to other fields, in which it is possible for the *differential facts* (economic, institutional or social) to be wielded by almost all the regions of Spain.

(d) The premise of the *centralist inertia* is rooted in a longstanding perception of the superior value of the central administration. This perception is the result not only of a tradition of authoritarian rule, which includes Franco's lengthy dictatorship (1939–75), but also of the Jacobin attitude imported from France and espoused by Spanish liberals throughout the nineteenth century. According to their view, state and central government, as well as nation and citizenry, were interchangeable concepts.

At the beginning of the decentralization process a significant number of politicians and state officials disregarded demands, needs and expectations of both regional and local administrations. They also tried, in covert ways, to discredit aspirations for home rule. But the decision of the Constitutional Court against the main provisions of the 'centralizing' LOAPA (see Chapter 2, p. 63) was a decisive setback to their attempts at 'harmonization'. Nevertheless, since then the devolution of powers has not been entirely free of interference and resistance from the higher echelons of bureaucracy. This is a result of the ingrained centralist mentality, still extant among central bodies and institutions in Spain, which sees the 'home rule all round' process as entailing the dismantling of the unitary state.

The very term 'state' is ambiguously employed in the text of the 1978 Constituion. In some articles (1, 56, 137 and, significantly, in Title VIII) the intention is for the term to denote the entire organization of the Spanish legal–political system. Thus, the term covers the regional administrations as well as the other agencies and administrative bodies which compose the entire structure of the state. In other constitutional articles (3.1, 149 and 150) the state is considered to be synonymous with the institutions of the central administration, together with their peripheral administration, which may on occasions clash with autonomous administrations. The Constitutional Court's judgment on 28 July 1981 clarified the semantic conflict by asserting that the state must be regarded as a composite whole including all the institutions of central, regional and local governments. Whatever the case, a certain mentality persists among some politicians and opinion leaders which regards *Comunidades Autónomas* as politically dependent on the central administration. This is considerably aggravated by the absence of lateral territorial representation, and especially by the political paralysis of the Senate. The reform of the Upper House (see Chapter 4, p. 134), with a view to eliminating serious misunderstandings, is an urgent matter. *Centralist inertia*, therefore, continues to act as a traditional inhibitor of Spain's spontaneous inclination towards the self-government of the nationalities and regions that constitute it.[31]

(e) The foundations for the principle of *democratic decentralization* were laid down, paradoxically, by Francoism. A unitary concept of Spain taken from the totalitarian ideas and values of some of those who had 'won' the Civil War (1936–39) had been imposed through a defence of Spanish nationalism. In the eyes of those who had 'lost' the war, however, all things 'Spanish' came to be tainted with Franco's cultural genocide, repression and reinvention of history. As a consequence, many of the democratic forces were suspicious of the 'Spanish'. Throughout the Franco era, 'Spanish' symbolism had tried to hide the plural reality of Spain.

The democratic opposition forces to Franco's regime articulated a strategy of political action which amalgamated both the struggle for the recovery of democratic liberties and the quest for the decentralization of power. The quest for democracy and territorial home rule thus went hand in hand.

Particularly in the so-called 'historical nationalities' (the Basque Country, Catalonia and Galicia) the struggle against dictatorship was a reaction against Francoist attempts to destroy the ethnoterritorial markers (such as language, cultural traditions or self-governed institutions). In fact, the ideology of home rule and political decentralization spread all over Spain and became a key element in the interparty political negotiations during the transition to democracy (1975–79).

The rise of demands for regional self-government during the 1970s and 1980s was due largely to a desire to establish democratic institutions, which brought decision-making closer to the people. Since then, the existence of democracy and freedom in Spain is inexorably linked to the continued protection and survival of power in a decentralized form, and the autonomy of the nationalities and regions.

If the institutional mechanisms of *democratic decentralization* have been erratic, it is as a result of the ambiguity of many of the clauses of the Constitution. It is also a consequence of the fact that those who negotiated and those who wrote the Constitution did so in an excessively legalistic style. It is certainly true that the ultimate form of the *Estado de las Autonomías* could not be precisely predetermined by mere legal parameters. But these deficiencies cannot hide the political feeling that the existence of democracy and freedom in Spain is inexorably linked to the continued legitimacy of power in a decentralized form and to the autonomy of the country's regions.

(f) The principle of *comparative grievance* determines the mobilization patterns of the nationalities and regions in Spain to a large extent. In accordance with this, the exercise of the right to autonomy legitimately practised by the regions compels them to claim the same degree of autonomy as the 'historical nationalities'. This is a principle they actively apply to themselves. None of these regions wants to be left behind. This principle conflicts with the premise of the *differential fact* claimed by the Basque Country, Catalonia and Galicia. Perceptions of *comparative grievance* and the *differential fact* cannot easily be translated into legislation reflecting social realities with varying aspirations for the degree of self-government to be achieved.

A reinterpretation of the popular saying 'coffee for all', expressed in the early stages of the decentralization process,[32] is required. However, it should not be thought of as a neo-centralist strategy that seeks to homogenize the political status of all 17 *Comunidades Autonómas*, thus spoiling the principle of the *differential fact*, but as a claim for a fair share, voiced by all the regions (apart from Catalonia and the Basque Country) which want the same treatment.

Indeed, many regions were encouraged by the leading parties (principally UCD and PSOE, in the early 1980s) to participate in the then nascent decentralization process. These parties had taken part in the *Pactos Autonómicos* (Autonomical Pacts) of 1981 with the aim of 'co-ordinating' the development of the *Estado de las Autonomías*. Once the decentralization process had made substantial headway and entered a more mature stage, the system still had to contend with the potentially disruptive forces of grievance, levelling and differences, which threatened its stability. Leading members of the main Spanish political parties in the 1990s (PSOE and PP) insisted on a 'homogenization of the Autonomies' (Eguiagaray, 1993: p. 99) and on the 'spreading out of responsibilities' (Rajoy, 1993: p. 48). However, perceptions such as *comparative grievance* and the *differential fact* are not easily extensible to positive legislation in that they reflect social realities that are not necessarily quantifiable in financial or institutional terms.

Comparisons may be made from perspectives such as that found in Catalonia, a 'rich' community where the perception of a *comparative fiscal grievance* has traditionally manifested itself in the form of a strong argument in support of political Catalanism. This perception is based on the idea, shared by a considerable number of Catalans, that their community receives much less from the central administration than their total contribution to the Spanish Treasury.[33] This feeling of financial discrimination has not only been perceived as an obstacle to the later development of Catalonia, but, significantly, it has been traditionally interpreted as the negligence of an inefficient state apparatus, which also fails to promote the growth of other less developed regions in Spain.[34]

In a country where grudges and envies are inherent features shared by all its idiosyncrasies, the zealous desire not to get left behind or be neglected could hardly fail to play a major role in the development of the most ambitious and innovative project in contemporary Spanish political history. In this sense, as the *Estado de las Autonomías* gradually takes shape, the *Comunidades Autónomas* keep an eye on each other and scrutinize, both formally and informally, the transfers and delegations of power which might entail a position of 'privilege' of one given community over the others.

(g) The principle of *interterritorial solidarity* is laid down in the 1978 Constitution (Article 2) as fundamentally necessary to guarantee the integration and interrelation of the Spanish nationalities and regions. From a more mundane point of view, the principle refers to the transfer of funds from the richer to the poorer regions of Spain, with the aim of attaining a minimal level of basic services state-wide, together with a fair and adequate distribution of the financial burdens.

The Constitution states (Article 40) that the three levels of public power (central, regional and local) must seek to balance out the rates of income, both regional and personal, attending to the modernization and development of all economic sectors, with the ultimate aim of bringing the standard of living of all Spaniards up to the same level (Article 130). It also stipulates that the state should guarantee the effective application of the solidarity principle through seeking an economic balance among the Spanish *Comunidades Autónomas*, so that differences between their statutes of autonomy may in no case imply economic or social privileges (Article 138).

With the gradual development of the 'home rule all round' process in Spain, nationalities and regions came to see territorial autonomy not merely as the means for bringing institutional decision-making closer to the citizens. They – particularly the economically poorer territories – also laid emphasis on the constitutional principle of interregional solidarity. The *Fondo de Compensación Interterritorial* (Interterritorial Compensation Fund) was established to ensure the application of the constitutional solidarity principle (Article 158). But this institutional formula has proved unable to even out differences in territorial wealth. The less developed communities have not been able to raise their capacity for investment in a significant way, in part because the funds available are modest but also because there are no clear criteria for positive discrimination designed to channel resources towards these communities. The poorer *Comunidades Autónomas* have a better chance of obtaining funds for regional and structural development from the European Community.[35]

Differences in management capacity, however, have brought about an incentive for the less developed regional administrations to catch up with those more advanced in new policy design and provision. A 'demonstration effect' regarding the implementation of policies by the *Comunidades Autónomas* is noticeable, together with policy transfers in those areas of their competence.[36]

It is unreasonable to expect that income levels will balance out automatically across the regions of Spain as a result of an improved management of the poorer communities and towns. Equally, there is no reason to doubt that this would effectively contribute to a closer convergence. Nor can it be argued that the action of free market forces produces a 'natural' levelling of territorial imbalances. This is a sophistry that has no basis in economic reality. On the other hand, it is often the case that central government intervention in the economy often reflects the interests of regional elites, co-opted at the request of the administration. Examples of such practices are legion throughout the political history of Spain in the nineteenth and twentieth centuries, as in other south European countries.[37] Only through the concerted action of the central, regional and local administrations will it be possible to maintain adequate levels of interterritorial solidarity in accordance with the potential of each region's civil society.

(h) The political pressure exerted upon central power by both Basque and Catalan nationalisms contributed decisively in 1978 to the establishment of a constitutional accommodation which recognized the internal plurality of Spain (Conversi, 1997). Since then, and during the continuing decentralization process, the rule of *spatial centrifugal pressure* has been repeatedly and generally applied by ethnoterritorial political elites. It has been used not only as a vehicle for negotiation, but also to dissuade certain politicians and higher civil servants of the central administration from reverting to centralizing tendencies.

The continuous and active presence of representatives of the Catalan and Basque nationalist parties in the Spanish parliament has been crucial in the consolidation of an *autonomist* vision of the state with respect to the political relations between the three levels of government. What is more, the increasing relative power of regional or federated organizations linked to national coalitions and parties has also contributed decisively to the federalization of politics in Spain. The electoral success of new regional parties has reinforced the crucial importance of the spatial element in Spanish politics. After the 2000 general election, nine out of the 12 parties with parliamentary representation in the Spanish Chamber of Deputies were sub-state nationalists or regionalists (34 MPs in total). These parties collected 11 per cent of the popular vote (for the electoral results during 1977–2000, see Table 2.3, p. 62)

The relative power of those regional and federated branches of the main Spanish political parties has increased noticeably in both the internal processes of party policy-making and the leadership contest. The federal organization of the Socialist Party (PSOE) and the United Left (IU), and the political agreements established by the Popular Party (PP) and PSOE with regionalist and nationalist regional parties (PA in Andalusia, PAR in Aragon, UPN in Navarre) have also greatly contributed to Spaniards becoming accustomed to the federalization of politics.[38]

The centrifugal effects of political negotiation on a territorial level in Spain tend to be multiplied by the bilateral relations between central and regional administrations. The practice of bilateralism, combined with comparative grievance, entails major difficulties for the *Estado de las Autonomías*, given that the 17 *Comunidades Autónomas* will exert centrifugal pressures of every kind over questions of common interest.

Intergovernmental co-operation of considerable political value has been initiated by sectorial conferences involving the central government and the *Comunidades Autónomas* (see Chapter 4, p. 139). Even at the level of consultation, these conferences are vital for the articulation of policies discussed, agreed by consensus, or only partially agreed. The prolonged absence of legislative requirements which systematize federal practices in Spain could in the long run get in the way of the consolidation of the Spanish *Estado de las Autonomías*.

(i) The rule of the *ethnoterritorial mimesis* has been the main factor responsible for 'tuning' the decentralization process in Spain. Nationalities and regions are constitutive units of the Spanish state. However, there is a clear asymmetry where the legitimacy of their political claims is concerned. According to the referential mechanism of the ethnoterritorial mimesis, the 'historical nationalities' (the Basque Country, Catalonia and Galicia) aimed at replicating the powers and symbols of the Spanish central state (their own police force, official visits to foreign places, public policies in the field of education, health and social policy, external and ornamental signs such as the flag, the anthem, and so forth). On deploying their political claims during the 1980s, a second group of *Comunidades Autónomas* with 'earlier' aspirations for home rule (Andalusia, Canary Islands, Navarre, Valencia)[39] have attempted to 'imitate' the institutional outlook of the 'historical nationalities'. A third group of 'late-comer' regions in the home rule process of decentralization (Aragon, Asturias, the Balearic Islands, both Castiles, Extremadura, Murcia) have struggled not to feel discriminated against by the achievements of those 'early rising' regions referred to in the second stage of the mimetic sequence. Ethnoterritorial mimesis has also applied to those communities with less well-defined ethnoterritorial identities.[40]

From the perspective of administrative organization, the

Comunidades Autónomas have chosen to reproduce the state to scale instead of reducing the state apparatus, both at the central and regional levels.[41] For this reason, a large number of the criticisms directed towards the persistence of a costly and inefficient regional replication of the central administration could be extended to public agencies of the *Comunidades Autónomas*, and in particular to the relations between these institutions and local councils.

In line with the concept of *ethnoterritorial mimesis*, it could be argued that Basque nationalism, especially in its most separatist forms, has played with the idea of setting up an independent state for the Basque Country. Given the peculiar confederation of its provincial *historical territories*,[42] such a state, paradoxically, would be structured very much like plural Spain. Modern political Catalanism, for its part, wants an independent fiscal system rather like the quota mechanisms currently operating in the Basque Country, if not simply a greater degree of financial autonomy. Galicia would probably follow Catalonia in having more power transferred from central state institutions. It should be noted, however, that the *mechanicity* of the mimetic process would remain relative to the extent to which citizens of the Basque Country identified themselves as Spanish, at least to some significant degree, and that *Catalanisme* maintained its tradition of being an inclusive nationalism which seeks to reform Spain as well as Catalonia. The strength of radical nationalism in Galicia does not seem to indicate anything like the collapse of a popular desire to belong to Spain as a whole.

However, nationalists in the Basque Country, Catalonia and Galicia have insisted on the idea of a 'shared sovereignty' within the Spanish state. On 16 July 1998 the 'Declaration of Barcelona' was signed by the Basque Partido Nacionalista Vasco (PNV), the Catalan Convergència i Unió (CiU), and the Galician Bloque Nacionalista Galego (BNG). They claimed the establishment of a confederal model of political accommodation in Spain.[43]

(j) The rule of the *inductive allocation of powers* sets the pace of the construction of Spain's *Estado de las Autonomías*. This rule, which is implicit in the provisions of Title VIII of the 1978 Constitution, draws attention to the fact that the division of powers between the three territorial levels of the administration is a matter yet to be completed.[44]

Essentially, the Spanish decentralization process has followed an open model of territorial structuring which only the passage of time has gradually defined, as indeed it will continue to do. It must be remembered that during the transition to democracy this was one of the thorniest issues on which to reach agreement, and therefore required complete consensus.

The fine-tuning of the federalizing technique for the distribution of political powers and financial resources, together with the general objective of reconciling both the highest level of decentralization and the necessary intergovernmental co-ordination, remains an enduring challenge for the consolidation of the Spanish *Estado de las Autonomías*.

The degree of heterogeneity among the 17 *Comunidades Autónomas* has levelled over time, although the decentralization process is far from complete. In contrast to the traditional philosophy upon which federal states such as Germany, Australia, the United States or Switzerland have been modelled and built, the decentralization process in Spain can only be regarded as complete once a period of intergovernmental familiarity has elapsed. When this situation has been achieved, a constitutional revision should functionally incorporate these divisions of powers so as to avoid the great political difficulties that would have occurred had the process developed inversely. At the same time, the process of European convergence will exercise considerable influence in the 'final' distribution of regional powers and responsibilities.

The gradual allocation of powers between the three layers of governments and the eventual constitutional review would seem to be the best route to federalization as it avoids the dangers of territorial de-structuring. (This is what happened with the case of *cantonalismo* during the Spanish First Federal Republic of 1873.)[45] In fact, the ideological dichotomy between federalism 'from the top' or 'from below' has become rather obsolete, as demonstrated by countries with long-standing historical federal experiences, which were consolidated by developing either of the two alternative modes. In different contexts and conjunctures the political initiative for the building of federal systems has remained with any of the three levels of government (central, regional, local). However, the essential feature of the federal formula has remained unchanged: compound government legitimized by a territorial pact between unity and diversity.

In Spain the absence of an enlightened and commanding central elite has gone hand in hand with a constant affirmation of ethnoterritorial diversity. The federalization of the *Estado de las*

Autonomías must not be confused with the unfolding of more or less sophisticated constitutional governing techniques. It is largely a matter of finding a political place for the vitality of its constituent units and of institutionalizing the free and natural understanding in which its citizens and peoples engage daily.

In sum, territorial politics in Spain can be regarded as the expression of a mode of *multiple ethnoterritorial concurrence* that relates sub-state mobilization with the interplay among Spanish regions and nationalities. Spain has faced the turn of the millennium with much of its ancestral legacy undamaged by the powerful solvents of early modernity. The working out of federal arrangements, which could accommodate the asymmetrical relationships that exist among constituent units, is a formidable challenge. Recent steps taken in such a direction have resolved a long-standing conflict through negotiation and agreement. In Chapter 4 some of the most pressing reforms to be confronted are analysed further.

NOTES

1. Lenin, 1917: p. 227. Note the use that Lenin makes of England when referring to the United Kingdom.
2. Castilian, or Spanish (as it is usually referred to elsewhere), is the official language of the Kingdom of Spain. Approximately a quarter of the Spanish population of 40 million is bilingual. The vernacular languages are also official in their respective territories: Catalan (spoken by 4.2 million in Catalonia, 2.1 in Valencia, 0.2 in the Balearic Islands and 0.05 in Aragon); Basque (0.7 million in the Basque Country and 0.05 in Navarre); Galician (2.3 million). Other official languages, as declared in their regional statutes of autonomy, are Bable (spoken by 0.4 million in Asturias) and Aranese (0.004 in Catalonia). (Data collected from Sanmartí Roset, 1997: p. 67.) There are also a number of dialects of the aforementioned languages widely spoken in other regions (Andalusia, Canary Islands, Extremadura, Murcia).
3. The traditional political and economic noncongruence in Spain has been translated into a permanent rivalry between centre and periphery (Giner and Moreno, 1990). Historically, this dichotomy has been reflected in two main alternative models of state organization: centralist–authoritarian and decentralized–democratic. On the types of economic and political noncongruence, see P.A. Gourevitch (1979).
4. An internal cohesion which goes beyond the common institutional and political framework. According to Francisco Pi i Margall, 'if nations had no other cohesive strength than the political ... they would all be in pieces. Bonds a hundred times stronger make possible their survival: the community of history and sentiment, civil relations and economic interests' (1911: pp. 286–7).
5. An idea to be understood with reference to Spain and not to the whole of the Hispanic world.

6. Furthermore, during the nineteenth century for most of the progressive democratic parties the replacement of an obsolete and oligarchic monarchy was their main priority. State organization and internal plurality was considered a secondary concern.

7. According to Stein Rokkan,

> the decisive breakthrough toward unification and centralization came during the reigns of Philip Augustus (1180–1223) and Louis IX (1226–70). The royal domain was extended to Normandy and Anjou, and later far into the south with the conquest of Toulouse in the wake of the war against the Albigensian heretics … At the end of the Hundred Years' War in 1453 the English had lost all their territories on French soil except Calais and the process of consolidation and unification could get under way with renewed force. (Flora *et al.*: p. 217)

8. It is not easy to draw a line between the two concepts of patriotism and state nationalism. The former implies a loyalty to a lifestyle, a language and the culture of the country of reference. These elements could also be shared by the notion of state nationalism. However, the country of reference can be a minority nation within a compound state, such as the UK. It can be argued, in this respect, that those Scottish and Welsh soldiers serving with the British army in various wars during the last two centuries showed in the first place a sentiment of patriotism for their respective nations (Scotland and Wales).

9. In 1945 Robert McIntyre obtained for the Scottish National Party (SNP) the Motherwell parliamentary seat. In 1966 the Welsh nationalist Plaid Cymru won the Carmarthen by-election. A year later, the SNP did the same in the Hamilton by-election. In 1998, and as a consequence of renewed demands for home rule, a Scottish parliament 'reopened' in Edinburgh along with other devolutionary reforms.

10. The absence during the eighteenth and nineteenth centuries of Spanish influential philosophers and political thinkers comes as no surprise. This pattern has remained the same during the twentieth century, with the exception of Ortega y Gasset.

11. A notion put forward by economic ideas such as 'cumulative imbalance' and 'spatial polarization' (Myrdal, 1957; Perroux, 1964).

12. During this period the manufacturing industries fuelled the Catalan economy and the number of immigrants from Valencia and Aragon exceeded those Catalans who emigrated (mainly) to Cuba, Argentina and Uruguay. (Data reproduced in this section has been taken from Moreno, 1986).

13. While in 1846 Catalan textiles were 70 per cent more expensive than English products, in 1878 the difference reached 159 per cent (Izard, 1970, 1979).

14. Early political Catalanists failed to understand that the Catalan society reproduced some incongruities between modernity and traditionalism that hindered the possibility to 'catalanize' Spain as a whole, as expressed by the philosopher Miguel de Unamuno.

15. The leftist parties changed their Jacobin tendencies, in part, after the First World War. In its 1918 Congress, the Spanish Socialist Worker's Party (PSOE) passed a motion to recognize the right to self-government of the 'Iberian nationalities' in a 'republican confederation' (Carretero, 1988).

16. Many of these were no more than counties or even more local in character.

17. To quote Pi i Margall: 'What should it matter if here in Spain, Catalonia,

Aragon, Valencia and Murcia, both Andalusias, Extremadura, Galicia, Leon, Asturias, the Basque Provinces, Navarre, both Castiles, and the Canary Islands, should recover their autonomy?' (1911: p. 91).

18. Following this line of argument, the Catalan thinker asserted that 'each nation thinks as it speaks and speaks as it thinks' (1917: p. 83).

19. As José Antonio Maravall pointed out, as early as the seventeenth century, and under the Bourbon monarchy's policy of imposing the French idea of a single central language, the suspicion-free cohabitation which had been commonplace in the Spanish kingdoms, and later under a single monarchy in Spain, was broken: 'To refer to the case of Spain, the dominions of Portuguese, Castilian and Catalan overlap, and over them hovers the common reference to Spanish' (1986: I, p. 469).

20. Some historians call it 'homogeneity in diversity', which is supposed by historiography to have existed since the early Middle Ages. Saint Isidoro (570–636) had implied such a notion in his expression '*mater Hispania*' (Moreno Alonso, 1984).

21. These historians consider that Spanish nationalism, together with the Catalan, Galician and Basque nationalisms, the nationalist movements in Andalusia and the Canary Islands, and the other regionalists, share a common legacy and origins. For an 'archaeology' of Spanish nationalism, see Juaristi (1992).

22. Once the liberal regime in Spain made explicit its intentions, the only people to rebel against this confused programme were the federal republicans. Incipient Spanish federalism began to manifest itself in the ideas and actions of those who called themselves Democrats around 1840.

23. The quotations in this section corresponding to the conservative politician have been taken from the work of Manuel Moreno Alonso (1984: pp. 79–83). This work contains an extensive and useful historiographic revision of Spanish nationalisms in the nineteenth century.

24. Cánovas del Castillo himself was against free enterprise because he thought it endangered a nation's internal life. For much the same reason he believed international law to be infeasible.

25. Let us remember that in order to strengthen Catalan national consciousness, Enric Prat de la Riba stated that '[it was necessary] to know that we were Catalans and nothing but Catalans … [This] second phase of the process of Catalan national assertion was done with hate, not love' (1917: pp. 40–1).

26. For a discussion on the theory of the 'external adversary', see Solé Tura (1985).

27. According to Karl Popper a situation of concurrence can and ought to be explained as an unintentional consequence (usually unavoidable) of the human actions (conscious and planned) of the competitors.

28. Axioms, premises, principles and rules should not be regarded as the constituent parts of a philosophical syllogism or as propositions in some logical proof.

29. For instance, on the occasion of the 1992 Olympic Games in Barcelona, the Catalan government of the Generalitat financed full-page advertisements in the *Financial Times* with the aim of drawing attention to the idea that the city's geographical location is in Catalonia, further placed in a peninsular and European context. Similarly financed publicity has appeared since in other international media, including a Website on the Internet.

30. During the period of democratic transition after the death of the dictator, the leaders of the political groups representing the interests of the Catalan and

Basque territories were the only ones standing for territorial distinctiveness to participate in the various stages of interparty negotiation. Among other agreements, they signed the *Pactos de la Moncloa* in October 1977. This pact set up a crucial plan of political and economic action for the first years of the return to democracy after the dictatorship.

31. According to Juan José Lucas, president of the Castile and Leon regional government and member of the Popular Party, the state was reluctant to reform the old centralizing bureaucratic apparatus: 'There was no desire to substitute the centralist state by a [decentralized] autonomical state, and [as a result] we have to deal with two overlapping state organizations' (1993: pp. 68–70).

32. Or the 'cheese-board theory', at some point alluded to by the then Minister for the Regions, Manuel Clavero. By this, the rights and powers of the *Comunidades Autónomas* did not need to be seen as something to be hastened, but as something from which every party could take whatever it wished (Platón, 1994: p. 104).

33. At the time of the tenth anniversary of Catalonia's Statute of Autonomy, Ferran Font, president of the Economy and Finance Commission of the Catalan parliament, wrote: 'Catalonia is tied to financial agreements which its Autonomous Government accepted merely to avoid death by suffocation'. See 'The Development of the Statute of Autonomy' (*La Vanguardia*, 23 July 1989).

34. However, the region of Madrid pays more in taxes than any other *Comunidad Autónoma*. Madrid has around five million inhabitants, compared with Catalonia's six million. Madrid's net contribution to the Spanish Treasury is 10 per cent of its GDP, compared with 5 per cent of Catalonia's.

35. Nationalities and regions have claimed a right to participate in the planning and management of such funds as a logical feature of their self-governing powers. Thus, the distribution of moneys from the European Cohesion Fund has been effected under territorial criteria.

36. The 'Family Minimum Income Programme' provides an illustration of this. It was introduced in the Basque Country in March 1998 to combat poverty and situations of social exclusion, and constituted a precedent in the subsequent programmes of minimum income benefits implemented in all 17 *Comunidades Autónomas*. Although showing a degree of diversity in policy design and coverage, schemes of 'minimum income' developed by the Spanish 'historical nationalities' and regions aim at combining cash benefits with policies of social insertion (primarily employment promotion and vocational training schemes) (Moreno and Arriba, 1999).

37. The case of the Italian *Mezzogiorno* illustrates policies involving inefficiency and wastefulness, with the associated activities of the Mafia. The political reaction to this situation can be seen in the electoral success of the Lega Nord in the northern regions of Italy during the 1990s (Aguilera de Prat, 1999).

38. In addition to the fusion of the regional PP group in Navarre and the Unión del Pueblo Navarro, other groups have obtained parliamentary representation in Madrid, or in their regional parliaments. Among these, the following may be mentioned: Chunta, Coalición Canaria, Convergencia de Demócratas de Navarra, Extremadura Unida, Partido Andalucista, Partido Aragonés, Partido Regionalista de Cantabria, Partido Riojano, Partido Socialista de Mallorca, Partiu Asturianista, Unión Alavesa, Unión Mallorquina,

Unión para el Progreso de Cantabria, Unión del Pueblo Leonés, and Unión Valenciana.

39. In 1984 Joan Lerma (president of the Valencian government) already considered that there were not three 'historical nationalities', but six *Comunidades Autónomas* with different levels of powers: 'they are allowed to get to the same place, and in particular I have to emphasise that the legal treatment for Catalonia and the Basque Country is the same as that for Galicia, and also for Andalusia, for the Canaries and for ourselves [the Valencians]' (*La Vanguardia*, 16 April 1984).

40. Certain areas lacking in self-governing experience suddenly professed aspirations to autonomy. Cantabria, La Rioja and the province of Madrid became uniprovincial autonomies although they had never had a tradition of self-government.

41. According to Eliseo Aja (1988, 1999), the *Comunidades Autónomas* have not moved towards a reorganization adequate to their new powers, and have maintained similarities with the state structure. Nevertheless, economy and administrative rationality appear to demand a different approach, one which adjusts the organization of a region to its particular characteristics and dimensions.

42. The seven Basque territories claimed by the nationalists to constitute the Basque Country are Araba (Alava), Gipuzkoa (Guipuzcoa) and Bizkaia (Biscay), integrated in Spain, Lapurdi (Labourd), Benafarroa (Lower Navarre) and Zuberoa (Soule), in France, and Nafarroa (Navarre), also in Spain.

43. In November 1999, however, CiU signed a document prior to the re-election of Jordi Pujol as president of the Generalitat in order to secure the support of the PP members in the Catalan parliament. CiU reaffirmed its commitment to comply with the Spanish constitutional order. In this context, the Barcelona Declaration appeared to be rather symbolic.

44. Even in February 1984, the Spanish government declared that it did not know what the different levels of administration would look like by the end of the decentralization process (*El País*, 15 February 1984). Such a statement, which acknowledged the absence of a clear-cut constitutional division of powers in the three-tier system of government in Spain (local, regional and central), could have been made 15 years later.

45. In 1868, before his 'federalist disappointment', the Catalanist Valentí Almirall considered that, given the historical characteristics of Spain, 'the federal Constitution must be completed before the particular [constitutional statutes] of the [constituent] territories' (reproduced in Trías Vejarano and Elorza, 1975: p. 446).

4

The Federalizing *Estado de las Autonomías*

Spain today is a state for all Spaniards, a nation-state for a large part
of the population, and only a state but not a nation for important
minorities.

(Juan Linz)[1]

After approval by popular referendum of the 1978 Constitution,[2] the
expression 'Estado de las Autonomías' became popular in the daily
use not only of politicians, lawyers and the media, but also of the
citizenship at large. Experts on devolution and the decentralization of
power have also coined such an expression outside Spain. Indeed, the
contribution of the 'autonomical formula' to the theoretical debate on
the territorial organization of contemporary democracies has been
significant. Both its originality and relative success in devising the
bases for a democratic territorial articulation of Spain have attracted
the interest of politicians and political researchers alike. However, the
'autonomical formula' cannot be considered as a theoretical
construction *in vacuo*. Its closely conceptual link with federalism is
undeniable.

After the gradual inception of the Statutes of Autonomy in the 17
Comunidades Autónomas, there has been an intensification of
suggestions in line with a 'federal reading' of the 1978 Constitution.
The federalizing nature implicit in the internal logic of the *Estado de las
Autonomías* is assumed by a growing number of political analysts and
opinion leaders. In fact, the federalization of Spain is the most
desirable option for both ethnoterritorial accommodation and
intergovernmental relations in Spain.

The beginning of the process of devolution of power after the
death of dictator Franco was troublesome and complex. The
interparty political consensus was established along functional
'top–down' criteria, instead of by horizontal negotiation among the
Spanish territories involved. But the end result of the ongoing 'home

rule all round' process ought to be one of a gradual federalization and an extension of federal-like political practices.

In this chapter a sociological reality of the foremost importance in the Spanish context is analysed: dual identity. This manner of self-identification by a majority of Spaniards implies shared loyalties to both the central state and meso layers of government. Dual identity is at the root of the federalizing rationale of the *Estado de las Autonomías*. Later on, those areas susceptible to reform for the consolidation of the federal *modus operandi* are examined. We shall also consider the reform of the Senate as a genuine federal chamber and the institutionalization of federal practices, with special reference to intergovernmental relations. Finally, we shall reflect on how the cosmopolitan vocation of the Spanish mesogovernments is related to the process of European convergence based on the principles of territorial subsidiarity and democratic accountability.

DUAL IDENTITY AND SHARED LOYALTIES

Spain offers a striking example of the shortcomings of some theories of modernization, namely diffusionist functionalism. According to such a paradigm the diffusion of cultural and social structural values, together with modernization and economic development, should have provoked progressive cultural, political and economic integration, thus replacing territorial cleavages with a set of functional and economic conflicts, primarily class conflicts.

Indeed, the processes of state-formation and nation-building, accelerated by the development of industrial capitalism in Europe during the nineteenth century, contributed to the enforcement of central authority upon peripheral regions or subordinated groups. Integration, or rather assimilation, has been referred to as the operation by which communities which are socially and culturally heterogeneous transfer their loyalty to a wider state political system. Industrialization, urbanization and social communication were identified as significant developments of national integration, also labelled as 'modernization' in general terms. However, the cornerstone of national integration was to be the creation of a common national identity throughout the territory that was under the central state authority.

The case of Spain shows the lack of a single and all-embracing national state identity extended throughout the country. Spain's multiple ethnoterritorial identities are indicative that the problems derived from a lack of internal accommodation are exclusive not only to the countries that have recently achieved independence. In fact, the persistence of a dual identity or compound nationality reflects the ambivalent nature of the internal ethnoterritorial relations that have existed within Spain throughout its long and complex history.

In modern times, the state-formation experience has not extended to a successful integration of all the territories (that is, the minority nations and regions) within the domain of Spain. Central state institutions have at times enforced their authority, adopting dictatorial and despotic programmes of standardization. The result has been the recurrence of the 'national question', which we might also define as the 'question of nationalities'.

The concept of dual identity or compound nationality concerns the way in which citizens identify themselves in sub-state minority nations or regions. It incorporates in variable proportions the regional (ethnoterritorial) ascriptive identity and the national (state) identity. As a result of this, citizens share their institutional loyalties at both levels of political legitimacy without any apparent fracture between them.

The quest for self-government by meso-level communities is in full accordance with the variable manifestation of such duality in citizens' self-identification: the more the primordial ethnoterritorial identity prevails upon modern state identity, the higher the demands for political autonomy. Conversely, the more characterized the state-national identity is, the less likely it would be for ethnoterritorial conflicts to occur. When two communities (ethnoterritorial and state-national) identify themselves exclusively with respect to each other, the result of such antagonism will also tend to be exclusive. At the extreme, complete absence of one of the two elements of dual identity would lead to a sociopolitical fracture in the plural state. In such a situation, demands for self-government would probably take the form of a claim of the right for independence. In other words, when citizens in a sub-state community identify themselves in an exclusive manner, the institutional outcome of such antagonism will also tend to be exclusive (Moreno, 1986).

Dual identity is a key concept for the understanding and assessment of politics and policies in contemporary Spain. It also provides a useful methodological tool for the measurement and interpretation of the degree of internal consent and dissent in decentralized Spain.

The task of identifying and measuring the notion of dual identity/compound nationality is far from simple. The changing nature implicit in such a duality complicates matters. Thus, positive perceptions on the action of the Spanish state by members of the *Comunidades Autónomas* can result in a loosening of their self-ascribed regional identity and a corresponding reinforcement of their sense of membership within the Spanish nation-state, and vice versa. Obviously, the dual identity concept modifies its constituent elements according to subjective perceptions and evaluations. The reinforcement of one identity upon the other may well result in the complete disappearance of such a duality as it now stands.

The existence of this compound nationality in most of the Spanish *Comunidades Autónomas* had its institutional correlation in the setting-up of regional legislatures and governments during the 1980s, which have not only preserved ethnoterritorial identities but have also projected the political aspirations of these sub-state communities. Since the approval by popular referendum of the 1978 Constitution, such cultural diversity has been greatly encouraged by the governments of the *Comunidades Autónomas*, which have given priority to cultural, educational, linguistic and mass media policies (Giner and Moreno, 1990). The role of these self-governing institutions in the creation and re-creation of regional identities is very important. Further, common elements of language and history in two or more *Comunidades Autónomas* make the task of interpreting the interplay of identities in boundary regions even more complex (for example, *Països Catalans* referring to Catalonia, the Balearic Islands and Valencia, or the cases of the Basque Country and Navarre).

In all 17 *Comunidades Autónomas* there is a high proportion of citizens who claim some form of dual identity. The questions addressed to them in successive surveys[3] were as follows:

> *In general, would you say that you feel ...*
> 1. Only Basque, Catalan, Galicia, etc.?
> 2. More Basque, Catalan, Galician, etc. than Spanish?
> 3. As much Basque, Catalan, Galician, etc. as Spanish?
> 4. More Spanish than Basque, Catalan, Galician, etc.?
> 5. Only Spanish?
> 6. Don't know?
> 7. No answer?

FIGURE 4.1: SELF-IDENTIFICATION IN SPAIN (1990–95)

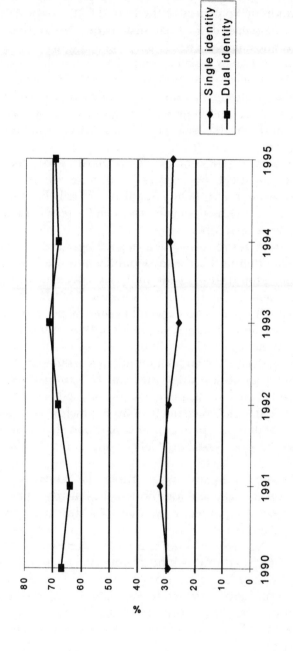

N = 56,298; 1990, N = 3,585; 1991, N = 11,924; 1992, N = 10,796; 1993, N = 10,795; 1994, N = 10,798; 1995, N = 8,400
(N = Number of people surveyed)
Source: Elaboration by Moreno, Arriba and Serrano (1998) of CIRES data (1990–95).

As shown in Figure 4.1, aggregate data in percentages concerning self-identification by Spaniards in the period October 1990–June 1995 indicate that a degree of duality had been expressed by around 70 per cent of those questioned. This duality corresponds to categories 2 ('More Basque, Catalan, Galician, etc. than Spanish'), 3 ('As much Basque, Catalan, Galician, etc. as Spanish') and 4 ('More Spanish than Basque, Catalan, Galician, etc.'). However, differences are noticeable in some nationalities and regions (for example, La Rioja, Navarre, Extremadura and Galicia show percentages of dual identity higher than 75 per cent).

Approximately 30 per cent of all Spaniards expressed a single identity with respect to either national/state or regional/ethnoterritorial dimensions ('Only Spanish', or 'Only Basque, Catalan, Galician, etc.'). The consistency in the results provided by CIRES periodical surveys is striking.[4]

Table 4.1 data reproduces data regarding all 17 *Comunidades Autónomas*. Note that in the Basque Country and the Canary Islands single regional/ethnoterritorial identity is higher than 20 per cent. Likewise, in Galicia, Catalonia, the Balearic Islands and Asturias, single regional self-identification is higher than 10 per cent of the total of survey respondents. Spanish single identity is more significant in Castile–La Mancha.

In order to gain a better understanding of the fluctuating nature of Spain's multiple identities, categories can be grouped as 'regional' (value 1, 'Only Basque, Catalan, Galician, etc.', and value 2, 'More Basque, Catalan, Galician, etc. than Spanish'), as 'equal' (value 3, 'As much Catalan as Spanish'), and as Spanish (value 4, 'More Spanish than Basque, Catalan, Galicia, etc.', and value 5, 'Only Spanish').

Equal identity in Spain, as a whole, is prevalent. In some *Comunidades Autónomas* equal identity reaches nearly 75 per cent (La Rioja), or above 50 per cent (Andalusia, Murcia, Extremadura, Navarre and Aragon).

'Don't know/No answer' figures are considerably lower than the usual figures produced in this kind of survey. This finding seems to suggest that Spaniards are far from indifferent to the cultural and institutional implications of self-identification and the process of decentralization. The only exception is the Basque Country (6 per cent), where the climate of political violence must have had an obvious impact.

129 of 200

TABLE 4.1
SELF-IDENTIFICATION BY COMUNIDADES AUTÓNOMAS (1990–95)

A. Vertical percentages

	Andalusia	Aragon	Asturias	Balearic Islands	Basque Country	Canary Islands	Cantabria	Castile and Leon	Castile-La Mancha	Catalonia	Extrem.	Galicia	La Rioja	Madrid	Murcia	Navarre	Valencia	TOTAL
Only *	5.6	4.9	11.3	11.9	26.8	21.7	3.4	3.1	2.4	12.5	7.5	15.4	2.9	2.3	3.4	9.7	2.5	5,006 (8.9%)
More * than Spanish	18.1	12.9	21.2	10.8	19.9	25.6	6.6	8.5	4.4	18.9	14.6	21.1	8.3	6.1	9.7	26.5	8	8,390 (14.9%)
As * as Spanish	57.5	50.4	45.6	41.2	30.8	34.4	40.9	44.2	41.8	38.9	53.6	47.9	73.5	43.4	54.3	50.8	43.6	26,055 (46.2%)
More Spanish than *	7.4	6.8	6.5	4.9	6.3	3.5	12.7	10.8	7.6	9.8	8.5	6.8	7.6	7.4	10.5	5.1	10.9	4,689 (8.3%)
Only Spanish	9.4	22.4	12.1	29.9	10	11.2	34.6	30	41.2	16.7	12.8	6.7	5.1	36.2	19.8	5.5	32.5	11,574 (20.5%)
Don't know	2	2.6	3.3	1.3	6.2	3.6	1.8	3.4	2.6	3.2	3.0	2.1	2.4	4.6	2.3	2.4	2.5	686 (1.2%)
TOTALS (No. of people surveyed)	1,825	345	310	205	592	382	144	720	464	1,703	294	793	75	1,305	278	136	1,034	56,400 (100%)

* = Basque, Catalan, Galician ...

(Table 4.1 continued)
B. Aggregated vertical percentages

	Andalusia	Aragon	Asturias	Balearic Islands	Basque Country	Canary Islands	Cantabria	Castile and Leon	Castile-La Mancha	Catalonia	Extrem.	Galicia	La Rioja	Madrid	Murcia	Navarre	Valencia	TOTAL
Single identity	15	27.3	23.4	41.8	36.8	32.9	38	33.1	43.6	29.2	20.3	22.1	8	38.5	23.2	15.2	35	16,580 (29.4%)
Dual identity	83	70.1	73.3	56.9	57	63.5	60.2	63.5	53.8	67.6	76.7	75.8	89.4	56.9	74.5	82.4	62.5	39,134 (69.4%)
Regional identity	23.7	17.8	32.5	22.7	46.7	47.3	10	11.6	6.8	31.4	22.1	66.5	11.2	8.4	13.1	36.2	10.5	13,396 (23.8%)
Equal identity	57.5	50.4	45.6	41.2	30.8	34.4	40.9	44.2	41.8	38.9	53.6	47.9	73.5	43.4	54.3	50.8	43.6	26,055 (46.2%)
Spanish identity	16.8	29.2	18.6	34.8	16.3	14.7	47.3	40.8	48.8	26.5	21.3	13.5	12.7	43.6	30.3	10.6	43.4	16,263 (28.8%)
Don't know	2	2.6	3.3	1.3	6.2	3.6	1.8	3.4	2.6	3.2	3.0	2.1	2.4	4.6	2.3	2.4	2.5	686 (1.2%)
TOTALS	9,346	1,808	1,634	1,041	3,584	2,021	761	3,764	2,372	9,126	1,519	4,574	409	6,851	1,402	751	5,431	56,400 (100%)

Notes:
Single identity includes 'only*' and 'only Spanish'.
Dual identity includes 'more* than Spanish', 'as* as Spanish' and 'more Spanish than*'.
Regional identity includes 'only*' and 'more* than Spanish'.
Equal identity includes 'as* as Spanish'.
Spanish identity includes 'only Spanish'.

Source: Elaboration by Moreno, Arriba and Serrano (1998) of CIRES data (1990–95).

Some *Comunidades Autónomas* may be labelled as 'exclusivist' (Basque Country and Canary Islands), and some others as 'balanced' (Catalonia and Asturias). Those *Comunidades Autónomas* with a level of single ethnoterritorial identity noticeably higher than the rest of the *Comunidades* are referred to as 'exclusivist'. 'Balanced' refers to those *Comunidades* where single ethnoterritorial and Spanish categories are on even terms, alongside an important manifestation of 'equal' identities. The *españolistas* communities include regions where Spanish identity is predominant with percentages over 40 per cent (both Castiles, Cantabria, Madrid and Valencia).

We shall now turn to an examination of the case of Catalonia, a historical nationality where demands of self-government have been intense for more than a century, and which has paved the way for home rule aspirations of other *Comunidades Autónomas*. The Catalonian example serves to demonstrate in a wider context the importance of the duality in citizens' self-identification within the context of Spain's internal politics.

The Catalan case

By the time of Franco's death (1975), the popular aspirations for home rule were widely expressed in the Catalan principate. In the campaign for the first general election held in Spain since February 1936 (which took place on 15 June 1977), 13 out of the 20 electoral Catalan candidatures committed themselves to home rule. (Note that 80 per cent of the elected candidatures to the Congress of Deputies – Lower House – and all but one of the elected candidates for the Senate – Upper House – were committed to political autonomy for Catalonia.)

The parties which explicitly define themselves as such cannot be sole claimants to the 'national' or 'nationalist' label. Both PSC (Partit dels Socialistes de Catalunya, integrated within the Spanish PSOE) and PSUC (Partit Socialista Unificat de Catalunya, brother organization of the Spanish Communist Party) have been not only Catalan national organizations but also the main instruments in the achievement of self-government in Catalonia. Note also that Catalan nationalists of the coalition CiU have steadily refused secessionism. Catalan nationalism has always attempted to influence Spanish politics and has repeatedly avoided limiting itself to mere regional activities.

The compatibility of identities is the most characteristic feature of Catalonia, which can be labelled as a 'balanced' *Comunidad Autónoma*.

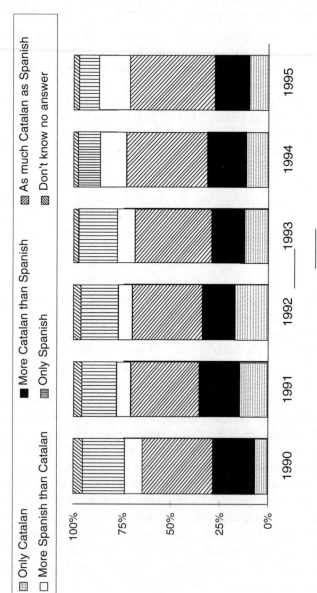

FIGURE 4.2: SELF-IDENTIFICATION IN CATALONIA (1990–95)

Legend:
- Only Catalan
- More Spanish than Catalan
- More Catalan than Spanish
- Only Spanish
- As much Catalan as Spanish
- Don't know no answer

N = 9,126; 1990, N = 570; 1991, N = 2,262; 1992, N = 1,711; 1993, N = 1,734; 1994, N =1,726; 1995, N = 1,123
(N = Number of people surveyed)
Source: Elaboration by Moreno, Arriba and Serrano (1998) of CIRES data (1990–95).

It is clearly shown in the percentages for the aggregate data of the period 1990–95: (1) 'Only Catalan, 12.5 per cent; (2) 'More Catalan than Spanish', 18.9 per cent; (3) 'As much Catalan as Spanish', 38.9 per cent; (4) 'More Spanish than Catalan', 9.8 per cent; (5) 'Only Spanish', 16.7 per cent; (6) Don't know/No answer, 3.1 per cent (Figure 4.2 illustrates the evolution during 1990–95).[5]

A multivariate analysis allows the possibility of gaining further insights in the available data (Moreno, Arriba and Serrano, 1998). The independent variables that have been taken into account were 'place of birth'; 'education'; 'social class'; 'income'; 'economic activity'; 'size of town'; 'occupation'; 'ideology'; 'age'; and 'religion' (see Methodological Appendix). As a preliminary finding, both place of birth of the parents of the respondents surveyed and the competence in the use of the Catalan language can be regarded as two important indicators to be assessed in future studies.[6] However, the variables cited offer a set of data that is relevant in order to carry out interpretations always subject to further contrast. Categories of identities were grouped as follows:

(a) Catalan identity ('Only Catalan' and 'More Catalan than Spanish'); Spanish identity ('Only Spanish' and 'More Spanish than Catalan'), and Equal identity ('As much Catalan as Spanish').
(b) Exclusive identity ('Only Spanish' and 'Only Catalan'), and Dual identity ('More Catalan than Spanish', 'As much Catalan as Spanish', and 'More Spanish than Catalan').

Results of two segmentation analyses[7] are highly illustrative of the way in which self-identification by Catalan citizens relate to cultural, economic, social and political circumstances of the citizens surveyed.

Analysis (a) (Tree-diagram 4.1)
The variable 'place of birth' appears to be the most relevant.[8] Almost 10 per cent of respondents born outside Catalonia expressed a 'Catalan identity' as compared to 41.2 per cent of those born in Catalonia. 'Spanish identity' was prevalent among 51 per cent of immigrants, in contrast to the 15 per cent of respondents born in Catalonia. Note that the latter group also incorporates a high percentage of 'equal identity' (40.7 per cent). This feature can be interpreted as a reflection of certain traditions of political tolerance and social integration from the native population with regard to the immigrant population.

TREE-DIAGRAM 4.1: PERCENTAGE OF CATALAN AND SPANISH SELF-IDENTIFICATION

CATALAN IDENTITY/EQUAL IDENTITY/SPANISH IDENTITY

31.36   38.87   26.5

(N=9,126)

BORN OUTSIDE CATALONIA
9.92 / 35.26 / 51.0

(N=2,853)

BORN IN CATALONIA
41.26 / 40.67 / 15.15

(N=6,219)

LOWER EDUCATIONAL LEVEL
9.0 / 36.11 / 52.3

(N=2,188)

MIDDLE EDUCATIONAL LEVEL
11.7 / 31.88 / 50.69

(N=436)

HIGHER EDUCATIONAL LEVEL
15.28 / 33.62 / 38.4

(N=229)

LOWER EDUCATIONAL LEVEL
35.6 / 46.27 / 16.36

(N=3,019)

MIDDLE EDUCATIONAL LEVEL
44.2 / 36.2 / 15.8

(N=2,374)

HIGHER EDUCATIONAL LEVEL
53.0 / 32.8 / 8.7

(N=826)

18–30 YEARS OF AGE
5.3 / 18.8 / 67

(N=94)

31–44 YEARS OF AGE
6.1 / 32.7 / 58.3

(N=437)

45 YEARS AND OVER
9.9 / 38.0 / 49.9

(N=1,657)

18–44 YEARS
26.1 / 49.9 / 22.6

(N=1,327)

45 YEARS AND OVER
43.1 / 44.0 / 11.4

(N=1,629)

NON-ACTIVE
50.2 / 31.8 / 15.7

(N=223)

UNEMPLOYED
31 / 54.7 / 2.3

(N=42)

EMPLOYED
55.7 / 31.5 / 6.4

(N=826)

LOWER & LOWER MIDDLE CLASS
36.3 / 39.6 / 21.3

(N=718)

MIDDLE CLASS
47.1 / 36.1 / 13.4

(N=1,493)

UPPER & UPPER MIDDLE CLASS
52.7 / 22.7 / 14.1

(N=163)

Notes: The rest of the percentages (up to 100 per cent) correspond to the responses 'Don't know' and 'No answer'.

N = Number of people surveyed.

Source: Elaboration by Moreno, Arriba and Serrano (1998) of CIRES data (1990–95).

When compared with the often-uneasy relationships between native and immigrant sectors of population in other parts of Europe (for example, Bavaria, Flanders, northern Italy), Catalonia offers an example of a high degree of social integration between natives and immigrants. Both collectives seem to be interwoven in various degrees and manifestations. Integration and tolerance are among the main features present in Catalonia's social life. There is a widespread assumption that internal differences are articulated in a common project, and that syncretism is a constituent element of Catalonia's national character. However, some nationalists are of the opinion that those Catalans showing 'equal' identities should opt in the future for a higher degree of 'Catalanness': 'Patriotic bigamy is not a good solution for the problems of survival of the stateless nations'.[9]

The second most relevant variable is education. Note that while citizens born in Catalonia are over-represented in high educational levels, those born outside Catalonia are concentrated primarily in low levels. A pattern shared by both immigrant and autochthonous collectives is that Catalan identity increases with the level of education. The role played by the intelligentsia and other professional elites in the diffusion of national sentiments is a well-known sociological fact. Numerous studies have insisted on the importance of the educational system in the consolidation and reproduction of national consciousness. Likewise, population groups with better access to formal instruction are more inclined to 'nationalistic' views in the context of minority nations within Western plural states. This feature is also applicable in the Spanish context.

Catalan has been often considered as a language of 'culture', which has traditionally conveyed the transmission of autochthonous idiosyncrasies. It comes as no surprise that those Catalans with higher degrees of formal education also show a greater disposition to 'Catalan identity'. On the other hand, CIRES data also confirm that individuals with a low level of education, the unskilled labour force and the unemployed, tend to adopt a 'Spanish identity' position.

A greater degree of 'Catalan identity' is also noticeable with ageing (in both immigrant and native cases, correlative with the level of education). This association seems to support the view that socialization forces are mainly responsible for identity formation. Degrees of 'equal identities' are evenly represented in most sub-groups, with the exception of the higher degree expressed by the native population already mentioned.

Note that early Catalan nationalism was mainly attributed to the political mobilization of Catalonia's bourgeoisie and middle classes during the second half of the nineteenth century (Solé Tura, 1967). 'Social class' is, thus, a relevant variable to be taken into consideration in the case of Catalonia. This observation seems to be corroborated by the analysis of the CIRES data. An increase in the importance of 'Catalan identity' is correlative to ascent within the social class structure. With regard to the predominance of 'Catalan identity' within the autochthonous population, it is possible to identify two groups: (a) those with higher levels of education (and employed); and (b) those upper-class groups with secondary education levels. These findings seem to underline the important role played by the collective internalization of historical events and by ideological traditions in the development of national identities.

Analysis (b) (Tree-diagram 4.2)
Yet again, the first and foremost segmenting variable is that related to place of birth. A pattern clearly emerges by which citizens born in Catalonia demonstrate a higher degree of dual identity. Apart from this finding, no other disparities are worth mentioning with respect to 'duality' as regards other variables. However, two peculiarities can be pointed out.

(1) Immigrants under 30 years old with a low level of education represent the group with the least degree of 'dual identity'. They tend to identify themselves exclusively as 'only Spanish' or 'only Catalan'. Likewise, the degree of duality for those citizens born outside Catalonia also increases with ageing. This indicator is consistent with the patterns of inclusion visible in Catalan society regarding immigration.

(2) With relation to the native population, duality increases inversely from higher to lower social classes. In other words, better-off citizens (also, in many cases, with higher levels of formal education) tend to be less 'dual' and more Catalan in their self-identification. (Note, however, that percentage differences are small.) This seems to corroborate the importance of the Catalanist tradition in contemporary manifestations of self-identification.

As far as 'dual identity' is concerned, the two most heterogeneous groups are: (a) lower and lower-middle classes of native Catalans (75.5 per cent of whom identify themselves in the three dual categories); (b) the 18–30 age group of citizens born outside Catalonia (38.3 per cent of whom expressed a degree of 'duality'). In this latter group processes of socialization and integration have little or no effect.

TREE-DIAGRAM 4.2: 'DUALITY' OF SELF-IDENTIFICATION BY CATALANS

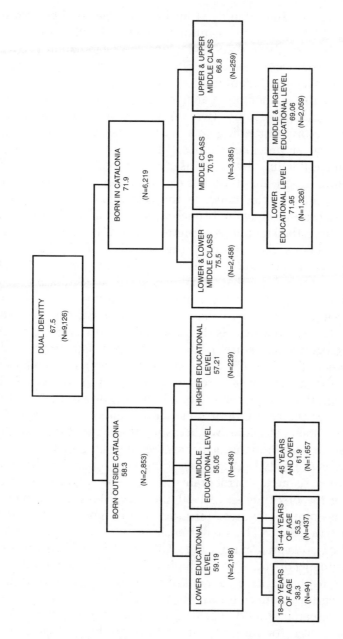

Notes: The rest of the percentages (up to 100 per cent) correspond to the responses of 'Don't know' and 'No answer'.

N = Number of people surveyed.

Source: Elaboration by Moreno, Arriba and Serrano (1998) on CIRES data (1990–95).

Self-identification and electoral behaviour

How do levels of 'dual identity' translate into electoral behaviour? The answer to this question cannot be univocal following survey analysis. In fact, available data for making cross-tabulation between these two variables is lacking. The establishment of a direct correlation between self-identification and voting patterns cannot be deduced from the segmentation analyses given. There is no question that the examination of these two variables would provide fruitful explanations. Notwithstanding this, and taking into account some partial findings of previous studies (Moreno and Arriba, 1996), a degree of 'tactical voting' by Catalans can be hypothesized.

Depending upon the type of election, there is a small but significant swing of votes between the two main Catalan political parties. The electoral behaviour of such voters is 'dual' and 'tactical'. In Catalan elections they tend to give preference to CiU while in Spanish and local elections they support the socialists. Table 4.2, which includes the electoral results produced in Catalonia during 1977–99, illustrates this point. Note that a relatively small but significant sector of electors votes differently according to the nature of the election (local/municipal, Catalan parliament, or Spanish parliament). Note also that 'duality' reaches its highest ratios with respect to the ideology categories of 'centre' (77.6 and 65.6 per cent, respectively) and 'centre-left' (75.4 and 65.7 per cent, respectively). It is a plausible hypothesis that a number of voters, who assigned themselves to the two ideological categories mentioned, have shown their voting preferences for the centre-right nationalist coalition Convergència i Unió, in the Catalan elections, while casting their votes for the centre-left socialists in both local/municipal and Spanish elections.

The results of the 1999 Catalan election were somewhat different, although they seem to corroborate the key role played by 'dual' electors. For the first time since 1980, the socialists won this type of election in popular votes (around 6,000 votes more than Convergència i Unió).[10] The small transfer of votes which took place between the two main political forces (CiU and PSC–PSOE), precisely in those segments of voters with a higher degree of dual identity, can be regarded as the decisive element in the variation of an otherwise consistent electoral pattern throughout the 1977–99 period.

Further research should substantiate these interpretations. Such studies are crucial for the purpose of distinguishing electoral sub-systems. In Spain, political colouring of local, regional and central

TABLE 4.2
ELECTORAL RESULTS IN CATALONIA, 1977–99
(SPANISH, CATALAN AND LOCAL ELECTIONS)

Year	PSC–PSOE	CiU	IC/EU (PSUC)	ERC	PP (AP)	Others
1977 (Spanish)	28.4	16.8	18.2	4.5	3.5	28.6
1979 (Local)	26.6	18.6	20.2	3.8	1.3	29.5
1979 (Spanish)	29.2	16.1	17	4.1	3.6	30
1980 (Catalan)	22.3	27.6	18.6	8.8	2.3	20.4
1982 (Spanish)	45.1	22.2	4.6	4	14.4	9.7
1983 (Local)	41.9	23.1	13.5	2.6	8.8	10.1
1984 (Catalan)	30	46.6	5.5	4.4	7.7	5.8
1986 (Spanish)	41	32	3.9	2.7	11.4	9
1987 (Local)	36.9	32.6	10.2	2.4	5.6	12.3
1988 (Catalan)	29.9	46	7.8	4.1	5.3	6.9
1989 (Spanish)	35.3	32.5	7.3	2.7	10.6	11.6
1991 (Local)	37	33.8	9.4	7.1	6.2	6.5
1992 (Catalan)	27.5	46.2	6.5	8	6	5.8
1993 (Spanish)	34.8	31.8	7.5	5.1	17	3.8
1995 (Catalan)	24.8	40.9	9.7	9.4	13	2.2
1995 (Local)	32.9	30	11.9	6.3	12.2	6.7
1996 (Spanish)	39.4	29.6	7.6	4.2	18	1.2
1999 (Local)	37.3	26.5	8.4*	7.7	10.9	9.2
1999 (Catalan)	37.9	37.7	2.5**	8.7	9.5	3.7

*   IC (6.4 per cent) and EU (2.0 per cent) votes are aggregated.
** Iniciativa per Catalunya (IC) formed a coalition with the socialists and the
   independent candidates *Ciutadans pel Canvi* (Citizens for the Change), with
   the exception of the constituency of Barcelona. EU received 1.4 per cent of the
   votes and did not get parliamentary representation.

PSC–PSOE: Catalan federated branch of Spanish socialists (left-to-centre).
CiU: Centre-right Catalan nationalist coalition.
IC/EU/PSUC: Catalan communists and left coalitions. (In 1999, the coalitions IC
   and EU contested the elections separately.)
ERC: Centre-left Catalan pro-independence party.
PP/AP: Spanish Popular Party (right-to-centre).

Source: Spanish and Catalan Ministries of the Interior.

institutions is increasingly dependent on the changing electoral support for parties operating at the various levels of government. Multiple identities seem to have a significant input in the way electors cast their votes. Undoubtedly, this 'tactical voting' will have far-reaching implications for the general governance of Spain and, in particular, with respect to the processes of policy-making and implementation. The achievement of a culture of intergovernmental relations in the three-tier system of government in Spain appears to be one of the main political challenges of the years to come.

THE INSTITUTIONALIZATION OF FEDERAL PRACTICES

The federal idea has adopted various institutional forms throughout its modern political history. The confusion between federalism and federation has been the origin of serious misunderstandings. In the Spanish case, the cantonalist experience of the First Federal Republic (1874), or the attempt to establish a federation of territorial units from below, thwarted the federalist option for a considerable period of time. This happened in a country in which the particular historical background and internal heterogeneity made it an ideal case for the development of federalist ideology and practices, and in particular of a type of devolutionary federalism.

Spain has an internal plurality somewhat similar to that of countries with a federal state organization. Some of them, such as the United States, have a much weaker ethnoterritorial composition, although their numerous ethnic minorities are socially distinguishable in each of the states of the union (Afro-Americans, Amerindians, Anglos, Asians, Germans, Hispanics, Irish, Italians, Jews, Slavs). Others, as in the case of ethnically homogeneous Germany, base their federal internal logic on intergovernmental relations of a co-operative nature. Both cases represent the disparity of territorial arrangements in federal-like political systems around the world.

In general, one should recognize two major features of federal states to be distinguished from those that are merely decentralized or regionalized: (1) the right to self-government of each political unit; and (2) the possibility of direct participation in the decision-making process of the state as a whole. To some extent, the *Estado de las Autonomías* incorporates certain elements of these *intra* and *inter* dimensions. Thus, although the *Comunidades Autónomas* have the self-governing possibilities of the first federal condition, the second is not altogether satisfied. The reason is the Senate, whose function is still not entirely clear, and the reform of which is discussed below.

The 1978 Constitution embodies a latent form of asymmetrical federalism that is reflected in a technique of legislative dissociation and execution at different levels. The 'open contract' nature reflected in the constitutional provisions guarantees the right of autonomy to be exercised by the Spanish nationalities and regions and the plural composition of the *Estado de las Autonomías*, but also left open the gradual consolidation of intergovernmental arrangements.

In accordance with its political dynamic and projection, the model of the *Estado de las Autonomías* should be viewed as a preliminary stage to a type of asymmetrical federalism in the manner of multiple ethnoterritorial concurrence discussed in the previous chapter. The two principal features of this process of federalization are (a) political asymmetry and administrative heterogeneity, and (b) the provisional nature of the participation of *Comunidades Autónomas* in state actions (Senate and intergovernmental relations). We shall now consider each of these features, and focus upon the most significant circumstances. (Note that this is not intended to be an exhaustive revision of a long list of constitutional elements or political arrangements, but only of those considered paramount for future developments.)

Asymmetry and heterogeneity

From the first stages of the process of devolution of powers in post-Francoist Spain, both *de jure* and *de facto* asymmetries have become an additional stimulus to the markedly concurrent nature of political relations between the central state and the *Comunidades Autónomas*. Early on, there was reason to expect a statutory and territorial asymmetry owing to the diverse inputs exerted by regional actors, elites and institutions. As a result the *Comunidades Autónomas* were constituted as historical nationalities (Catalonia, Galicia and the Basque Country), nationality according to Article 151 (Andalusia), nationality according to 143 (Valencia),[11] regions under 143,[12] *fuero* community (Navarre).[13] Other territorial units include provinces with *fuero* status, provincial *diputaciones*, *cabildos*,[14] island councils,[15] and municipalities, to mention the most characteristic.

The transfer of powers and responsibilities from the central administration to the new administrations of the *Comunidades Autónomas* was such that it was almost inevitable that representatives of both sides would be involved in bilateral political practices. Asymmetry of power in the nationalities and regions has developed alongside a basic administrative heterogeneity among multi- and uniprovincial communities. This has caused a territorial and political overlap that has often upset relations between local governments and the *Comunidades Autónomas*, on the one hand, and the latter and the bodies of the state administration that operate in their territory, on the other.

The problem is one of territorial and political overlap. Moreover, while both the old uniprovincial *Comunidades Autónomas* (Asturias, the Balearics, Navarre) and the new ones (Cantabria, Madrid, Murcia, La Rioja) have been able to adapt comfortably to their new modes of self-administration from their previous and now extinct provincial councils, the remaining ten *Comunidades Autónomas* have been burdened with two political and administrative sub-levels (provincial and local).[16] Both these levels of government are fully constitutional and are legitimized by electoral processes distinct from those of the *Comunidades Autónomas*.[17] Local governments, *cabildos* and island councils contribute, therefore, to the heterogeneity that is reflected in the variety of political institutions. Attempts in recent years have been aimed at reducing the administrative overlap of autonomous provincial agencies and offices sharing the same tasks of government.

Provinces and local councils

The Franco regime maintained the arbitrary provincial administration introduced by Javier de Burgos in 1833, following the model of the French *départements*. In 1927 the number of Spanish provinces rose to 50. The governments of the provinces, or *diputaciones*, acted basically as agents of central government and carried out functions as political controllers of towns and smaller communities. These, in turn, were empowered to deal with most local activities such as town-planning, sanitation and recreation. Members of city and town councils were appointed directly by the central authorities until the late 1960s, when some were allowed to be partially 'elected' by municipal residents.

In 1900, the number of municipalities – the areas to which local/city councils correspond – was 9,287. This figure dropped in 1975 to a total of 8,194 of which three-quarters (6,000 approximately) had fewer than 2,000 inhabitants. In the early 1960s the two main Spanish cities, Madrid and Barcelona, were awarded special charters granting them additional fiscal powers and responsibilities over urban planning, the water supply, transport and sanitation (among others).[18] As far as the regions were concerned, no political or administrative arrangement was introduced during the Franco dictatorship.

The 1978 Constitution protects the local integrity and autonomy of the provinces for the management of their respective interests. But their political existence as levels of intermediate government between local councils and *Comunidades Autónomas* is not merely old-fashioned, one and a half centuries after their establishment. Their existence brings about a further element in which the continuity of the so-called 'peripheral state administration' lingers on. The agencies and offices, which owe their origins to the hypercentralist Francoist state, have been languishing and living off the general state budget, awaiting their transferral to regional administrations, if not in some cases generating antagonistic relations with the latter. However, some adjustments have been implemented in order to avoid administrative overlapping. The political demotion of the once powerful *gobernadores civiles* (civil governors),[19] and the consolidation of the *delegados del gobierno* (government delegates)[20] can be regarded as a significant step towards the rationalization of the state administration according to territorialization of the *Estado de las Autonomías*.

The modernization of provincial administrations and their adaptation to regional reality should not necessarily entail their complete disappearance as administrative entities providing public services (Carrillo, 1997). They belong to a historical legacy and constitute an institutional heritage that is deeply rooted in certain parts of Spain. This is particularly relevant in larger *Comunidades Autónomas*, such as Andalusia, Aragon, Castile and Leon, Castile–La Mancha, Galicia, Valencia, or those with provincial political traditions, such as the Basque Country. In this last community, the various cultural and social realities possess political referents of the first order in their provincial historical territories. However, it would perhaps be appropriate to grant the provinces a greater involvement in the political life of the *Comunidades Autónomas* through the transfer of their legal statutes to the autonomous legislative framework. This would undoubtedly require a constitutional reform guaranteeing their participation at state level through and in conjunction with regional and local representatives (Upper House, or Senate, and intergovernmental relations). In any case, and given the advanced maturity of the decentralization process, continuing to grant to the provinces a greater electoral representation in the Senate reflects an inconsistent political choice.

Regional economic disparity

De facto economic asymmetries have had decisive repercussions for the decentralization process, and are associated with numerous arguments relating to the practice of interregional solidarity and the equal sharing of financial burdens. There is considerable regional economic disparity in Spain, although it is not as extreme as the difference between the north and south of Italy, to compare with a geographically and politically proximate case.

In general, territorial imbalances nonetheless provide a battery of arguments to justify those aspirations towards homogenization put forward by advocates of a neo-centralist Spanish nationalism. But there are also alternative views. For example, there are suggestions that Catalonia could disappear as a nation if it continues to be tied to Spain. The argument runs that between the public moneys collected and spent in Catalonia there is a difference of some 600,000 million pesetas (around 3,500 million euros).[21]

Since 1980, and together with the general decentralization process in Spain, regional disparity has shrunk modestly in figures, but significantly in its direction (see Table 4.3). In the period 1980–90, gross available family income in Extremadura, Spain's poorest region, rose by four percentage points with respect to its comparison with the richest, Madrid. Over the same years, in the second poorest region, Castile–La Mancha, income increased by 12 per cent over the growth in Catalonia, the second richest community by income in Spain.[22] Another study confirms that regional GDPs of poorer *Comunidades Autónomas* have somewhat caught up with those of richer ones (Bosch and Castells, 1997). During the period 1989–95, the regions with higher annual growth were the Canary Islands (8.3 per cent), Andalusia (7.8 per cent) and Galicia (7.1 per cent), as compared with the more sluggish Catalonia and Valencia (both at 6.5 per cent). It will still be necessary, however, to examine data over longer periods of time to confirm the redistributive and balancing effects of the decentralization process.

TABLE 4.3
EVOLUTION OF THE GROSS AVAILABLE FAMILY INCOME
IN THE SPANISH *COMUNIDADES AUTÓNOMAS*

Comunidad Autónoma	1980	1990	% Increase 1980–90 (1980 = 100%)
Andalusia	465,072	579,742	25
Aragon	652,890	657,032	1
Asturias	589,240	694,957	18
Balearic Islands	711,003	759,455	7
Basque Country	672,202	771,551	15
Canary Islands	483,985	597,782	24
Cantabria	692,892	646,227	–7
Catalonia	667,996	850,264	27
Castile and Leon	600,894	674,709	12
Castile–La Mancha	405,646	563,913	39
Extremadura	399,842	513,635	28
Galicia	544,427	621,442	14
La Rioja	593,225	678,100	14
Madrid	711,254	880,131	24
Murcia	535,142	613,337	15
Navarre	695,805	818,776	18
Valencia	580,261	649,444	12
Spain	585,007	698,201	19

(Spanish pesetas, per capita, 1986 constant prices.)

Source: Pena Trapero (1995).

Basically, there are two different systems of finance for the *Comunidades Autónomas*: the special regime and the common regime.[23] The first is applied to Navarre and the Basque Country and the second to the rest. The Navarran and Basque communities enjoy a fiscal 'independence' in which they collect their own taxes for personal income, companies and VAT.[24] A previously agreed quota is transferred by the Navarran and Basque executives to the central state Treasury. These transfers represent a compensation for Spanish common expenditure, and to cover the costs of running those state administrative bodies located in Navarre and the Basque Country.

Until 1994, the 15 *Comunidades Autónomas* run under the fiscal common regime had obtained their main financial resources through the concession and management of certain taxes (judicial acts and municipal taxes, luxury and heritage taxes, inheritance tax and transfers, gambling taxes), from their share in the domestic income of the whole state, as well as from European funds.[25] After an agreement of the Council for Fiscal and Financial Policy on 7 October 1993, the *Comunidades* under the common regime came to receive 15 per cent of the total personal income tax collected in their own territory. Later on, such percentage rose to 30 per cent for the period 1997–2001, although not all the *Comunidades Autónomas* accepted the calculations for the implementation of this arrangement. Note that such a percentage compares with the 46 per cent of the states of the United States, the 34 per cent of the Canadian provinces or the 29 per cent of the German *Länder*. Most significantly, it indicates a change of approach in the financing of the *Comunidades Autónomas*.

The impact of the reforms on the financial resources of the 15 common regime *Comunidades Autónomas* will be moderate in the foreseeable future. The political cost for the autonomous executives will be minimal, given that it can be seen as a continuation of taxes previously conceded. Many autonomous governments continue to display 'blame avoidance' practices, and they point to the central administration for their own political failures, alleging 'limited' financial resources. Given the fact that many responsibilities in the running of their governmental responsibilities are shared with the central authorities, it is always possible for the *Comunidades Autónomas* to consider the central state as the 'scapegoat'.

Although the LOFCA (Ley Orgánica de Financiación de las Comunidades Autónomas (Organic Law of the Autonomous Community Finance)) grants the *Comunidades Autónomas* a certain freedom to place surcharges on personal income tax, the Spanish mesogovernments have shown reluctance to take this option given its probable unpopularity. One of the consequences of these practices is the great difficulty for many voters to judge and ascribe political responsibility in central, regional or even local spending. It also emphasizes the instrumental role of central government in budgetary distribution, creating more confusion for the electorate and limiting the exercise of financial autonomy by the *Comunidades Autónomas*.

The concurrent nature of ethnoterritorial relations in Spain undoubtedly spurs the comparatively poorer *Comunidades Autónomas* to develop. This is the case despite the fact that the instruments designed to reduce imbalances in the quality of services and in investment capacity (the Interterritorial Compensation Fund) are inadequate. The dual tax-collection systems for the *Comunidades Autónomas* constitute an important *de jure* asymmetry. Both factors generate a degree of uncertainty and institutional turbulence with respect to the provisional nature of the system and the concept of the fiscal co-responsibility of nationalities and regions with the Spanish Treasury.

The asymmetrical system of regional financing implies further difficulties for attaining a certain degree of horizontal equalization foreseen in various constitutional clauses. In particular, it raises questions with respect to the general desire for greater fiscal efficiency and interterritorial solidarity. In September 1994, the President of the Catalan Autonomous Government, Jordi Pujol, graphically complained in the Senate about the burden of interterritorial solidarity for Catalonia: for every 100 pesetas handed over to the state Treasury, Catalonia got 70 back. The state invested 55,000 pesetas per capita in Catalonia, while in other 'fast route' *Comunidades Autónomas* (for example, Andalusia, Galicia) investment reached 85,000, and 114,000 in those of the 'slow route'.

The financing issue is one of the thorniest for its direct implications in the level of self-government of the *Comunidades Autónomas*, as well as for the difficulty it entails for the conciliation of the views and interests of the 17 nationalities and regions. It seems as if the alternative to a method of fiscal co-responsibility would be one of 'tributary confederation' along the lines of those enjoyed by Navarre and the Basque Country. That is to say, the *Comunidades Autónomas* would collect most of the taxes and would then pay the state previously agreed sums or quotas for the general state budget. This possibility is desirable in so far as it would be clearer for the citizens to assess expenditure responsibilities by mesogovernments of the *Comunidades Autónomas*. However, it would also require greater specification where the principle of solidarity is concerned, in the form of explicit transfer requirements between rich and poor communities. All things considered, asymmetries in the income-raising and the spending capacities of nationalities and regions could further reinforce the concurrent nature of the Spanish model and thus improve public efficiency.

Political singularity of the 'historical nationalities'

The main source of asymmetry in the *Estado de las Autonomías* lies in the role of the 'historical nationalities', where nationalist parties constitute major political forces. Political asymmetries are also common to federal systems, posing challenges of various sorts in accommodating their constituent units. Federalism should not, therefore, be considered as an instrument for concealing cultural, social and political diversity. It is better equipped as a vehicle of institutional organization for the integration of internal plurality by democratic means.

The way in which federalization in Spain can be fully established points to an asymmetry not so much in the *de jure* element as in the *de facto*. If, on the one hand, the provisions of the Constitution laid down unequal legal procedures for access to the exercise of the principle of territorial autonomy, on the other hand the internal logic of the system has induced a greater degree of equality in powers and responsibilities laid down in the 17 statutes of autonomy. Both a sense of 'comparative grievance' and a practice of 'ethnoterritorial mimesis' implicit in the mode of multiple concurrence previously analysed (Chapter 3, p. 101) have played an important part in the equalization of powers and competencies.

The rejection of regional interdiscrimination in the exercise of self-government and the desire that has emerged in certain *Comunidades Autónomas* not to be left behind have been the principal causes of this levelling of governmental responsibilities. In any case, the *de facto* asymmetry will have to take on board the differential political weight of minority nations, such as the Basque Country, Catalonia and Galicia, in the general governance of Spain. Other *Comunidades Autónomas* will not easily accept an advantageous position in terms of the degree of home rule to be exercised regarding governmental functions. However, there is no reason why powers of the 'historical nationalities' relating to competencies in the domains of their 'differential facts' could not be increased. Such powers would cover areas such as civic relations, culture, education, language or public administration.

The reform of the Senate

Both the 'founding Fathers' of the 1978 Constitution and most of the existing parliamentary parties support a constitutional reform to make the Senate the representative territorial chamber of the citizens of the *Comunidades Autónomas*, thus becoming the principal body of horizontal participation in the running of state affairs.[26] Parliament would thus be constituted by the Congress of Deputies (Lower House), representing Spanish citizens as a whole, and the Senate (Upper House), representing Spanish citizens through their autonomous nationalities and regions. This would be a fundamental step towards the federalization of Spain.

It is highly probable that the limited degree of enthusiasm raised by the constitutional reform proposal is associated with the mistrust of political groups to create a party-wide consensus similar to that achieved during the transition to democracy.[27] The tense climate of party political confrontation in the 1990s has hindered the viability of the proposal. It has also not been considered an urgent priority on the political agenda of party leaders. The day-to-day affairs of parliament have delayed a reform that is essential to breathe new life into Spanish politics. A system that fails to integrate all of its state levels, including the territorial, inevitably invites social apathy and political indifference. The values of the party-wide agreement that made the 1978 Constitution possible are to be revitalized. Otherwise, that occasion can be seen as the exception to a rule in which upheavals and fractures have been the main features during nineteenth- and twentieth-century Spanish politics.

The *Estado de las Autonomías* in Spain dealt well with the early stages of the decentralization process and the distribution of political power. The later stages involve the integration of the plurality of nationalities and regions in parliament. For this purpose a transformation of the *Estado de las Autonomías* is necessary through a 'federal reading' of the Constitution. This implies its eventual reform and the corresponding ratification of the parliamentary agreements between the political parties by public referendum.

Electoral constituencies
The disappearance of the provinces as constituencies for the election of senators is a *sine qua non* for the genuine territorialization of the Senate. As a consequence, representatives in the Upper House would be elected directly by the citizens of their *Comunidades Autónomas*. This could take place at the same time as general elections. Alternatively, senators could be elected indirectly by the regional parliaments from among their members. The assignation of seats in the Senate would

proportionally reflect political preferences in each *Comunidad Autónoma*. Also, it would be necessary to assign a common minimum number of representatives for each regional constituency, before allocating any additional members according to population.[28]

All of these options entail decisions of considerable political weight, and are supported by the experiences of several countries with federal systems (Austria, Canada, Germany, India or Switzerland).[29] Further complementary measures not directly related to senatorial territorialization could well be introduced. For example, the direct election of representatives to the Upper House could be combined with the maintenance of a majority system by which the elected candidates would be those obtaining the largest number of votes in their regional constituencies. This measure would almost certainly invigorate the electoral process for the Senate, and would make room for less party-bound voting combinations, avoiding the rigidity of the fixed party lists in operation for elections to the Spanish Lower House, or Congress of Deputies.

It would be inadequate to use the same procedure in the case of an indirect party-proportional election by members of the regional parliaments. It is obvious that this choice, in line with the Bundesrat system in Germany where the weight of the *Länder* executives is decisive, would indeed produce a greater fluidity and consonance between Senators and regional parliaments.[30] However, in the case of Spain, if senators were to be elected from among the members of regional parliaments, a contradiction of legitimacy would arise because regional MPs were elected to debate and legislate on questions strictly pertaining to their regions. To whom would members of an Upper House elected in this way be accountable? Such a democratic deficit could only be sorted out by having senators bowing mechanically to party discipline.

If one accepts the notion of a Senate constituted by the *Comunidades Autónomas*, then senators should be elected according to territorial electoral processes taking place in different dates on a regional basis. In such a case the Upper House would not be dissolved at the same time as the Lower House, and would be subject to constant renovation of its members. Alternatively, it could also be argued that if the Senate represented Spanish citizenship at large, decision-making processes in both Houses would be in line with each other and would more closely reflect the changes in perceptions and expectations in Spanish society.

Functions and powers

Responsibilities of a federalized Senate should be about regional specialization. That is, the Upper House would deal with matters directly affecting the competence and rights of the *Comunidades Autónomas*. Its legislative sphere of influence could be extended to local government to ensure a greater territorial coverage. European Union regulations concerning the powers of autonomous regions or local councils would also become integrated into its legislative commitments. In any case, the limits to such a specialization would be determined by the impossibility of pre-establishing the limits of state legislative activity concerning region-specific matters. Practically all state legislative activity is in some way tied to regional interests, including that relating to the exclusive powers of the state.

Interrelations and interdependence among regions, rights and jurisdictions are multiplied in countries of multiple concurrence such as Spain. It is not possible to draw precise boundaries between the three tiers of government, namely central, regional and local. This is an unavoidable fact not only in federations and federal systems but even in centralized countries with varying degrees of administrative deconcentration. A political understanding that legal texts can hardly reflect is therefore essential. Long-winded and complex constitutional texts frequently do nothing more than increase confusion in their aim to be explicit and to provide accurate definitions. Canada's constitutional rearrangement offers a typical example of such a problem. Belgian federal reform illustrates an instance of how broad agreements are later transformed into legal text.[31]

It has been a major political weakness that since 1978 the Senate has merely doubled the legislative functions of the Congress of Deputies. Its value has been basically instrumental, offering the parties of government and opposition a second chance to agree on legislative projects or to introduce amendments where legislative readings in the Lower House were hurried or superficial. This has contributed to its poor political reputation and to its low estimation among the populace with respect to its place and function. The continuing existence of institutions without a clear meaning is an invitation for increasing the lack of public interest in political life.

Although in cases of discrepancy between the Houses the Congress of Deputies has the last word, it would be convenient to empower the Senate in questions which particularly concern it, namely those which are specifically regional. Otherwise, the institutional role of the Senate would be clearly subordinate, and in the eyes of citizens its contribution to Spanish public life would be much as it has been since the beginning of the decentralization process: that is, practically non-existent.

Review of nominations

In addition to its territorial concerns, the Senate ought to take up other functions in order to enhance its tasks as a representative institution of political control. Among such additions should be included the power to review candidates' suitability for constitutional posts (Royal House, Council of State, General Council of the Judiciary, Ombudsman, Constitutional Court, Accounts Court). Other government nominations of institutional relevance should be also reviewed by the Senate (State Attorney, Governor of the Bank of Spain, and high posts of the armed forces and state security forces).

The political experiences of other federal institutions, such as the case of the United States Senate, cannot be treated as exact analogies for the Spanish case. But they can certainly act as useful referents for future reform. In a country like Spain, with a gloomy tradition of inquisitorial practice and pathological envy, the 'test' of the political suitability of candidates to constitutional bodies and to positions of high responsibility would involve a risky parliamentary exercise. Perhaps party tactics would not shy away from preferences and phobias in assessing candidates' suitability. On the other hand, it would also be worth considering the effects of the political dignity obtained by candidates occupying major posts through parliamentary support. Senate judgements would not be an antidote for the appearance of political scandals, but they would reduce their potentially destabilizing effects. Furthermore, it would reinforce the central role of parliamentary activity and make incursions into the monopoly of the media on public control of political life.

To sum up, the atrophy of the Senate as a territorially based chamber, constitutes a dangerous invitation to the dismantling of the autonomous regional web. A renewed cross-party consensus is required to ensure a constitutional adaptation to the federalization of a heterogeneous reality. Such an agreement would have to precede its legal formalization. Constitutional engineering is in itself sterile and inconsequential. In Spain the tradition of laying down agreements which have no basis in reality has been an obstacle to the consolidation of democratic values. The greediness of the centre towards the periphery may have been the most evident of the misguided tendencies of the country's political modernization.

Intergovernmental relations

The process of Spanish decentralization has now been going on for 20 years. The level of home rule achieved by the *Comunidades Autónomas* is considerable compared to the federal-like systems of other countries. However, the institutional involvement of the *Comunidades Autónomas* in state-wide decision-making is somewhat provisional in character. The general political consensus, intergovernmental co-operation and consociational practices in Spain have been left unaided by the institutional liaison mechanisms available. Several factors have contributed to these institutional shortcomings, and we shall now identify and discuss the four main ones.

(1) *The inadequacy of the Senate as a territorial chamber.* This is surely a major drawback in the functioning of the *Estado de las Autonomías.* The main reforms to be accomplished have been already examined in the previous section.

(2) *The discretion of the* conferencias sectoriales *(sectoral conferences).* In these conferences high-ranking official and political representatives of both central government and *Comunidades Autónomas* meet to discuss sectoral matters in order to maximize intergovernmental co-operation and to avoid conflicts. In 1982 the first *conferencia sectorial* was established: the *Consejo de Política Fiscal y Financiera de las Comunidades Autónomas* (Council for Fiscal and Financial Policy of the Autonomous Communities). In 1989 there already existed 17 forums. Ten years later, 24 sectoral conferences have been set up: agriculture, civilian protection, consumer affairs, culture, drugs, education, environment, European affairs, fiscal and financial policy, fisheries, health, infrastructure, industry and energy, labour, public housing, public personnel, research and development, social affairs, telecommunications, tourism, traffic, transport, universities, and water.

At first, the *Comunidades Autónomas* were reluctant that the sectoral conferences could be transformed into institutional mechanisms controlled by the central administration in order to intervene in areas of power of regional competence.[32] Gradually such uneasiness has paved the way for an increasing mutual trust. However, these conferences are not institutions for joint decision-making.[33]

Meetings and contacts are irregular and do not always respond to an already fixed agenda. Co-operation seems to depend a great deal on the personal attitudes of the political officials involved and on the political mood in general.[34] The exchange of information, nevertheless, is an important element. Some analysts regard the sectoral conferences as mechanisms of 'institutional courtesy' (Grau i Creus, 2000), while others see them as evidence of the shift from competitive regionalism to co-operative federalism,[35] along the lines of the German model (Börzel, 1999).

It is a simplification suggestive of desire over intellect to impose a model of intergovernmental co-operation based in homogenizing values of federative reliance, as in the case of the German *Bundestreue*, and to make it fully operative in Spain in the short-term future. Behind the ideas of some Spanish advocates of the model of co-operative federalism, usually regarded as a type of executive federalism, is still latent the 'centralist inertia' analysed in Chapter 3, p. 95. In the gradual process of federalization in Spain the most compelling element to be aware of is the concurrent nature of internal ethnoterritorial relations. Political complexity cannot become synonymous with inefficiency (Kincaid, 1995). To put it another way: the shortest route is not always a straight line. In complex decision-making processes the temptation towards simplification often ends in misunderstanding.

That is why nationalist and regionalist parties prefer to engage themselves in negotiations with the political party in power in central government. Intergovernmental relations are very dependent on the colouring of the political party in charge of the different levels of government. Consequently, most of the conflicts are political rather than policy-oriented. That is why 'bilateralism' is still the preferred manner of reaching political agreements rather than the institutionalization of multilateral intergovernmental relations.

(3) *The persistence of arbitrariness in bilateral relations between the central government and the* Comunidades Autónomas. This is to be understood in the terms described earlier, namely the political negotiations between the parties in power at the centre and periphery. In order to secure majorities in the Spanish parliament or at the regional legislatures, the parties in office engaged in political transactions with far-reaching implications for the governance of the country as a whole. The agreements reached between the PP (Spanish government) and the Basques (PNV) and Catalan nationalists (CiU)

during the term of office 1996–2000 illustrate these practices of bilateralism.

At other levels of government, pacts and agreements have taken place among parties with a diversity of interests and have concentrated more in common policy aims. This has not always been the case as regards central and regional levels. In fact, parties in opposition at the Spanish level have favoured alternative policies while being in government at the regional level. For example, when the modifications for the financing system started in 1993 (15 per cent of the income tax to be ceded over the *Comunidades Autónomas*), the minority PSOE government was supported by the Catalan nationalists (CiU). The modifications were rejected by those *Comunidades Autónomas* governed by the PP, which contested before the Constitutional Court the governmental decision previously discussed at the sectoral conference (Council for Fiscal and Financial Policy). In 1996 the situation was reversed. The minority PP government was supported in the Spanish parliament by the Basque, Canary and Catalan nationalists (PNV, CC and CiU). The reforms of the system aimed at raising the percentage of income tax to be handed over to the *Comunidades Autónomas* (30 per cent). Soon after, the three *Comunidades Autónomas* controlled by the PSOE appealed to the Constitutional Court, while the *Comunidades Autónomas* which had contested the previous reform had to withdraw their existing appeals by virtue of party discipline.[36]

The territorialization of politics in Spain has manifested itself in the proliferation of regionally based parties and the compounded representation on party systems and government formation on the regional level (Pallarés *et al.*, 1997; Hamann, 1999). Internal asymmetries in Spain have also expressed themselves in a wide and varied mosaic of political parties. Even the political organizations receiving state-wide public support have structured themselves in line with the federal texture of Spain. This aspect brings about a further element of 'pork-barrel politics'[37] to a system where the territorial dimension has become decisive.

After the 1999 regional elections, the political map of the *Estado de las Autonomías* was substantially modified. A higher degree of heterogeneity in the composition of the three-tier system of government was also introduced. At the meso-level, the PP representatives controlled nine *Comunidades Autónomas* in coalition with regional forces in two of them (the Canary Islands and Navarre).

Six other *Comunidades* had PSOE governments in coalition with other parties, mainly nationalist or regionalist (Andalusia, Aragon, Balearic Islands). Finally, a coalition of nationalists (PNV and EA) governed the Basque Country, and the CiU formed a government with the support of the PP and the *ad hoc* abstention of the ERC (centre-left independentists).

It comes as no surprise that when bilateral political negotiation is not successful, the parties involved contest governmental decisions and pieces of legislation before the Constitutional Court. This has often constituted a perversion of the system.

(4) *The role of the Constitutional Court in the delimitation of powers among the three layers of government.* The arbitrating responsibility of the highest Spanish tribunal has been of paramount importance for the subsequent implementation of the *Estado de las Autonomías*. It has among its powers the authority to decide on legal conflicts between the state (central government) and the *Comunidades Autónomas*, or even conflicts among the latter. Let us remember that, according to the 1978 Constitution, there is a need for partisan compromise on the nomination of candidates to the Constitutional Court. This circumstance has provided the latter with a great deal of authority and independence. Based on this legitimacy, central and regional governments have appealed to the Court, and have accepted its judgement when the option of a bilateral political negotiation was not possible. On many occasions the challenge to a piece of national or regional piece of legislation has served the purpose of 'gaining time' in order for further political negotiations to take place between the parties involved. This goes some way to explaining why the number of contested laws by either central or regional governments has decreased sharply in recent times.

In 1993 the number of challenges submitted to the *Tribunal Constitucional* were only 12 as compared to 131 in 1985. The level of constitutional conflict over competencies has been high in comparison to other European countries (about 960 challenges in the period 1981–97). However, these figures are somewhat misleading if we take into account the particular characteristics of the process of decentralization in Spain: namely, the inductive manner in which powers have gradually been allocated among the three-tier system of government. Indisputably, the institution enjoying the highest interparty agreement for the solving of conflicts has been the *Tribunal Constitucional*.

On the more technical issue of the *ultra vires*, or legislation passed beyond the scope of the responsibilities in each level of government, the *Tribunal Constitucional* has carried out a crucial function in the gradual delimitation of powers. Challenges to laws, decree laws and legislative decrees, either by the Spanish or the regional parliaments, have been judged by the Court in a manner that confirms the federalizing trend towards the 'sharing of rule' between central and regional levels (Agranoff and Ramos Gallarín, 1997).

It now seems clear that the capacities of the *Tribunal Constitucional* as the interpreter and arbiter of power-sharing are somewhat exhausted. Most contested competencies and powers have been already resolved. Future developments in the process of the federalization of Spain will depend more on the will of the political parties to engage and work out new constitutional settings rather than their resorting to the *Tribunal Constitucional* as the trouble-shooting institution.

In the immediate future, intergovernmental relations will become absolutely decisive in the process of federalization of the *Estado de las Autonomías*. Administrative and political processes will be more laborious than those hierarchically determined in unitary centralized states. But they will enjoy a greater degree of legitimacy as well as greater effectiveness. In Spain, the absence of an enlightened and authoritative elite, and of a centralizing political leadership, has gone hand in hand with a constant affirmation of ethnoterritorial diversity. The federalization of the *Estado de las Autonomías* must not be confused with the unfolding of more or less sophisticated constitutional governing techniques. It is largely a matter of finding a political place for the vitality of its constituent units and of institutionalizing the free and natural understanding with which its citizens and peoples engage in daily life.

Europeanization and the growing degree of interdependence in the world economy have had a major impact on the Spanish central, meso and local levels of government. The Spanish *Comunidades Autónomas* have repeatedly shown a European vocation and a cosmopolitan approach towards the development of their potentialities. This is another crucial aspect that will condition the future federalization of Spain, and one which we will now examine.

MESOGOVERNMENTS AND THE NEW COSMOPOLITAN
LOCALISM IN EUROPE

At the turn of the millennium demands by mesogovernments for a greater say in the running of their own affairs have come to the fore of political life in many plural societies. However, the nation-state is not only subject to pressures from 'below' but also from 'above'. Among the latter, economic globalization and the transfers of state power to both markets and supranational institutions stand out.

The nation-state has constituted the central arena of economic life during the last two centuries. At present, it often attends as a spectator the world-wide representation of virtual financial transactions. The one-time powerful economic policies established at the national level are now severely restricted by those decisions taken by international trusts, pension funds or 'whitened' capital from transnational organized crime. Furthermore, globalization also affects other factors of production, such as components of industrial goods made in third-party countries, as well as the increasing legion of stateless workers.

Globalization brings with it a transfer of authority and power from the states to the markets. New rules of global markets and corporate strategies of multinational companies have had a growing impact in setting the pace of both international and national patterns of economic development. Obviously, such markets' rules and strategies are not territorially 'neutral'. In any consideration of the most profitable portfolios for investment, local incentives play an important role. But less tangible factors, such as institutional and political stability, social cohesion or cultural and political affinities between place of origin and destination are also crucial.

National governments negotiate among themselves in order to establish wide frameworks of economic transactions (General Agreement on Tariffs and Trade, European Monetary Union, International Monetary Fund, Common Market of South America, North American Free Trade Agreement, World Trade Organization). In parallel they also negotiate with firms, and try to adjust to the consequences of the relationships between firms. State sovereignty is becoming more nominal than real. Furthermore, the capabilities of national governments to pursue economic policies different from those of their neighbouring countries are severely curtailed.[38]

Given this context of internationalization, the role played by the mesogovernments is acquiring relevance in most aspects of contemporary life. Mesogovernments are no longer dependent on those programmes of rationalization carried out during the nineteenth and twentieth centuries by central bureaucracies and elites. Their own entrepreneurs, social leaders and intelligentsia have taken up many of the initiatives and roles once the exclusive province of those 'enlightened' actors who held the reins of power of their nation-states. Positions of political influence are now more evenly distributed in central, meso-level and local institutions. Co-option of regional elites to the central institutions of government are no longer the exclusive routes available to 'successful' political careers.

In Europe, meso-level communities are taking up initiatives and leading roles in many areas of social life. They have developed a new *cosmopolitan localism* that combines, on the one hand, an active opposition to the centralized model of the unitary state and, on the other, a mobilization of sub-state identities coupled with an active supranational participation (Moreno, 1999).

The case of plural Spain offers an example of how multiple identities and political loyalties can be accommodated allowing ethnoterritorial co-operation and agreement among its constituent nationalities and regions. Multiple concurrence of territorial interests cannot only overcome conflicts but can also provide a deepening of democracy by means of greater access of civil society to political decision-making. This is aimed at adapting economic, political and social lives to the relative obsolescence of the nation-state.[39]

European *cosmopolitan localism* mainly concerns medium-sized polities within or without the framework of a state. Thus it can be detected in minority nations (Basque Country, Catalonia, Scotland), small nation-states (Czech Republic, Luxembourg, Slovenia), and also in regions (Brussels, Languedoc, Veneto) and conurbations (Berlin, London, Paris). Meso-level communities seem to follow a pattern of re-creating those political communities which flourished as far back as the medieval period (the Italian city-states, the Hanseatic League, principalities). However, and in contrast with the Renaissance period, there is now a common institutional tie inherent in the process of Europeanization.

The supranational framework provided by the European process of convergence brings with it a 'new' element of further cosmopolitanism to meso-level communities and conurbations. At one point, and in the face of hard economic competition from other world regions, some analysts proposed the very idea of a 'fortress

Europe'. According to this view, the secession from the international world arena would preserve the maintenance of the European welfare regimes. An economic 'wall' around EU member states would guarantee the social rights achieved by generations of Europeans. It would also stimulate balanced growth, which in turn would create new employment coupled with job-sharing and the reduction of working time. Immigration would be tightly regulated. Undoubtedly, this option would mean a U-turn in the cosmopolitan approach of the European culture and a radical mutation in its value-system. Besides, the current level of Europeanization makes the establishment of a strategy for achieving a monolithic autarchy infeasible. The very idea of a 'fortress Europe' cannot be embraced as a workable scheme.

What is acquiring major relevance in the political life of Europe is the role of the meso-level. Among others, two factors can be identified as having greatly contributed to enhance its significance: (a) the reassertion of sub-state identities; and (b) the implementation of the principle of subsidiarity. Let us briefly review both elements.

(a) *The reinforcement of sub-state identities* has provided civil societies with a more participatory and active role. Examples in Western Europe do not refer solely to electoral deviations from national patterns (for example, CiU–Catalonia, CSU–Bavaria, Lega–Northern Italy, SNP–Scotland). Social movements and local entrepreneurs have found a more flexible context for action. Central state apparatuses are often clumsy and inefficient in dealing with bottom–up initiatives. Thus, conurbations and metropolitan areas are well equipped for some innovation policies in a more adaptable context to the changing needs laid down by the information age. Metropolitan Madrid or Milan and its urban satellites can be regarded as instances of re-creating local civic cultures alongside their cosmopolitan traditions. These conurbations are in a position similar to other meso-level communities (regions and minority nations) as regards the running of their own affairs, and the development of their potentialities beyond the *dirigiste* control of central state institutions.[40]

Many signs seem to indicate the rise of a European type of communitarianism, which should be regarded as quite distinct from that which has developed in some local communities in America (Etzioni, 1993). In the case of the United States, many of the communitarian experiences can be seen as reactions to specific social cleavages and social fractures (the criminalization of social life), as an instrumental means of socialization in response to urban constriction (suburban isolationism), or as alternative lifestyles to dominant values (possessive individualism). From this perspective US communitarianism is socially defensive.[41]

In the European Union, territorial identities are mainly proactive. They are not mere mechanisms of response for controlling the informational avalanche generated by the telecommunications revolution. The reinforcement of sub-state territorial identities is deeply associated with powerful material and symbolic referents of the past (culture, history, territories). They seem to have engaged in a process of innovation departing from a common ground, and which seeks to overcome the de-naturalizing effects of global hyper-modernity.[42] However, their manifestations do not take refuge in a reactive parochialism. They emerge, therefore, as 'project identities' characterized by proactive attitudes.[43]

(b) *The principle of subsidiarity* was enshrined in the Treaty of European Union of 1992, known as the Treaty of Maastricht. It provides for decisions to be taken transnationally only if local, regional or national levels cannot perform better. In other words, the preferred locus for decision-making is that closer to the citizen, and as local as possible. State political elites, reluctant to further the process of European institutionalization, interpreted the subsidiarity principle as a safeguard for the preservation of traditional national sovereignty and, consequently, the powers to intervene centrally. The case of the United Kingdom is paradigmatic in this respect. According to such interpretations, the legislative supremacy of Westminster should be preserved from supranational intervention and regulation originated at the 'federal' institutions of the European Union. Likewise, the devolution of power from the centre of the British state to the constituent nations of the United Kingdom, and to amalgamated local authorities such as the former Greater London Council, could not have been denied on the same grounds. Paradoxically, anti-European advocates of the national interpretation of the principle of subsidiarity refused to accept the latter sub-state understanding of the same principle.

The rationale implicit in the principle of subsidiarity favours the participation of sub-state levels of government in the running of public affairs, although global levels are also to be taken into account. At the same time, it encourages intergovernmental co-operation on the assumption that the role of the nation-state is to be less hierarchical than it has been previously. Territorial identities are intertwined in a manner that expresses the degree of citizens' loyalties towards the various sources of political legitimization: municipalities, regions, nations, states and European Union. Accountability and territorial institutions should therefore reflect the political expression of people's identities and democratic participation.

Immigration from non-EU countries has certainly had an impact on the growing sentiments of xenophobia in Europe. Nevertheless, immigrants willing to take on those values of civic pluralism and tolerance find no major difficulties integrating into the economic and social life at their first 'port of entry', that is, local and meso communities.

In the case of Spain, the process of 'home rule all round' has considerably allowed the extension of *cosmopolitan localism*. This is reflected in both societal interests aimed at developing a sense of community, and at participating actively in international spheres. There is, thus, a growing congruence between the particular and the general. Note that all Spanish mesogovernments have made explicit their European vocation. They all share the desire of the majority of Spaniards for a EU that would be not only the main economic institutional locus in the medium-term future but which would also provide the legitimizing bases for an embryonic European citizenship.

The majority of the EU peoples have internalized European institutions, albeit rather loosely and gradually. The European Court of Justice, the Schengen Agreement, and the inception of the euro currency can be regarded as steps, uneven but clear, towards the idea of European transnationalization. Even areas such as those concerning social policy and welfare development – the traditional domain of national intervention – are being viewed gradually from a supranational perspective, together with an understanding of the increasing role to be played by mesogovernments.

Needless to say, all these processes in Europe are taking place in a period of relatively stable economic growth characterized by the absence of wars between the once powerful colonial nation-states. Some authors hold the view that together with globalization the potential for a pessimistic scenario is just around the corner (Chomsky, 1994). The latent possibility of rivalries between the nation-states, trade conflicts between world regions, or the growth of religious fundamentalism and xenophobia are potentially explosive. Alternatively, a move towards a new form of civilization capable of revitalizing the old federalist congruence between unity and diversity by means of political pacts appears to be a reasonable challenge for this emerging *cosmopolitan localism*.

NOTES

1. Reproduced from two of his publications (1973: p. 99 and 1975: p. 423).
2. On 6 December 1978 the Spanish Constitution received 87.9 per cent 'yes' votes, 7.8 per cent 'no' votes, and 4.3 per cent null or blank votes. As much as 32.9 per cent of the registered electorate abstained from voting.
3. For details see the Methodological Appendix. This section and the subsequent reference to the case of Catalonia is based on a piece of research undertaken with my colleagues Ana Arriba and Araceli Serrano, which was published in the journal, *Regional and Federal Studies*, 8, 3: pp. 65–88.
4. Note that the maximum deviation in the surveys is a four-point percentage. Although Fig. 4.1 reproduces aggregated data, the same percentage consistency is observable on analysing results by regions.
5. As also happens in the Spanish context as a whole, data from the Catalan case shows a degree of consistency of the values produced in each of the self-identification categories throughout the period under analysis. Slight annual variations are of little relevance.
6. Note that interpretations have been carried out taking into account secondary data produced by the Centro de Estudios de la Realidad Social (CIRES) during the 1990–95 period, and which do not include these two variables.
7. The segmentation analysis allows the construction of models where a considerable number of variables are taken into account. It also makes possible the setting of basic typologies with regard to the variable being used (Escobar, 1992). Associations among different variables are worth exploring. However, the analyses concentrated on those with a higher degree of concomitance in the various levels of segmentation. These variables are reproduced in Tree-diagrams 4.1 and 4.2
8. Let us remember that since the beginning of the century, but mainly from the 1960s onwards, immigration from poorer regions of Spain has been very important in Catalonia. Between 1900 and 1950, three-quarters of all the demographic growth in Catalonia was due to immigration. In 1975, 38.3 per cent of Catalan residents had been born outside Catalonia. In the period 1941–80, as many as 1,655,149 immigrants established themselves in Catalonia. They were mostly job-seekers, non-skilled and with low degrees of formal education, and from other parts of Spain. At present, around a third of all legal residents in Catalonia are immigrants. However, it would be wrong to speak of a homogeneous social group or category *vis-à-vis* native Catalans (Miguélez and Solé, 1987).
9. This was the opinion of Joaquim Triadú i Vila-Abadal, member of the executive committee of the nationalist party, Convergència Democràtica de Catalunya (*El País*, 26 October 1996).
10. Nevertheless, the coalition Convergència i Unió obtained one more parliamentary seat than the electoral platform led by the Socialists (see Table 4.1).

11. The self-denomination *nacionalidad* appears in the Statute of the Comunidad de Valencia, which obtained its autonomy through the application of Article 143 of the 1978 Constitution.
12. Among those granted autonomy through Article 143, some define themselves as *historical regional entities* (the Balearic Islands, Cantabria, Extremadura, La Rioja, Murcia). In other autonomy statutes there are concepts such as *historical entity* (Aragon) or references to a *historical and cultural origin* of the provinces constituting the region (Castile and Leon). The rest have avoided categorization (Asturias, Castile–La Mancha, Madrid).
13. The Comunidad Foral de Navarra was 're-established' according to the provisions of the Ley Orgánica de Reintegración y Amejoramiento del Régimen Foral.
14. These correspond to each of the Canary Islands (Fuerteventura, Gran Canaria, Hierro, La Gomera, La Palma, Lanzarote and Tenerife).
15. Or *consells* of the Balearic Islands (Mallorca, Minorca and Ibiza/Formentera).
16. In the case of Catalonia we should also include a fourth level, that of the *comarques* (counties).
17. In Spain there are four major types of elections for public office: Spanish general elections, to the Congress of Deputies and the Senate; meso-level elections, held independently in each *Comunidad Autónoma* to elect members of the regional parliaments and governments; local elections, held state-wide (though not in seven of the uniprovincial communities) to elect representatives of provincial and local councils; and European elections, held in unison with the rest of the EU countries, to elect representatives to the European Parliament. Often, when appropriate, combinations of these are held simultaneously.
18. The conurbation of Barcelona and its surrounding municipalities saw the creation of a multi-purpose metropolitan authority in 1974. In 1986 the metropolitan county of Barcelona, which comprised not only the city of Barcelona but also 27 municipalities, had a population of 3,025,666 inhabitants. This figure compared with that of 3,058,182 for the city of Madrid. However, the nationalist-controlled Generalitat was uneasy about the powers concentrated in this socialist-controlled metropolitan authority, and decided to suppress it.
19. The *gobernadores civiles* were mostly in charge of public safety, and law and order. During Francoism, their most visible task was none other than political repression.
20. They are appointed by the central government in order to direct state administration in each of the 17 *Comunidades Autónomas* and to co-ordinate it, whenever necessary, with the region's own administration (Art. 154 of the 1978 Constitution).
21. However, these allegations do not take into account both commercial and financial cash-flows. In 1993 they favoured Catalonia by one billion pesetas of commercial surplus and 0.9 billion regarding the difference between Catalan deposits in Spanish banks and the credits obtained from these in Catalonia (around 6,000 million and 5,400 million euros, respectively). In fact, industrial development both in Catalonia and the Basque Country during the twentieth century has been possible mainly as a result of savings made in Spanish agricultural regions, and channelled to these nationalities, dominated by an entrepreneurial spirit unlike the rest of Spain (data published in *El País*, 12

February 1993).

22. According to Pena Trapero's data (1995), gross available family income in constant pesetas for Extremadura in 1980 was equivalent to 56 per cent of that of Madrid's, increasing to 58 per cent by 1990. With respect to Catalonia, the income for Castile–La Mancha increased from 61 per cent in 1980 to 66 per cent in 1990.

23. The Canary Islands have some fiscal prerogatives inherited from the past and because of their location far away from the peninsula.

24. At the end of 1996 an agreement between the Basque Nationalist Party and the Popular Party established that the Basque fiscal authorities could also collect the 'special taxes' (on petrol, tobacco and spirits). Soon after, Jordi Pujol also claimed for Catalonia the power not only to collect but also to legislate for such 'special taxes'. On 23 November 1998 Pujol made proposals for the Generalitat to collect all taxes in Catalonia after the year 2002. The transfer of fiscal competencies to the Basque Country and Catalonia was seen to compensate for the political support provided by both Basque and Catalan nationalists to the minority PP government in the Spanish parliament.

25. In 1995 the *Comunidades Autónomas* managed 10 per cent of the moneys transferred from the European Cohesion Funds received for infrastructure and transport, and 40 per cent of those for the environment.

26. 'The Senate is not and ought to be the chamber of representation of the *Comunidades Autónomas*, and the Senate is and ought not to be a duplication of the Congress of Deputies [Lower House]' (Portero Molina, 1995: p. 82).

27. Since 1994 some reforms have been introduced in the Senate in line with a further territorial specialization. The creation of the *Comisión General de las Autonomías* (General Committee for the Autonomies) was regarded as a stepping-stone towards a gradual federalization of the Senate. However, reforms are still lingering and have primarily dealt with formal internal processes of the Upper House.

28. In accordance with federalist 'orthodoxy', the composition of the territorially based chamber invariably over-represents the least populated regions. Federations impose maximum limits on the criterion of proportionality in some cases. In the United States, for example, citizens in Vermont amount to no more than 0.2 per cent of the country's population, and California 11 per cent, yet each has its two members in the Senate, regardless of their respective populations. All US states have the right to elect the same number of senators independently of their specific demographic weight. This is also the case in Australia (Burgess and Gagnon, 1993; de Villiers, 1994).

29. In Germany, representation of the *Länder* in the Bundesrat varies between three, four or six members. In Austria and India, although the smaller units are over-represented, there is greater adjustment to demographic correlation. Of the 26 cantons in Switzerland, six are considered 'half-cantons' and elect only one representative to the Council of States, as compared to two elected by each of the others.

30. Nonetheless, in the German case there is no strict proportionality in the nomination of representatives to the Bundesrat. The *Land* of North Rhine Westphalia, with a population of 17 million (equivalent to five new *Länder* of the extinct German Democratic Republic), has six representatives for the 23 of those nominated in the east German states. Notwithstanding, the four most populous western *Länder* in 68 seats of the Bundesrat have obtained a political

guarantee which affords them a strong position to exercise veto (*Sperrminorität*) (Sturm, 1994).

31. In the case of Belgium, territorial interests are formally incorporated into the federal executive on the basis of territorial quotas in the composition of the government (Peeters, 1994). As regards the Canadian case, interstate institutions rely on agreements often reached informally. The main difficulty that Canada has faced regarding its internal accommodation has precisely been the infeasibility of implementing mega-constitutional reforms such as the Lake Meech Accord (1988) or the Charlottetown Accord (1992) (Gagnon, 1994, 1998; McRoberts, 1995).

32. Once the dominant actor of the system, now the role of the central administration has become that of a 'middleman' or broker within a highly decentralized state (Bañón and Tamayo, 1997).

33. Multilateral agreements (*convenios*) are a euphemism to describe a joint decision by more than one *Comunidad Autónoma* with the central government. Out of the 424 agreements signed in 1994, 145 were signed bilaterally by a single *Comunidad Autónoma* and the central government. Of the remaining 279 *convenios*, 237 were bilateral adhesions of other *Comunidades* to a pre-existing *convenio*. As a matter of fact, only 11 were multilateral agreements *in sensu strictu*, and were signed by the 15 *Comunidades Autónomas* of the fiscal 'common regime' (Basque Country and Navarre excluded) (Grau i Creus, 2000).

34. Further to the *convenios*, the *Juntas de Cooperación* (bilateral commissions) are another instrument of intergovernmental relations in Spain. They serve as informal platforms for sorting out conflicts over powers, for the discussion of *convenios*, and for the exchange of information. Yet again, they cannot be regarded as joint-decision mechanisms (Börzel, 1999).

35. This would be the result of the Europeanization of policy issues. Certainly, multilateral intergovernmental co-operation in Spain is more effective when European as opposed to domestic issues are involved.

36. Another example is provided by the socialist-controlled *Junta* in Andalusia, which in 1999 decided to subsidize autonomously the cost of some medicines of the social security whose co-payment had been increased by the PP government in Madrid.

37. This expression should not be understood only as an illustration of the practices of politicians and government officials to dip for 'pork', or funds for regional and local projects, from the national treasury. It also implies the support from regional parties sought by national parties to stay in power in the central state.

38. Even in France, where indicative planning was used by the state as a powerful instrument to beat the business cycle, the experience of the Mitterrand government in the early 1980s showed the infeasibility of implementing economic policies independently of the fashion adopted by most of the European governments of the time: 'Neither the control over interest rates nor the country's balance of payments [is] left under the authority of governments. Even competition policy, like property rights and protected financial services, may come under pressure to conform to standards set outside the state' (Strange, 1995: p. 299).

39. Immanuel Wallerstein, pioneer of the world-system approach that emphasizes a global rather that a state-centric perspective (1974), has also

underlined the growing importance of the local dimension and households as 'part and parcel' of the world economy, and as basic units of production (Wallerstein, 1984).

40. A different issue is the location of central bureaucracies, or 'eurocracies', as is the case of Brussels. Officials of the central institutions cannot refrain from the perception that capital cities are the true representation of the nation-state or, in the case of Belgium's capital, of the European Union as a whole.

41. Other functional identities, such as those related to cultural forms, gender, religion and individual sociobiological conditions, can also be interpreted as new forms of 'resistance' (Kilminster, 1997).

42. Denaturalizing is used here to mean the deprivation of the rights of citizenship within an established democratic polity.

43. According to Manuel Castells (1997), 'project identities' do not seem to originate from the old identities of the civil societies in the industrial age, but from the development of current 'resistance identities'. This argument is rather circular as regards its territorial dimension. In the case of the United States sub-state spatial identities are not commensurable with the type of identities deeply rooted in the *Volkgeist* of the diverse European peoples.

Conclusion: Unity and Diversity in Spain

The Estado de las Autonomías has, to a large extent, transcended patterns of internal confrontation in Spain. It has also reactivated a regional creativity smothered by centuries of (failed) forced uniformity and lingering institutional decay. The deep and widespread process of decentralization can be regarded as one of progressive federalization in line with the asymmetrical nature of Spain's composition. It serves the purpose of accommodating a long-standing diversity within unity of a state member of the European Union.

As in other plural states, regional devolution in Spain seeks to articulate a response to the stimuli of the diversity or plurality of society, comprising minority nations and regions with differences of language, history or traditions. Let us remember that Spain was constituted as the first modern state in Europe by means of a dynastic union under the Catholic Kings in the second half of the fifteenth century. As a consequence, its constituent territories maintained their political existence. Besides, the incorporation of such territories into the Hispanic monarchy was achieved centuries before the processes of national homogenization carried out by other European monarchies.

During modern times, Spain has often been under the rule of weak conservative or reactionary governments. There has also been a lack of congruence between political and economic powers, which has nourished centrifugal tendencies. Such tendencies manifested in armed conflicts and civil wars such as the Revolt of the Reapers (1640–52), the War of Spanish Succession (1701–14), or the Carlist Wars (1833–40, 1846–48 and 1872–75).

A great deal of the strength shown by minority and peripheral nationalisms in Spain has been a consequence of the weakness of central government. In fact the last *autonomist* upsurge in Spain has been, to a great extent, the result of the inefficient and sordid centralism of Franco's dictatorship. After this last attempt of despotic national consolidation, Spain faced the political challenge of integrating the legacy of its historical diversity. Since the transition to democracy, and the approval by popular referendum of the 1978 Constitution, territorial politics in Spain have developed according to a mode of *multiple ethnoterritorial concurrence*. This relates sociopolitical ethnoterritorial mobilization to the interplay among Spanish nationalities and regions pursuing political and economic power, as well as to the achievement of legitimization for their institutional development.

Dual identity, or compound nationality, is a sociological reality that is at the root of the federalizing rationale of the Estado de las Autonomías. This manner of self-identification by a majority of Spaniards implies shared loyalties to both central state and meso-levels of government. This concept of dual identity is very useful for the understanding and assessment of politics in contemporary Spain. It also provides a useful methodological tool for the measurement and interpretation of the degree of internal consent and dissent in the process of federalization in Spain. This gradual process is somewhat provisional owing to problems of accommodation of the 'historical nationalities' (the Basque Country, Catalonia and Galicia), and the articulation of the horizontal participation of the *Comunidades Autónomas* in the general governance of the country (reform of the Senate and the institutionalization of intergovernmental relations). If these reforms were to succeed in Spain, the political gravity in the centre–periphery political relationship could in no way be placed exclusively in the centre. Let us not forget that in Spain all non-democratic regimes have been centralist and have neglected the economically powerful periphery in the general process of political decision-making.

All things considered, the pillars of civic culture in Spain appear at present to consolidate the tendency towards agreement and the toleration of dissent. The legacy of past civil confrontations is still considerable. Besides, the effect of political violence in the Basque Country continues to be the negative referent in the generally peaceful cohabitation of the Spanish territories and peoples. An expression of the modernizing character of home rule demands by the *Comunidades Autónomas* is their European vocation, which is symptomatic of a general desire to leave behind the long stagnation of the Franco era and to develop a new form of *cosmopolitan localism*.

This is in line with the increasing role of mesogovernment in the process of Europeanization, which in turn is the result of a reassertion of territorial identities together with the implementation of the principles of subsidiarity and democratic accountability.

The process of federalization in Spain will involve *de facto* arrangements of power delimitation in its three-tier system of government (local, intermediate and central) before its federal-like arrangements take shape within the European Union. Once this situation has been achieved, a constitutional revision should functionally incorporate these divisions of powers, thus avoiding the great political difficulties which would have occurred had the process developed inversely.

The values that matter most in democratic life are those that favour agreement and understanding and reject intolerance. Beyond party interests, Spaniards are committed to paving the way towards a common future placed somewhere between the possible, the probable and the desirable. The ultimate challenge for Spain lies in finding the right way of living with its unity and diversity simultaneously. Its political future depends on it.

Methodological Appendix

CIRES DATA

The Spanish Centre for Studies on Social Reality (Centro de Estudios de la Realidad Social: CIRES) provided research teams with data from national surveys. From October 1990 until June 1995, 46 surveys were carried out by CIRES on a monthly basis (except for the summer months) covering several monographic questions. The monthly sample size was 1,200 adults aged 18 and over. (Note: The sample for June 1991 was 2,400.) The survey poll is representative of the Spanish population over 18. Monthly samples are random and stratified by regions (*Comunidades Autónomas*) and municipalities according to size.

The periodical repetition of part of the questionnaire allows data aggregation for statistical purposes. In this way, larger samples can be obtained with a higher degree of reliability, and population areas such as Catalonia can be also analysed. For our purposes, data from 46 survey polls have been aggregated, resulting in a sample of 56,400 cases. The size of the Catalan sample is 9,126 cases.

This appendix analyses the identity expressed by Catalan citizens based on the question addressed to them in the successive polls, which is reproduced as follows:

In general, would you say that you feel …
1. Only Catalan?
2. More Catalan than Spanish?
3. As much Catalan as Spanish?
4. More Spanish than Catalan?
5. Only Spanish?
6. Don't know?
7. No answer?

For the purpose of our study, answers have been aggregated according to the following categories:

(a) single identity (values 1 and 5);
       dual identity (values 2, 3 and 4);
              (values 6 and 7 have been aggregated);
(b) Catalan identity (values 1 and 2);
       shared identity (value 3);
       Spanish identity (values 4 and 5);
              (values 6 and 7 have been aggregated).

SEGMENTATION ANALYSIS

Segmentation analysis is based on the *chi-square* research technique. It allows the selection of relevant variables and provides a description of the differences that diverse sample groups can manifest in a given category.

A number of independent variables are selected as predictors, along with the dependent variable subject of study. Population is divided into homogeneous groups, different from each other with respect to the dependent variable to be measured. Within a dependent variable, subjects are classified within groups with characteristics significantly different and based on the chi-squared statistical logic for the selection of the best available predictors (CHAID). This technique carries out the merging by categories of those independent variables with a similar profile in relation with the dependent variable. A first segmentation is carried out with the best predictor, and successive segmentations with the resulting groups follow. The test is continued only if resulting differences are statistically significant (Escobar, 1992).

The variables used as predictors in our segmentation research are:

• Place of birth (born 'in Catalonia' or 'outside Catalonia');
• Educational level ('lower', 'middle' or 'higher');
• Social class ('lower', 'lower middle class', 'middle class', 'upper middle' or 'upper'). This is a subjective indicator (self-perceived);
• Occupation ('non-active', 'unemployed' or 'occupied');
• Age (four categories: 18–30, 31–44, 45–64, 65 and over);
• Religion ('no or little practice', 'middle', and 'active');

- Size of the place of residence ('less than 5,000', '5001–50,000', '50,001–250,000', and '250,000 and over');
- Sex;
- Economic sector ('primary', 'secondary' and 'tertiary');
- Ideology ('extreme right', 'right', 'centre', 'left' and 'extreme left');
- Monthly income ('less than 75,000 ptas', 'less than 150,000 ptas', 'less than 275,000 ptas', and 'less than 450,000 ptas').

References

Agranoff, R. (1993), 'Intergovernmental Politics and Policy: Building Federal Arrangements in Spain', *Regional Politics and Policy: An International Journal*, 3, 2, pp. 1–28.

Agranoff, R. and Ramos Gallarín, J.A. (1997), 'Toward Federal Democracy in Spain: An Examination of Intergovernmental Relations', *Publius: The Journal of Federalism*, 27, 4, pp. 1–38.

Aguilera de Prat, C.R. (1999), *El cambio político en Italia y la Liga Norte*. Madrid: CIS–Siglo XXI.

Aja, E. (1988), 'Propuestas para el desarrollo del Estado de las Autonomías', in Ll. Armet (ed.), *Federalismo y Estado de las Autonomías*. Barcelona: Planeta, pp. 141–65.

—— (1999), *El Estado Autonómico. Federalismo y hechos diferenciales*. Madrid: Alianza.

Anderson, B. (1983), *Imagined Communities: Reflections on the Origins and Spread of Nationalism*. London: Verso.

Anti-Federalists versus Federalists. Selected Documents (1967), ed. J.D. Lewis. San Francisco, CA: Chandler.

Armet, Ll. *et al.* (1988), *Federalismo y Estado de las Autonomías*. Barcelona: Planeta.

Balcells, A. (1983), *Historia contemporánea de Cataluña*. Barcelona: Edhasa.

Bañón, R. and Tamayo, M. (1997), 'The Transformation of the Central Administration in Spanish Intergovernmental Relations', *Publius: The Journal of Federalism*, 27, 4, pp. 85–114.

Banton, M. (1983), *Racial and Ethnic Competition*. Cambridge: Cambridge University Press.

Barth, F. (ed.) (1969), *Ethnic Groups and Boundaries: The Social Organization of Cultural Difference*. Boston: Little, Brown.

Bendix, R. (1962), *Max Weber. An Intellectual Portrait*. Garden City, NY: Doubleday.

—— (1964), *Nation-building and Citizenship. Studies of Our Changing Social Order*. New York: John Wiley.

Beramendi, J.G., Máiz, R. and Núñez, X.M. (eds) (1994), *Nationalism in Europe. Past and Present* (2 vols). Santiago: Universidade de Santiago de Compostela.

Beramendi, J.G. and Núñez-Seixas, X.M. (1995), *O nacionalismo galego*. Vigo: Edicións A Nosa terra.

Berlin, I. (1976), *Vico and Herder: Two Studies in the History of Ideas*. London: Hogarth Press.

Börzel, T.A. (1999), 'The Domestic Impact of Europe. Institutional Adaptation in Germany and Spain', PhD thesis. Florence: European University Institute.

Bosch, N. and Castells, A. (1997), 'La reforma del sistema de financiación autonómico: Implicaciones financieras', in *Informe Pi i Sunyer sobre Comunidades Autónomas 1995–1996*. Barcelona: Fundació Carles Pi i Sunyer d'Estudis Autonòmics i Locals.

Bottomore, T. (ed. and trans.) (1978), *Austro-Marxism*. Oxford: Clarendon Press.

Brass, P.R. (1991), *Ethnicity and Nationalism. Theory and Comparison*. New Delhi: Sage.

—— (1994), 'Elite Competition and the Origins of Ethnic Nationalism', in J.G. Beramendi *et al.* (eds), *Nationalism in Europe. Past and Present*, Vol. I. Santiago: Universidade de Santiago de Compostela, pp. 111–26.

Burgess, M. (1993), 'Federalism and Federation: A Reappraisal', in M. Burgess, and A.-G. Gagnon (eds), *Comparative Federalism and Federation: Competing Traditions and Future Directions*. London: Harvester Wheatsheaf.

Cadalso, J. (1978), *Cartas marruecas. Noches lúgubres* (2nd edn). Madrid: Cátedra.

Cambó, F. (1927), *Por la concordia*. Madrid: Compañía Ibero-Americana de Publicaciones.

Carr, R. and Fusi, J.P. (1979), *Dictatorship to Democracy*. London: George Allen & Unwin.

Carretero, A. (1988), 'Socialismo y federalismo en España', in Ll. Armet *et al.*, *Federalismo y Estado de las Autonomías*. Barcelona: Planeta, pp. 51–73.

Carrillo, E. (1997), 'Local Government and Strategies for Decentralization in the State of Autonomies', *Publius: The Journal of Federalism*, 27, 4, pp. 39–64.

Castells, M. (1997), *The Information Age: Economy, Society and Culture*.

Vol. II: *The Power of Identity*. Cambridge, MA: Blackwell.

Castro, A. (1984), *España en su historia. Cristianos, moros y judíos* (3rd edn). Barcelona: Crítica.

Chomsky, N. (1994), *World Orders, Old and New*. London: Pluto Press.

Coakley, J. (1994), 'Approaches to the Resolution of Ethnic Conflict: The Strategy of Non-Territorial Autonomy', *International Political Science Review*, 15, 3, pp. 297–314.

Cohen, A.P. (1992), *The Symbolic Construction of Community* (1st edn: 1985). London: Routledge.

Cohn, S. (1982), 'Michael Hecter's Theory of Regional Underdevelopment: A Test using Victorian Railways', *American Sociological Review*, 47, pp. 477–88.

Connor, W. (1984), *The National Question in Marxist–Leninist Theory and Strategy*. Princeton, NJ: Princeton University Press.

—— (1994), *Ethnonationalism. The Quest for Understanding*. Princeton, NJ: Princeton University Press.

Conversi, D. (1997), *The Basques, the Catalans and Spain. Alternative Routes to Nationalist Mobilisation*. London: C. Hurst.

Crick, B. (1989), 'An Englishman Considers his Passport', in N. Evans (ed.), *National Identity in the British Isles*. Coleg Harlech Occasional Papers in Welsh Studies, No. 3.

Cucó, A. (1971), *El valencianisme polític, 1874–1936*. Valencia: Garbí.

Dahl, R.A. (1957), 'The Concept of Power', *Behavioural Science*, 2, pp. 201–15.

—— (1968), 'Power', *International Encyclopaedia of the Social Sciences*, Vol. 12. New York: Macmillan, pp. 405–15.

—— (1971), *Polyarchy, Participation and Opposition*. New Haven, CT: Yale University Press.

de Blas Guerrero, A. (1991), *Tradición republicana y nacionalismo español (1876–1930)*. Madrid: Tecnos.

de Blas Guerrero, A. and Laborda Martín, J.J. (1986), 'La construcción del estado en España', in F. Hernández and F. Mercadé (eds), *Estructuras sociales y cuestión nacional en España*. Barcelona: Ariel, pp. 461–503.

de Madariaga, S. (1979), *España: Ensayo de Historia Contemporánea* (14th edn). Madrid: Espasa-Calpe.

de Riquer, B. and Ucelay-Da Cal, E. (1994), 'An Analysis of Nationalisms in Spain: A Proposal for an Integrated Historical Model', in J.G. Beramendi *et al.* (eds), *Nationalism in Europe. Past and Present*, Vol. II. Santiago: Universidade de Santiago de Compostela, pp. 275–301.

de Tocqueville, A. (1954), *Democracy in America* (original ms: 1832–40). New York: Vintage.

de Villiers, B. (ed.)(1994), *Evaluating Federal Systems*. Cape Town: Juta.

de Vos, G. and Romanucci-Ross, L. (eds) (1975), *Ethnic Identity: Cultural Continuities and Change*. Palo Alto, CA: Mayfield.

Deutsch, K.W. (1966), *Nationalism and Social Communication* (2nd edn). New York: MIT Press.

Díaz López, C. (1985), 'Centre–Periphery Structures in Spain: From Historical Conflict to Territorial Consociational Accommodation?', in Y. Mény and V. Wright (eds), *Centre–Periphery Relations in Western Europe*. London: Allen & Unwin, pp. 236–72.

Domínguez Ortiz, A. (1976), *Sociedad y Estado en el siglo XVIII español*. Barcelona: Ariel.

Duchacek, I.D. (1970), *Comparative Federalism: The Territorial Dimension of Politics*. New York: Holt, Rinehart & Winston.

Eguiagaray, J. (1993), 'El pacto autonómico', in N. Serra *et al.*, *Organización territorial del estado*. Salamanca: Ediciones Universidad de Salamanca, pp. 95–108.

Elazar, D.J. (1984), *American Federalism: A View from the States* (3rd edn). New York: Harper & Row.

—— (1987), *Exploring Federalism*. Tuscaloosa, AL: University of Alabama Press.

—— (1991), 'Introduction', in D.J. Elazar (ed.), *Federal Systems of the World: A Handbook of Federal, Confederal and Autonomy Arrangements*. Harlow: Longman, pp. ix–xxiii.

Elliot, J.H. (1970), *Imperial Spain (1469–1716)*. Harmondsworth: Pelican.

—— (1984), *Richelieu and Olivares*. Cambridge: Cambridge University Press.

Elorza, A. (1975), 'La primera democracia federal: Organización e ideología', in J.J. Trías Vejarano and A. Elorza, *Federalismo y reforma social en España (1840–1870)*. Madrid: Seminarios y Ediciones, pp. 75–243.

Epstein, A. (1978), *Ethos and Identity: Three Studies in Ethnicity*. London: Tavistock Press.

Escobar, M. (1992), 'El análisis de segmentación: concepto e implicaciones', Working Paper 1992/31. Madrid: CEACS–Instituto Juan March.

Etzioni, A. (1993), *The Spirit of Community. Rights, Responsibilities, and the Communitarian Agenda*. New York: Crown.

The Federalist Papers, Hamilton, A., Madison, J. and Jay, J. (1961) (1st edn: McLean, 1788). New York: Mentor.

Flora, P., Kuhnle, S. and Urwin, D. (eds) (1999), *State Formation, Nation-Building, and Mass Politics in Europe. The Theory of Stein Rokkan*. Oxford: Oxford University Press.

Fossas, E. and Requejo, F. (eds) (1999), *Asimetría federal y estado plurinacional. El debate sobre al acomodación de la diversidad en Canadá, Bélgica y España*. Madrid: Trotta.

Fundación BBV (1999), *Estudio de la renta en España (1955–1998)*. Bilbao: Fundación BBV.

Fusi Aizpurúa, J.P. (1989), 'La organización territorial del Estado', in J.P. Fusi (ed.), *Autonomías*. Madrid: Espasa-Calpe, pp. 11–40.

Gagnon, A.-G. (1994), 'Manufacturing Antagonisms: The Move Towards Uniform Federalism in Canada', in B. de Villiers (ed.), *Evaluating Federal Systems*. Cape Town: Juta, pp. 125–42.

—— (1998), *Quebec y el federalismo canadiense*. Madrid: CSIC.

Galligan, B. (1995), *A Federal Republic. Australia's Constitutional System of Government*. Cambridge: Cambridge University Press.

García de Añoveros, J. (1984), 'Autonomías, un proceso abierto'. Madrid, *El País*, 29–30–31 May 1984.

García Ferrando, M. López-Aranguren, E. and Beltrán, M. (1994), *La conciencia nacional y regional en la España de las Autonomías*. Madrid: Centro de Investigaciones Sociológicas.

Geertz, C. (1973), *The Interpretation of Cultures*. New York: Basic Books.

Gellner, E. (1983), *Nations and Nationalism*. Ithaca, NY: Cornell University Press.

—— (1987), *Culture, Identity and Politics*. Cambridge: Syndicate of the Press of the University of Cambridge.

Giner, S. (1980), *The Social Structure of Catalonia*. The Anglo-Catalan Society Occasional Publications, University of Sheffield.

—— (1984), 'Ethnic Nationalism, Centre and Periphery in Spain', in C. Abel and N. Torrents (eds), *Spain: Conditional Democracy*. London: Croom Helm, pp. 78–99.

Giner, S. and Moreno, L. (1990), 'Centro y periferia: La dimensión étnica de la sociedad española', in S. Giner (ed.), *España. Sociedad y política*. Madrid: Espasa-Calpe, pp. 169–97.

Glazer, N. (1997), *We are All Multiculturalists Now*. Cambridge, MA: Harvard University Press.

Glazer, N. and Moynihan, D. (1963), *Beyond the Melting Pot*. Cambridge, MA: MIT and Harvard University Press.

González Casanova, P. (1965), 'Internal Colonialism and National Development', *Studies in Comparative International Development*, 1, 4, pp. 27–37.

González Navarro, F. (1993), *España, nación de naciones. El moderno federalismo*. Pamplona: Ediciones Universidad de Navarra.

Gourevitch, P.A. (1979), 'The Re-emergence of "Peripheral Nationalisms": Some Comparative Speculations of the Spatial Distributions of Political Leadership and Economic Growth', *Comparative Studies in Sociology and History*, 21, pp. 303–22.

Grau i Creus, M. (2000), 'Spain: The Incomplete Federalism', in U. Wachendorfer-Schmidt (ed.), *Federalism and Political Performance*, London: Routledge.

Greenfeld, L. (1992), *Nationalism. Five Roads to Modernity*. Cambridge, MA: Harvard University Press.

Guibernau, M. (1999), *Nations without States*. Cambridge: Polity Press.

Hamann, K. (1999), 'Federalist Institutions, Voting Behavior, and Party Systems in Spain', *Publius: The Journal of Federalism*, 29, 1, pp. 111–37.

Hechter, M. (1975), *Internal Colonialism: The Celtic Fringe in British National Development 1536–1966*. London: Routledge & Kegan Paul.

—— (1983), 'Internal Colonialism Revisited', in D. Drakakis-Smith and S. Wyn Williams (eds), *Internal Colonialism: Essays Around a Theme*. Monograph No. 3, Developing Areas Research Group, Institute of British Geographers and Dept. of Geography, University of Edinburgh, pp. 28–41.

—— (1987), *Principles of Group Solidarity*. Berkeley, CA: University of California Press.

Hennessy, C.A.M. (1962), *The Federal Republic in Spain. Pi y Margall and the Federal Republican Movement, 1868–74*. Oxford: Clarendon Press.

Heywood, P. (ed.) (1999), *Politics and Policy in Democratic Spain: No Longer Different?* London: Frank Cass.

Hintze, O. (1975), *Historical Essays* (comp. F. Gilbert). New York: Oxford University Press.

Hirschmann, A.O. (1970), *Exit, Voice and Loyalty: Responses to Decline in Firms, Organisations and States*. Cambridge, MA: Harvard University Press.

Hobsbawm, E.J. (1990), *Nations and Nationalism since 1780: Programme, Myth and Reality*. Cambridge: Cambridge University Press.

Horowitz, D. (1985), *Ethnic Groups in Conflict*. Berkeley, CA: University of California Press.

Hroch, M. (1985), *Social Preconditions and National Revival in Europe. A Comparative Analysis of the Social Composition of Patriotic Groups among the Smaller European Nations*. Cambridge: Cambridge University Press.

Hunter, F. (1953), *Community Power Structure*. Chapel Hill, NC: University of North Carolina Press.

Hyslop, B.F. (1950), 'French Jacobin Nationalism and Spain', in E.M. Earle (ed.), *Nationalism and Internationalism*. New York: Columbia University Press, pp. 190–240.

Izard, M. (1970), *Revolució industrial i obrerisme. Les tres classes de vapor a Catalunya, 1869–1913*. Barcelona: Ariel.

—— (1979), *Manufactureros, fabricantes y revolucionarios. Las burguesías industriales catalanas y el control del poder en España, 1868–1875*. Barcelona: Crítica.

Jover Zamora, J.M. (1983), 'La época de la Restauración: Panorama político-social, 1875–1902', in M. Tuñón de Lara (dir.), *Historia de España* (Vol. VIII, 2nd edn). Barcelona: Labor, pp. 269–406.

Juaristi, J. (1992), *Vestigios de Babel. Para una arqueología de los nacionalismos españoles*. Madrid: Siglo XXI.

Keating, M. (1988), *State and Regional Nationalism. Territorial Politics and the European State*. Brighton: Harvester Wheatsheaf.

—— (1992), 'Regional Autonomy in the Changing State Order. A Framework of analysis', *Regional Policy and Politics*, II, 3, pp. 45–61.

—— (1996), *Nations against the State: The New Politics of Nationalism in Quebec, Catalonia and Scotland*. London: Macmillan.

Kilminster, R. (1997). 'Globalization as an Emergent Concept', in A. Scott (ed.), *The Limits of Globalization*. London: Routledge, pp. 257–83.

Kincaid, J. (1995), 'Values and Value Transfers in Federalism', *Publius: The Journal of Federalism*, 25, pp. 29–44.

King, P. (1982), *Federalism and Federation*. London: Croom Helm.

Krejcí, J. and Velímsky, V. (1981), *Ethnic and Political Nations in Europe*. London: Croom Helm.

Kymlicka, W. (1995), *Multicultural Citizenship: A Liberal Theory of Minority Rights*. Oxford: Oxford University Press.

—— (1998), *Finding our Way: Rethinking Ethnocultural Relations in Canada*. Oxford: Oxford University Press.

Lenin, V.I. (1917), 'Statistics and Sociology', in *Collected Works* (45 vols, 4th edn, 1977). Moscow: Progress Publishers.

Letamendía, F. (1994), 'On Nationalisms in Situations of Conflict (Reflections from the Basque Case)', in J.R. Beramendi, *et al.* (eds), *Nationalism in Europe. Past and Present* (Vol. I). Santiago: Universidad de Santiago de Compostela, pp. 247–75.

Linz, J.J. (1967), 'The Party System of Spain: Past and Future', in S.M.

Lipset and S. Rokkan (eds), *Party Systems and Voter Alignments: Cross-National Perspectives*. New York: Free Press, pp. 197–282.

—— (1973), 'Early State-Building and the Late Peripheral Nationalisms against the State: The Case of Spain', in S. Eisenstadt and S. Rokkan (eds), *Building States and Nations. Models, Analyses and Data across Three Worlds*, 2 vols. Beverly Hills, CA: SAGE, pp. 32–116.

—— (1975), 'Politics in a Multilingual Society with a Dominant World Language: The Case of Spain', in J.G. Savard and R. Vigneault (eds), *Les États multilingues: problems et solutions*. Quebec: Les Presses de l'Université Laval, pp. 367–444.

—— (1997), 'Democracy, Multinationalism and Federalism', Working Paper 1997/103. Madrid: CEACS–Instituto Juan March.

Livingston, W.S. (1952), 'A Note on the Nature of Federalism', *Political Science Quarterly*, 67, pp. 81–95.

—— (1956), *Federalism and Constitutional Change*. Oxford: Clarendon Press.

Llobera, J.R. (1994), *The God of Modernity. The Development of Nationalism in Western Europe*. Oxford: Berg.

López Aranguren, E. (1983), *La Conciencia Regional Española en el Proceso Autonómico Español*. Madrid: Centro de Investigaciones Sociológicas.

Lucas, J.J. (1993), 'Autonomía y transferencia de funciones', in N. Serra *et al.*, *Organización territorial del estado*. Salamanca: Ediciones Universidad de Salamanca, pp. 67–77.

McCrone, D. (1992), *Understanding Scotland. The Sociology of a Stateless Nation*. London: Routledge.

—— (1998), *The Sociology of Nationalism. Tomorrow's Ancestors*. London: Routledge.

MacKay, A. (1977), *Spain in the Middle Ages. From Frontier to Empire, 1000–1500*. New York: St Martin's Press.

McRoberts, K. (ed.) (1995), *Beyond Quebec: Taking Stock of Canada*. Montreal: McGill–Queen's University Press.

Máiz, R. (1994), 'The Open-ended Construction of a Nation: The Galician Case in Spain', in J.G. Beramendi *et al.* (eds), *Nationalism in Europe. Past and Present*, Vol. II. Santiago: Universidad de Santiago de Compostela, pp. 172–208.

—— (2000), 'Nationalism, Federalism and Democracy in Multinational States', in W. Safran and R. Máiz (eds), *Identity and Territorial Autonomy in Plural Societies*. London: Frank Cass.

Maravall, J.A. (1986), *Estado moderno y mentalidad social (Siglos XV a XVII)* (2 vols: 1st edn). Madrid: Alianza.

Marc, A. and Aron, R. (1948), *Principles du federalisme*. Paris: Le Portulan.

Mazzini, G. (1891), 'The Holy Alliance of the Peoples' (1849), in *Life and Writings of Joseph Mazzini* (6 vols: new edn, Vol. V, *Autobiographical and Political*). London: Smith, Elder, pp. 265–82.

Meinecke, F. (1970), *Cosmopolitanism and the National State* (trans. of *Weltburgertum und Nationalstaat*). Princeton, NJ: Princeton University Press.

Melucci, A. (1989), *Nomads of the Present*. London: Hutchinson Radius.

Miguélez, F. and Solé, C. (1987), *Classes Socials i Poder Politic a Catalunya*. Barcelona: Promociones y Publicaciones Universitarias.

Miliband, R. (1973), 'Poulantzas and the Capitalist State', *New Left Review*, 82, pp. 83–92.

Montagu, A. (1972), *Statement on Race* (3rd edn). New York: Oxford University Press.

Moreno, L. (1986), 'Decentralisation in Britain and Spain: The Cases of Scotland and Catalonia'. PhD thesis, University of Edinburgh.

—— (1994), 'Ethnoterritorial Concurrence and Imperfect Federalism in Spain', in B. de Villiers (ed.), *Evaluating Federal Systems*. Cape Town: Juta, pp. 162–93.

—— (1995), 'Multiple Ethnoterritorial Concurrence in Spain', *Nationalism and Ethnic Politics*, 1, 1, pp. 11–32.

—— (1997a), 'Federalization and Ethnoterritorial Concurrence in Spain', *Publius: The Journal of Federalism*, 27, 4, pp. 65–84.

—— (1997b), *Federalism: The Spanish Experience*. Pretoria: HSCR.

—— (1999), 'Local and Global: Mesogovernments and Territorial Identities', *Nationalism and Ethnic Politics*, 6, 3/4, pp. 61–75.

Moreno, L. and Arriba, A. (1996), 'Dual Identity in Autonomous Catalonia', *Scottish Affairs*, 17, pp. 78–97.

—— (1999), *Welfare and Decentralization*, EUI Working Paper EUF No. 99/8. Florence: European University Institute.

Moreno, L., Arriba, A. and Serrano, A. (1998), 'Multiple Identities in Decentralized Spain: The Case of Catalonia', *Regional and Federal Studies*, 8, 3, pp. 65–88.

Moreno Alonso, M. (1984), 'El sentimiento nacionalista en la historiografía española del siglo XIX', in *Nation et nationalités en Espagne, XIXe–XXe siècles* (Colloquium proceedings, 28–31 March 1984). Paris: Editions de la Fondation Singer-Polignac.

Myrdal, G. (1957), *Economic Theory and Underdeveloped Regions*. London: Duckworth.

Nadal, J. (1980), *El fracaso de la revolución industrial en España, 1814–1913*. Barcelona: Ariel.

Nairn, T. (1997), *Faces of Nationalism. Janus Revisited*. London: Verso.

Nash, M. (1989), *The Cauldron of Ethnicity in the Modern World*. Chicago: University of Chicago Press.

Newton, M. (1983), 'The Peoples and Regions of Spain', in D. Bell (ed.), *Democratic Politics in Spain*, pp. 98–131. London: Frances Pinter.

Olábarri Gortázar, I. (1985), 'Un conflicto entre nacionalismos: La "cuestión regional" en España, 1808–1939', in F. Fernández Rodríguez (ed.), *La España de las Autonomías*. Madrid: Instituto de Estudios de Administración Local, pp. 71–143.

Olson, M. (1982), *The Rise and Decline of Nations. Economic growth, Stagflation and Social Rigidities*. New Haven, CT: Yale University Press.

Ortega y Gasset, J. (1989), *España invertebrada. Bosquejo de algunos pensamientos históricos* (9th edn). Madrid: Espasa-Calpe.

Pallarés, F., Montero, J.R. and Llera, F.J. (1997), 'Non State-wide Parties in Spain: An Attitudinal Study of Nationalism and Regionalism', *Publius: The Journal of Federalism*, 27, 4, pp. 135–69.

Paterson, L. (1994), *The Autonomy of Modern Scotland*. Edinburgh: Edinburgh University Press.

Peeters, P. (1994), 'Federalism: A Comparative Perspective – Belgium Transforms from Unitary to a Federal State', in B. de Villiers, *Evaluating Federal Systems*. Cape Town: Juta, pp. 194–207.

Pena Trapero, J.B. (1995), 'Estudio de la distribución de la renta en España: 1970–1990'. Paper presented at II Simposio sobre Igualdad y Distribución de la Renta y la Riqueza. Madrid: Fundación Argentaria.

Pérez-Agote, A. (1994), 'Modelo fenomenológico-genético para el análisis comparativo de la dimensión política de las identidades colectivas en el Estado de las Autonomías', in J.G. Beramendi, *et al.* (eds), *Nationalism in Europe. Past and Present*, Vol. I. Santiago: Universidad de Santiago de Compostela, pp. 307–23 .

Perroux, F. (1964), *L'Economie du XXe siècle*. Paris: Presses Universitaires de France.

Phadnis, U. (1989), *Ethnicity and Nation-Building in South Asia*. New Delhi: Sage.

Pi i Margall, F. (1911), *Las nacionalidades* (4th edn) (1st edn: 1876). Madrid: Librería de los Sucesores de Hernando.

Platón, M. (1994), *La amenaza separatista. Mito y readlidad de los nacionalismos en España*. Madrid: Temas de Hoy.

Popper, K. (1976), 'The Logic of the Social Sciences', in T. Adorno *et al.*, *The Positivist Dispute in German Sociology*. London: Heinemann, pp. 87–104.

Portero Molina, J.A. (1995), 'Contribución al debate sobre la reforma del Senado', *Revista de Estudios Políticos*, 87, pp. 81–105.

Poulantzas, N. (1973), *Political Power and Social Classes*. London: New Left Books.

Prat de la Riba, E. (1917), *La nacionalidad catalana*. Valladolid: Imprenta Castellana. (1st edn in Catalan: Barcelona, L'Anuari de la Exportació, 1906.)

Pujol, J. (1980), *Construir Catalunya*. Barcelona: Pòrtic.

Rajoy, M. (1993), 'Los problemas de la organización territorial del estado después de los acuerdos autonómicos', in N. Serra *et al.*, *Organización territorial del estado*. Salamanca: Ediciones Universidad de Salamanca, pp. 41–53.

Renan, E. (1947), *Oeuvres complètes*. Paris: Calmann-Lévy.

Rex, J. (1986), *Race and Ethnicity*. Milton Keynes: Open University Press.

Riker, W.H. (1975), 'Federalism', in F.I. Greenstain and H.W. Polsby, (eds), *Cumulative Index, Handbook of Political Science*, Vol. 5. Reading, MA: Addison-Wesley, pp. 93–172.

Rokkan, S. and Urwin, D. (1983), *Economy, Territory, Identity. Politics of West European Peripheries*. London: Sage.

Roosens, E. (1989), *Creating Ethnicity. The Process of Ethnogenesis*. London: Sage.

Rudolph, Jr, J.R. and Thompson, R.J. (1992), *Ethnoterritorial Politics, Policy, and the Western World*. Boulder, CO: Lynne Rienner.

Safran, W. (1987), 'Ethnic Mobilization, Modernization, and Ideology: Jacobinism, Marxism, Organicism and Functionalism', *Journal of Ethnic Studies*, 15, 1, pp. 1–31.

—— (1991), 'State, Nation, National Identity, and Citizenship: France as a Test Case', *International Political Science Review*, 12, 3, pp. 219–38.

—— (1998), *The French Polity* (5th edn). Longman: New York.

Safran, W. and Máiz, R. (eds) (2000), *Identity and Territorial Autonomy in Plural Societies*. London: Frank Cass.

Sánchez-Albornoz, C. (1956), *España: un enigma histórico*. Buenos Aires:

Editorial Sudamericana.

Sanmartí Roset, J.M. (1997), *La políticas lingüísticas y las lenguas minoritarias en el proceso de construcción de Europa*. Victoria-Gasteiz: Instituto Vasco de Administración Pública.

Shils, E. (1975), *Center and Periphery: Essays in Macrosociology*. Chicago: Chicago University Press.

Smith, A.D. (1971), *Theories of Nationalism*. London: Duckworth.

—— (1986), *The Ethnic Origins of Nations*. Oxford: Basil Blackwell.

Solé Tura, J. (1967), *Catalanisme i Revolució Burgesa*. Barcelona: Ediçions 62.

—— (1985), *Nacionalidades y nacionalismos en España. Autonomías, federalismo, autodeterminación*. Madrid: Alianza.

Stalin, J. (1975), *Marxism and the National–Colonial Question*. San Francisco, CA: Proletarian Publishers.

Strange, S. (1995), 'The Limits of Politics', *Government and Opposition*, 30, 3, pp. 291–311.

Sturm, R. (1994), 'The Constitution Under Pressure: Emerging Asymmetrical Federalism in Germany?', paper presented at the 16th IPSA Congress, 21–25 August 1994, Berlin.

Sumner, W.G. (1940), *Folkways: A Study of the Sociological Importance of Usages, Manners, Customs, Mores, and Morals* (1st edn: 1906). Boston: Ginn.

Tamir, Y. (1993), *Liberal Nationalism*. Princeton, NJ: Princeton University Press.

Tarlton, C.D. (1965), 'Symmetry and Asymmetry as Elements of Federalism: A Theoretical Speculation', *Journal of Politics*, 27, 14, pp. 861–74.

Taylor, C. (1992), *Multiculturalism and 'the Politics of Recognition': An Essay*. Princeton, NJ: Princeton University Press.

Thom, M. (1995), *Republics, Nations and Tribes*. London: Verso.

Tilly, C. (1975), 'Western Statemaking and Theories of Political Transformation', in C. Tilly (ed.), *The Formation of National States in Europe*. Princeton, NJ: Princeton University Press, pp. 601–38.

Tönnies, F. (1957), *Community and Society* (trans. of *Gemeinschaft und Gesellschaft*). East Lansing, MI: Michigan State University Press.

Trías Vejarano, J.J. (1975), *Almirall y los orígenes el catalanismo*. Madrid: Siglo XXI.

Trías Vejarano, J. J. and Elorza, A. (1975), *Federalismo y reforma social en España (1840–1870)*. Madrid: Seminarios y Ediciones.

Trujillo, G. (1967), *Introducción al federalismo español*. Madrid: Edicusa.

Tuñón de Lara, M. (1986), *España: la quiebra de 1898*. Madrid: SARPE.

—— (ed.)(1983), *Historia de España* (10 vols). Barcelona: Labor.

van den Berghe, P.L. (1978), 'Race and Ethnicity: A Sociobiological Perspective', *Ethnic and Racial Studies*, 1, 4, pp. 401–11.

—— (1981), *The Ethnic Phenomenon*. New York: Elsevier.

Vidal-Folch, X. (ed.) (1994), *Los catalanes y el poder*. Madrid: El País/Aguilar.

Vilar, P. (1986), *Historia de España* (1st Spanish edn: 1978). Barcelona: Crítica.

Wallerstein, I., *The Modern World-System*: Vol. 1 (1974), *Capitalist Agriculture and the Origins of the European World-Economy in the Sixteenth Century*. New York: Academic Press; Vol. 2 (1980), *Mercantilism and the Consolidation of the European World-Economy, 1600–1750*. New York: Academic Press; Vol. 3 (1989), *The Second Era of Great Expansion of the Capitalist World-Economy, 1730–1840s*. London: Academic Press.

—— (1984), 'Household Structures and Labor-force Formation in the Capitalist World-Economy', in J. Smith, I. Wallerstein and H.D. Evers (eds), *Households and the World Economy*. Beverly Hills, CA: Sage, pp. 17–22.

Walzer, M. (1997), *On Toleration*. New Haven, CT: Yale University Press.

Watts, R.L. (1994), 'Contemporary Views on Federalism', in B. de Villiers (ed.), *Evaluating Federal Systems*. Cape Town: Juta, pp. 1–29.

Weber, E. (1976), *Peasants into Frenchmen: The Modernization of Rural France, 1870–1914*. Stanford, CA: Stanford University Press.

Weber, M. (1947), *The Theory of Social and Economic Organization*. Oxford: Oxford University Press.

—— (1961), 'Ethnic Groups', in T. Parsons (ed.), *Theories of Society*, Vol. I. New York: Free Press, pp. 305–6.

Index